"POVERTY OF AFFLUENCE" is nonfiction family ....on Valley. The family's agrarian roots and perspective give the reade. ...ew of Silicon Valley from the inside looking out rather stories about Silicon Valley from outside looking in.

From its origins as risk-takers along the Mediterranean trade routes at the time of Homer through its settling in the Santa Clara Valley, California and establishment of internationally successful fruit growing and real estate enterprises, the Mariani family's story is emblematic of the American success story. Specifically, it is the story of the origins and fulfillment of the entrepreneurial spirit that defined Silicon Valley and continues to nurture its growth.

It is also a deeply personal story addressing the challenges of losing a patriarch, sibling rivalry, sexual abuse, pain and forgiveness, fortunes gained and lost all woven in a series of life lessons between a roller coaster of adventures behind the Iron Curtain, working in leper colonies, three-legged horses, giant earthworm, beheadings, and revolutions.

In POVERTY OF AFFLUENCE, I follow the immigrant journeys of my distant and immediate ancestors as well as my journey all the while shedding light on the major trends and movements in the growth of the world around us. It's a story peopled not only by my family but by the major influencers such as David Packard, Steve Jobs, Bill Gates, Wozniak, Andy Grove, Gene Amdahl with whom we crossed paths. Embedded in these stories are different meanings behind poverty and the meaning behind affluence whether entertaining royalty, heads of state, celebrities or the gardeners and janitors. It is a universal story of the discovery of oneself through life lessons. In this way, the book provides a detailed fabric of Silicon Valley's culture and a rare, inside, panoramic view of a place that continues to enthrall in popular media and the imagination.

Poverty of Affluence:
The Story of the Mariani Family in California

by David W. Mariani

MARIANI

ISBN 978-1-7331461-2-8

Table of Contents

DEDICATION

This book is about living in the Santa Clara Valley during a now bygone era, described through the lens of my childhood and the lives of my parents and grandparents who arrived there in the late 1800s. Though it is not a book about the private life of my immediate family, my wife and children, I feel it is appropriate to dedicate this book to them. I have written all my life, but I live for them. I married over my head when I married my wife Arlene. I love her even more today than the day we fell in love and the day I married her. Without her constant support and patience with my on-again, off-again writing, and her ever present encouragement to write down my family's story in what is now known throughout the world as "Silicon Valley," this book would never have been written.

To my five daughters—Nancy, Molly, Janna, Julie, and Tracy—who lost their dad over the years when I was either working long hours, coming home late, or cloistered behind closed doors researching, collecting, and writing down our family memories, I regret the time lost. This book, in so many ways, is for you and your children.

ACKNOWLEDGMENTS

To the many family members who assisted me, I thank you. My aunts—Mathilda Sousa, Irene Perkov, and Winifred Thiltgen—my cousin Winifred Mardesich, and my nephew Dr. Thomas Osborne were especially helpful in researching our family tree. Without the extended family support and input, many of the stories told would be lost to the ages. I am particularly grateful to my mother Mary Frances, my wife's uncle Nick Scrabo, and grandmother Ann Skrabo Morey Goodwin. A special note of recognition goes to my cousin Andrew Mariani, who is a student of our family's history, and to my brother Richard Mariani, who took the time to research, in extraordinary detail, our family history in Croatia.

Finally, I am indebted to a dear friends, Dr. Jeffrey Lewis, Marilyn Dorsa, Christopher Bernard, John Swensson, Peter Verbica and Anne Marie Todd whom provided untold hours to read, edit, and make critical suggestions to earlier versions of this book.

Preface

Whenever I look back on my life, echoes keep ringing in my mind of my father's stories about his life, and my grandfather's stories about his father. Those stories prompted me to research the history of that branch of the Mariani family who settled in California in the 1880'ss and then search even further into our family's roots in Europe.[1]

My great-grandfather was a Croatian immigrant who settled in the 1800s in an area that, in the mid-twentieth century, when it was a world center for fruit cultivation and production, first knew fame as "The Valley of Heart's Delight." That same valley later became famous, for different, though, as we shall see, curiously related reasons, as "Silicon Valley." The historical significance of Silicon Valley is legendary worldwide, with many stories written about it from the viewpoint of outsiders "looking in." *Poverty of Affluence: The Story of the Mariani Family in California* is a firsthand account of how the Valley of Heart's Delight became Silicon Valley from the viewpoint of an insider "looking out."

In 1978 my dad dictated a short memoir, meant to be shared with our immediate family, that he titled "My Life and My Dreams" and which I frequently quote from in this book. It is an incomplete chronicle of his life, in which he describes both what he believed he got right and what he got wrong; he wanted his children to learn from his mistakes as well as from his successes. It is a snapshot of an extraordinary man living through extraordinary times in the twentieth century.

Dad unexpectedly died of a heart attack shortly afterward. As I sat and listened to the audiotapes on which he had recorded his memories, I was inspired to fill in the blanks he had left and to add my own memories. I began to write and reflect.

We are all products of our own unique life experience. It will be surprising if other members of the family have the same memories perspectives or conclusions. I did my best to maintain objectivity regarding our history. Nevertheless, inescapably, I told our story through the lens of the author.

The British writer Goronwy Rees defined his life as "only a succession of disjointed episodes." Rees saw his life story not as a continuous history, but "as a collection of short stories – a bundle of sensations, linked together by the accidents of memory." Similarly, my life has been punctuated by meeting a series of remarkable people who profoundly influenced me and became an integral part of my life experience. My reflections would not be complete without describing and including some of the people whose paths I have crossed in the Valley, because many of them - some unknown, some celebrated - imparted a piece of their lives to me, and many of them had a profound effect on the place we now call Silicon Valley.

The stories are often about various tug of wars between poverty and affluence and poverty of spirit that often comes from affluence. My hope is that the reader will also get an inside glimpse of Silicon Valley in the making through my descriptions of these people who have influenced my life.

It has been a great journey. I hope you enjoy the ride.

INTRODUCTION

The Truth is a Powerful Magnet

The truth is a powerful magnet which pulls at the jacket of steel most of us have around our hearts. Whether someone tells us of their journey to hell or heaven, if what he or she shares is true, chances are, we're going to listen with greater earnest. Christ asks his disciples to bring children to him; perhaps it's because children are natural truth tellers. The self-proclaimed Son of God was kind to children, thieves, tax-collectors, outsiders and whores and is followed by billions today. Maybe it's because He had little use for bull durham. Now, I'm no pastor – quite far from one. But, David Mariani was a seminarian in his early years. And, in his book *Poverty of Affluence* on the Mariani family, he masterfully demonstrates the child-like, and dare I say, Messianic, business of telling the truth. David doesn't flinch. There's something quintessentially divine in his writing because of this.

The Bay Area has its well-known heroes, and David Mariani's family's long-standing presence here means that the author rubbed elbows with many of them, including Packard, Jobs, Wozniak, Amdahl, Sobrato, Arriaga, and others. The genesis of David taking pen to paper was inspired by a conversation the author had with Packard at the technologist's Los Altos Hills' apricot orchard. He urged David to tell the story of Silicon Valley from the "inside looking out." Sometimes innocent suggestions end up having lifelong consequences, and for David, sharing an insider's perspective through a deeply personal book has become his life's work. Like the cap on the Washington Monument which was constructed out of the most precious metal of that era, David's effort marks a shining culmination of one man's comprehensive perspective on history, the present and where we may be heading.

Since I brought up heroes, it's only fair that I confess that I have a new one: Paul Mariani, David's plain-spoken dad. It's unequivocal that geniuses are at their best when they take the complex and make it simple. Paul Mariani exemplifies this when he advises his son, "If you buy a house first, you'll never be able to afford an orchard. But, if you buy an orchard first, you'll be able to buy a house." What a great piece of advice for young men and women. How I wish that I had access to this book in my twenties! Now, Paul Mariani had his missteps, including a contract to dispose of large quantities of coffee grounds, the perils of spontaneous combustion and giant earthworms. You'll have to read about it in David's book, because I'm not about to spoil the fun.

There is much adventure in *Poverty of Affluence* and wisdom, too. David as a young boy caught in a Latin American coup. A headline-grabbing burglary. Tales of kidnappers and turncoats. Of duplicitous bankers and damn good donuts. Of children left to fend on their own. Of Silicon Valley when it knew a simpler time. When women cut cots in the summer. When the bosom of the earth could breathe in neatly disced rows between the fruit trees

~ Peter Coe Verbica, Author of *Hard-Won Cowboy Wisdom (Not Necessarily in Order of Importance)*, *Left at the Gate and Other Poems*, and *Small Miracles*.

PART I

Chapter 1

Two roads diverged in a wood, and I—
I took the one less traveled by,
And that has made all the difference.

~Robert Frost

Being mortal, death stalks us like a silent shadow during the day and rests under our beds at night. Like a lamb sleeping with a freshly fed lion, we become acclimated to the beast's mercy. As years pass, death becomes uneasy and hungrier for us. In our youth, death watches us with patience, from a tree branch, from the blind of tall grass, from an embankment as we felicitously slake from the stream of life. For years, death's pining is muted, but, as I say, not always. There are startling instances when death reveals its nature. Such an event occurred to me recently. Caused all that is inside of me to awaken with alarm; forced me to review my life's experiences with an urgent and cold-eyed sobriety. You are the bystander, the passenger on a train I grab by the lapels with the urgency of one who knows he is pursued but has an urgent, essential message. And, as a well-known band artfully observes, "what a long, strange trip it's been."

At age twelve, as a young member of a global agricultural concern, I traveled to Brazil, Argentina, and Chile with my father, in his trademark dark suit and my mother, who, in spite of the humidity, preserved her magazine model's supernatural radiance. In Chile, a country which one writer describes as having the shape of a snake, I waved goodbye to my parents as they boarded a twin-propeller plane to return to America without me. Alone in a Latin American country subsequently infamous for its shallow graves of Pinochet's "missing," I would not see my parents again until the following year. Despite the political turbulence which drove Leftists to their guns and poets to their pens, it all seemed so normal at the time. I did not understand that some people live their entire lives never to travel beyond the county they were born.

In 1968, I was nineteen years old and traveled mostly alone, to Australia, Fijian Islands, China, Bali, Denpasar, Jakarta, Japan, Poland, England, East and West Germany, Switzerland, Italy, France, Austria, and Mexico. A young nomad with an old soul. I also journeyed to the former Soviet Union as a teenager. I visited Moscow's Saint Basil Cathedral and the Peterhof Palace of Leningrad and eventually exited the Soviet Union through the infamous "Check Point Charlie" in East Berlin. I was comfortable as a teenager to travel without my family but navigating behind the so-called "Iron Curtain" during the height of the Cold War forever changed me. Seeing the predominantly colorless soot laden buildings, grey clothing of the people, and razor-wired repression of Eastern Europe instilled in me a broader world view and reminded me how culturally myopic I had been. Arriving back into the West, it was as if Michelangelo himself had stepped from the Sistine Chapel to paint each building. The first thing I noticed leaving Communist-run countries was the wondrous blush of color.

The extensive traveling at an early age is not a boast. Instead, it is illustrative of a family with a cosmopolitan perspective with a strong philosophy of independence. We were taught at an early age to be self-reliant; to catch fish, you had better know how to string a pole; to raise an orchard, one needed to prepare and plant the soil. The Mariani family is an adventurous clan, in part, because our forefathers, many of whom were fishermen, became emboldened over generations. Forced to navigate the fickle seas of the Mediterranean, bravery became inbred out of necessity. Such role models, combined with a curious culture, gave us a global perspective of the world. Adventurousness has its risks. I am grateful to be able to tell my story after escaping a series of life and death challenges.

Recently, while visiting with friends in Ensenada, Mexico, around midnight, I decided to turn out some lights. As I flicked off a series of switches, the estate gradually became as dark as a mine. I do not recommend walking around in total darkness in an unfamiliar home. Tragedy struck. I fell back down a short set of cement stairs and landed on my neck and head at the bottom. The compression impact left me stunned as if I had been hit with a hammer. I lay in the quiet of the home in stark darkness, with everyone asleep on the other side of the house. Worse, I soon realized my arms and legs would not move on command. I became a prisoner in the jail of my own body.

The Ensenada accident left me spending about an hour in darkness crumpled on the floor and paralyzed. Foreboding emotions came flooding in as I realized I had no feeling in my arms and legs. My mind began to race. A wide range of thoughts, including future possibilities, and potential limitations went through my head. Scenes from the kinescope of my life oscillated before me. The deadly scorpions in Bali scuttling under me while I slept in a little hut in a leper colony now seemed trivial. I remembered the white fear when our landing gear would not deploy in our private aircraft while flying over our Texas ranch with an odd sense of detachment. I was about 30 years old at the time. It seemed so long ago, but now, it seemed like yesterday.

As I continued to lay in the darkness, searing chest pains began. I suppose the shock from fall was starting to wear off. The combination of my life's memories pulsing through my head and chest pains reminded me of my pulmonary arrest at age 40, and my heart attack at 41 came to mind. As the pain in my chest abated, I calmed down and tried to control my breathing – meanwhile, recollections continued to syncopate before me. Escaping Guatemalan armed rebels at age 22 brought back disturbing memories but strangely without the anxiety.

All of these previous "near misses" distracted me from the significance of feeling pain. I was getting my feeling back! My left hand was twitching. Apparently, I have nine lives and used up more than most.

The last time my life flashed through my head was when I nearly drowned in my thirties while scuba diving in Mendocino with a good friend John Vidovich. John saved my life. Because of John's heroic efforts, Thankfully, I live to tell these stories.

My adventure, however, begins with a series of bold migrations. Allow me to resurrect some of these intrepid ghosts at the beginning. Their lives provide a context for my thesis of poverty and affluence. It is from this contradiction that the amazing story of the Mariani Family thrives and blossoms.

Chapter 2

The Neretva Valley and the Island of Vis

The First and Second Migrations

Circa 350–1800s

For centuries the Mariani family made a living and raised families on a little island in the Adriatic Sea called Vis, in the town of Komiza, off the coast of what is now Croatia, due west of the city of Split. The Catholic Church in Komiza (a small harbor town and the island's principal municipality) maintains voluminous records of baptisms, weddings, death certificates, and graves going back centuries. Those records chronicle our family history, as well as that of other islanders. The Church's diligent record keeping preserve both our island's history and our family legacy.

An centuries old painting (exact date unknown) of the seaside church in Komiza

A photograph of the same church, taken in 2011, showing it virtually unchanged

The wrought-iron railing outside the church

Another old painting of the church.

(Made prior to photography, the two paintings show our local church and countryside during the time described in the Turkish documents mentioned in the text. Both paintings are by Marianis.)

Classic Croatian street masonry

As I researched, I came across one amazing story after another. And the journey kept taking me further back in time: the documents I found traced our family tree back to around 350 AD. The story of the forces that shaped the people and cultures of the Mediterranean and Adriatic, especially people like the Marianis, who lived along strategically important trade routes, provided fascinating insights into wars, intrigues, brutality, tragedy, and adventure. The stories I found described the secret caves of Komiza, possible secrets and mysteries behind the *Iliad* and *Odyssey* (for example, Vis may be the island of Issa or Lemnos mentioned in both of the Homeric poems), and more.

People living in or along the Adriatic during the tumultuous Middle Ages, from living on a major trade route and at a crossroads of many cultures, forged a collective consciousness of adventure and risk taking.

The Adriatic Sea was the most direct sea route between Constantinople and the Byzantine empire, on the one hand, and, on the other, the rich city of Venice and the eastern coast of Italy, the Dalmatian coast, and the belly of Europe, by way of what is today Trieste. Whoever controlled the Adriatic benefited from this vitally important trade route. The Island of Vis is located roughly midway between the coasts of Dalmatia and Italy. One result of this was that whoever maintained military presence on Vis controlled the Adriatic's trade routes. The island consequently became the ground-zero battle ground for control of the small but strategically vital sea. These forces, in part, shaped some of the reasons a small group of people migrated both to and from the island of Vis.

A combination of hope and fear, blended together to drive the family to migrate all over the world, including Santa Clara Valley. These migratory stories became part of the collective consciousness of the people who changed Santa Clara Valley into Silicon Valley.

"A Brief History of Time"

The Mariani family was first mentioned, by Venetian chroniclers, as rulers of the "Neretanis"[2] (inhabitants of the Neretva Valley) in 834–835 AD. The Marianis are referenced again in 1050 in a charter issued in favor of the Benedictine monastery of St. Mary on the Island of Tremiti, located in the Adriatic, north of the "heel" of the Italy's "boot."

The exact timing of the first migration by the Mariani clan to the Neretva valley is not known. However, based on Neretani records, and ancient Roman references to the Mariani family's presence, it is safe to say our family lived in the Neretva Valley for more than 800 years; perhaps longer. The family then migrated to the Island of Vis in the 1600s.

The two dominant religions in the eastern Mediterranean, Christianity and Islam, have been in frequent conflict from the Middle Ages down to early modern times. For generations after the Battle of Lepanto, in 1571, the Ottoman Empire was defeated by the Holy Alliance under Spain, an intense tug of war between East and West for control of the strategically important Dalmatian coast was ever present.

The Mariani family migration from Neretva Valley, after being settled there for 800 years, was presumably to escape constant pillaging by the Ottomans along the coast. It was during this tumultuous time in 1688 Nicolas Mariani (Marianovic(h),[3] began the diaspora from the Neretva Valley to Vis. Nicholas was born in 1671 in Dubrovacko-Neretvanska, Croatia. He was my great-great-great-great-great-grandfather.

However, migrating to Vis was like jumping from the frying pan into the fire. Nikolas left the center of epic battles and constant coastal plundering to Vis, ground-zero for control of the Adriatic. Vis was a grim place under Ottoman military occupation. Nikolas's motivation for migrating is not known; however, love or shame may have played a part.

Nikolas was a child himself when his own son was born, to an unknown spouse. He migrated to Komiza at age 17 with a 5-year-old son in tow. It is possible that the extreme shame associated with children born out of wedlock during the Middle Ages may have motivated Nikolas to move away with his son and from his community.

Mariani family history and Island folklore are replete with hints of royalty and aristocratic status. Genealogical records on Vis include clear references to a Count Mariani. (A "count" didn't necessarily mean royal lineage; it was often a title conferred upon someone for participating in important battles. Battlefield titles proliferated during this period.)

While living for centuries on Vis, our family had no royal courts to attend; they attended rather to their boats as lowly fishermen, and farmed poor-quality, rocky fields. It was a hard life. Third- and fourth-generation Mariani in California nevertheless tend to cling romantically to the Mariani coat of arms and enjoy, with misty eyes, our inferred royal roots from what is more akin to hubris than we might like to admit. The truth is that we were relatively poor farmers when my great-grandfather and grandfather migrated to California with less than $50 to their collective names.

Aside from noble ancestry, there are many tales of secrets, including ones about a black Madonna and about secret Christian treasures and sacred vessels on Vis, and also stories from the northern French / Austrian family lines of our family.

The reason for our third migration, *from* Vis, is not so speculative. My maternal great-grandfather, John Svilich, was born in 1861, when Vis was still under Ottoman control. In 1878, with the help of a coalition of Russians and Austrians, the Ottomans were finally forced off the Dalmatian coast and the island, only to be replaced by another tyrant. In 1882, an important development was initiated on the other side of the ocean, the Linz program. The Linz program was drafted by the radical George Ritter who ushered in the Austro-Hungarian Empire anti Dalmatia sentiment and moved in to occupy Dalmatia.

Panoramic view of Komiza Bay and a sheltered valley on the Island of Vis

The tyrannical rule of Austria-Hungary over the idyllic world of Komiza

became unbearable to my great-grandfather after he was conscripted into the Austro-Hungarian army and ordered to police, and take up arms against, his own people.

In 1889 my great-grandfather deserted and smuggled his way into America. This precipitated the third great migration of the Marianis, eventually to Santa Clara Valley in California just south of the young, romantic and exciting city of San Francisco.

There were five sons and two daughters born of Joseph and Vinka Mariani in the Dalmatian town of Komiza, on the island of Vis, now in Croatia, but at that time part of the Hapsburg Austrian Empire.

Paul Andrew Mariani, my grandfather, the third son, was born on July 22, 1885. The family had a vineyard, made wine to sell, and fished in the summer.

Near the vineyard the Svilich family had their home and when young Paul went to the vineyard with his father he made friends with a little girl named Victoria. He came to see her more often as he grew up and then she suddenly left in 1900 with her mother and sister Antionette, for an odd sounding place called California.

My grandfather followed, but not to escape tyranny; rather it was the result of a love story.

Chapter 3

Arrivals

Maternal Roots

Late 1800s

Little did my great-grandpa, John Svilich realize, when he fled to America, that it would be thirteen years before he saw his wife and his daughter Victoria as well as the child his wife was carrying at the time. John escaped Vis under a cloud of mystery and secrecy. Even his wife had no idea where he was going; all she had from him was a promise that he would send for her and the family after he became established in parts unknown.

In late 1889, John arrived in Portland, Oregon, as he had heard there were Croatians living in the area. Like most Croatians living on islands in the Adriatic, he was a skilled fisherman. For four months he worked, saving his money but also becoming homesick for his Croatian countrymen and culture.

Croatians at that time were also well known for their seamanship. (The Croatian island of Korcula notably claims to be the birthplace of the medieval seaman and voyager Marco Polo. (The celebrated traveler's birthplace is subject to vigorous debate by the Italians.) And, especially in the nineteenth century, Croatian sailors regularly jumped ship to find better opportunities rather than return to their war-ravaged lands. Often unknowingly, Croatian seamen on merchant ships were on a one-way trip to such places as New Orleans, San Pedro and San Francisco.

Not long after the California Gold Rush, by 1857 there were more than fifty Croatian businesses in San Francisco. And it was in San Francisco that the Slavonic Illyrian Mutual and Benevolent Society was formed; it was the first charitable organization of its kind in America.

California: Push and Pull

Croatians were attracted to California because of both '"push" and "pull" forces.

In Europe, from the sixteenth through the eighteenth centuries, land tenure in Europe was limited by the feudal system, and in the nineteenth century, it was still difficult, and in many cases impossible, for farmers, fishermen, and workers to acquire land in any way: by purchase, inheritance, the spoils of war, or by any other means.

In Croatia, and on the Island of Vis in particular, almost all farmers were tenant farmers and farmed for the owner "at will"; this meant that the landowner could kick them off the land at any time and for any reason. Naturally, this created a strong incentive for farmers to want to have legal possession of their own land.

However, Europe had been settled for centuries, and there was no frontier and so no new land to settle. At the same time, in most of Europe in the 1800s, selling land was a social embarrassment for most landowners. It was a sign of financial distress and akin to selling the family's silverware. Consequently, land and other forms of real property seldom came up for sale. This resulted in a cultural environment in which peasants—

the people who actually worked the land—had no opportunity to own it. A good example of this tradition is that our family home, built in the 1500s, is still owned today by members of our family lineage. In 500 years, it has never been put up for sale.

Thus, the idea of being able to purchase good land had incredible allure for the peasant class of Europe.

In the United States, plantation systems in the southeastern regions of the country were largely controlled by an elite aristocracy; there too, it was extremely difficult to buy land. Then rumors began to spread across Europe that in California there was so much territory available that it was possible for almost any man, if he just worked hard, to buy and own his own spread. This is a concept we take for granted today, but for the Europeans of that era, it was a novel, and seductive, dream.

The allure of being able to possess your own land was thus part of the "pull." In addition, there were forces that "pushed" people to migrate—to California in particular.

In 1851, French vintners excitedly discovered a new grape variety indigenous to California. The idea that the French (who often prided themselves on their skills in wine-making) might be able to make an exciting new wine from a mysterious, unknown grape from the New World caused great excitement. The idea was too much for the French to resist, so they brought rootstocks of the new grape back to France and began propagating and testing the grapes vigor in various regions of the country to determine the best soil and climatic conditions for its cultivation.

The grape is known today as the Concord grape, and it makes a truly awful wine, much to the disappointment of the French. But the bad wine made from the grape was the least of their worries, as a cataclysmic disaster had begun, of which they were not yet aware; a ticking time bomb had been set off, caused when they imported the new grape into Europe.

About five years after importing the grape from America, the French discovered they had also imported a disease caused by near-microscopic nematodes of phylloxera attached to the grape's roots. Whereas the Concord grape in America showed no ill affects from the phylloxera because it had developed a natural immunity over thousands of years of evolution, virtually all of the European grape varietals were susceptible. The result was that most of the grapes in Europe were soon wiped out.

Within ten years the wine industry in Europe was completely destroyed. However, the geological isolation provided by the French and Italian Alps safeguarded the vineyards of the Baltic regions. Croatia in particular was spared the scourge of phylloxera. The wine industry on the Dalmatian coast thrived, and for fifteen years there was a great demand for wines from Croatia, at high prices.

This led many Croatian landowners to replace their peasant farmers and plant new vineyards. Young vineyards need less labor for many years until the vines are mature enough to be harvested. This forced most of these peasants back to the sea to fish, in particular for sardines, the area's most plentiful fish.

In the meantime, the world came to understand the causes both of the collapse of the vineyards and of the Concord grape's immunity to phylloxera. Soon Europe and Californian vintners were grafting the surviving varietal grapes onto Concord rootstocks, and Europe, with California's help, successfully and rapidly re-established the cultivation of varietal grapes. In the 1880s, a massive replanting of varietals began to be harvested, creating an instant glut of wine grapes and a collapse of prices. At almost exactly the same time, sardines disappeared from the waters of the Adriatic because of over-fishing.

Facing the collapse of both wine prices and the fishing industry, the landless island peasants had few options.

The persistent reports that there were enormous tracts of land in California available for purchase added pull to push and started drawing a large influx of Croatian farmers and seamen to the west coast of America.

Santa Clara Valley and a Tradition of Mutual Aid

Santa Clara Valley in particular was especially attractive to the Slavic people. The fertile soil, ideal weather, and sheer quantity of land available was a dream come true for these immigrants.

Croatians were, of course, not the only cultural group attracted to Santa Clara Valley. Chinese, Japanese, Italian, Irish, and German immigrants also flocked to the Valley. It was one of the world's few truly egalitarian cultural environments in the late 1800s.

The valley was riddled with little family homesteads comprising of five- to ten-acre parcels. The more prosperous purchased and accumulated large land holdings, but the majority of farms and ranches were small family affairs.

The communities were made up largely of newcomers who quickly developed customs of mutual aid: If someone needed extra help, a neighbor would send over farm hands. If someone needed ladders or boxes or bins for harvesting, these would show up on the front porch as a loan from the neighbors. There were no fences; neighbors tended to trust each other and helped each other out as needed, a custom that prevailed for generations, with neighbors trusting and sharing and helping one another on each other's farms.

This trust spilled over to my grandfather's days in the early decades of the twentieth century. As part of his business, he purchased fruit for more than fifty years without the use of written contracts: his handshake was his contract. My cousin, George Sousa and partner in the dried fruit business, even in the 1950s and '60s, frequently traded hundreds of tons of fruit with our competitors over the phone. For example, if one packer's inventory was short of, say, peaches, but they had too many prunes—and we were short of prunes, with plenty of peaches—we would make a trade, with no paperwork other than internal inventory adjustments. Millions of dollars' worth of goods were exchanged through a discussion on the phone.

One day, when I first began working in the office, I looked out my window and saw one semi-truck after another suddenly come rolling into our receiving yard. And I could see semis leaving our plant, loaded with dried fruit. I asked George, "What are all these trucks doing—coming and going with full loads of fruit?" He said, simply, "We trade for fruit we need, and give our competitors the fruit they need to satisfy *their* customers." These "customers" were often the same customers that we were competing for! This amazing spirit of cooperation and unwavering willingness to give our neighbors a helping hand remains in my mind today. Notwithstanding the common prejudices and outright racism associated with the white/British-based immigrants in the area, the majority of the immigrants in the Valley were, by and large, tolerant of each other; more than tolerant, they openly went out of their way to help each other.

That was the Santa Clara Valley through the 1960s. With the emergence of Silicon Valley, Santa Clara Valley was about to experience the influx of a very different culture.

Before my great grandfather's [John Svilich] arrival to Santa Clara Valley, in the mid to late nineteenth century, Mateo Americh, a sailor from the Croatian island of Brac, and Mark Rabasa, pioneered early Croatian agriculture in Santa Clara and Pajaro Valley by the 1880s. (Later, Jack London, in his novel *Valley of the Moon,* described the Pajaro Valley as "New Dalmatia.")

John Svilich Comes to the Valley

Having heard, up in Portland, that Croatian countrymen were congregating near San Francisco Bay, together with rumors that just south of San Francisco the weather was like the mild Adriatic, in a land with a wonderfully arable soil, my great-grandfather migrated down to what is now known as Cupertino in late 1889.

Fishing was lucrative in the Pacific Northwest, so, every fishing season, John migrated back to Oregon, returning at the end of the season with his earnings so he could pay for the land and orchards he was investing in in the Valley. The Croatians have often viewed fishing as their livelihood and land and orchards as their savings account. At the same time, they never forgot their roots and cultural customs and practices.

Cupertino's appeal to John was for four primary reasons: one, a mild climate; two, fertile soil; three, as we will discuss later, soil that was *not rocky* (this is a serious, long-standing problem in Vis); and four, and most important, cheap land. Cupertino was located in a backwater between San Francisco and San Jose, though not far from either: in short, in the middle of nowhere. Ironically, the land in and around Cupertino was about the only land John could afford to buy. How cheap? Something my Grandfather Paul A. Mariani, Sr., once said might suggest an answer. He was asked his secret in business. "I saved money, and when I had an extra dollar, I would buy another acre of land in Cupertino."

Maternal lineage of Paul A. Mariani, Jr.'s family:

his mother was a Svilicić, buried at the Muster in Komiza.

My great grandfather finally saved enough money to afford to pay for safe passage for his wife and daughter in 1900.

For Great-grandma, it was bittersweet, mostly bitter. Great-grandma Slvilich remained mostly bitter throughout her adult life because she had been uprooted from Komiza, a small, mature, pastoral seaside town, making a comfortable living, going to a church that was a thousand years old, living within walking distance of charming cobbled streets, to come to settle in what she felt was a barbaric country. The nearest church was well over twenty miles away. In the wintertime, the horses had to pull the wagon taking Great-grandma through mud often high as the hubcaps, to get to Mission Santa Clara, which had given the valley its name. [4]

Great grandfather was just a farmer as agricultural work and agricultural investment seemed the natural thing to do in Santa Clara Valley, in fact in most of the United States, in those days. Approximately 41% of the American population worked directly in agriculture; over 70% were either directly or indirectly involved in feeding themselves and each other. And life on the farms was hard.

The photographs above show that life on the farm was hard work, but it would rapidly change, especially in the twentieth century.

Although my great grandfather and grandfather were always looking for better ways to accomplish farm tasks, harvesting, and packing through the use of clever technical devices, he could have had no concept of how technology born in the Valley where he had lived and worked for most of his life, and which would come to be known as "Silicon Valley," would, during his lifetime, transform not only agriculture, but the entire modern way of life in a way he would hardly be able to recognize.

Great-grandma Svilich considered much of the local "English settler" high society vulgar and uneducated. And a farm worker was clearly below her station in life. This was another reason she was bitter, living in the middle of nowhere, surrounded by what felt to her like a social and cultural vacuum.

Besides being angry about her circumstances, Great-grandma Svilich was angry about the local society and how it treated women. The turn of the twentieth century in Santa Clara Valley was an era when sons were in great favor and girls were primarily valued for domestic work. But it was also an era when women were becoming increasingly aware of their second-class status in society at large. The suffragists (then called "suffragettes") were becoming vocal in England and elsewhere, and their movement was having an effect in America and an influence on Victoria.

Chapter 4

The madness of love is the greatest of heaven's blessings.

Plato

A Romance

Djede and Victoria:

1800's – 1900

Although the Mariani family migration began with my great-grandfather John Svilich's bold escape from tyranny, the story of my paternal grandfather's migration began as a result of an epic love story between Paul and Victoria.

In the last 1800's John's Svilich called for his daughter, Victoria and his wife to America, leaving Paul behind, hearts were broken. The journey began for my grandfather following his love and his heart.

The families of Paul Mariani, Sr., and Victoria Svilich both grew up Island of Vis, one of a chain of islands in the Adriatic Sea, known as "the sea of a thousand islands." Paul was a tall with broad shoulders light hair and blue eyes. Victoria was also slender, graceful with flashing dark eyes: opposites attract.

Vis, is the beautiful with its white-sand beaches and stunning, aqua-blue waters. The respective families grew grapes for wine-making, lavender for the mainland oil market, olives, and a variety of vegetables; they fished, and they made wine and olive oil for the local island market. Small animals, such as goats, were kept on the ground floor of both family houses for heat. The heat generated by the animals heated the upper two stories during winter. Fireplaces were used sparingly, as trees are not abundant on the Island. The fireplaces doubled for the cooking. It was hardly a regal existence.

At the time of Paul Mariani Sr's arrival in California, the Mexican-American War was a now a dim memory, with California having joined the

Union, as a spoil of war from Mexico, in 1850; however, the same period marked the beginning of exponential population growth in the state as a result of a series of epochal events, from finding gold, silver, and quicksilver to ultimately something more enduring and of greater value: the establishment of agriculture.

My grandfather's migration to Santa Clara, while motivated out of love, was also motivated by broader social, historical, economic, and even geological phenomena. Joel Kotkin, an internationally recognized authority on global economic, political, and social trends, states, "With movement west into its wide expanses, America offered a welcome refuge for Europeans who sought freedom from the shackles of a still-entrenched feudal culture. America's persistent agricultural surplus and a general labor shortage during the colonial era made it possible for peasants who migrated to America to enjoy freedom from starvation, as well as higher wages, lower mortality rates, and a greater opportunity to own land."

Santa Clara Valley's soil was generally not as rocky, as it was on the Island of Vis, and so it was easier to cultivate and plant trees. And land in America was not automatically handed down to the first-born son. On Vis, if you were the second son, you were landless and worked for your older brother. Even with the prospects of a dim future, and of leaving the only home he knew, it was not until Djede fell in love that he listened to his heart and moved to venture to an unknown land.

Paul Mariani Sr. was a tall, broad-shouldered, strong-willed man's man; he also was a softhearted, soft-spoken gentleman all his life. My earliest recollection Paul Mariani Sr was that he wore a woolen-tweed the three-piece suit over long-john underwear [modern day "onesie's"] year-round. He walked with a limp and used a cane.

While living in San Francisco, he saw a young child flying down one of the hills of San Francisco out of control on a scooter heading towards an intersection with heavy traffic. He jumped in front of the scooter to stop the pending catastrophe. The little child's wagon came crashing into his outstretched leg. He stopped the wagon and saved the little boy's life. His heroic effort was at the expense of damaging his growth plate in one leg. He grew several inches after the accident. To compensate, he had a custom-made shoe with a 2.5-inch thick sole to minimize his limp. Djede was always courageous, principled, with a distinct sense of justice. He also responded to injustice, although not always wisely.

Back in Djede's home town of Komiza, there was no elementary school on the Island. However, just off the coast from Komiza lay an island called Biševo, with a one room school house. Paul attended this school, commuting to and from the island daily by boat. On one occasion, during Paul's third year at the school, a schoolmaster came down unduly hard with a whipping on a classmate and friend of Paul's for a minor infraction. Paul perceived the schoolmaster's actions as cruel and unjust. He had been taught at home that all actions, good or bad, had consequences. So he wanted the schoolmaster to know that being cruel had consequences—at least, that was Paul's reasoning for opening the door of the schoolmaster's personal aviary and letting the schoolmaster's entire collection of rare birds go free. The schoolmaster was particularly incensed because the collection had been three decades in the making. The schoolmaster saw to it that Paul never went back to school—that was the end of his formal education, at age 9.

Many years later, Djede spoke with me about this incident and discussed the lesson he had learned: that retaliation was different from defending someone or righting a wrong. Djede lamented that many groups in the Balkans had never learned the lesson he learned from releasing the birds: that righting a wrong with a wrong is also wrong. I didn't appreciate his point until many years later, when I read my dad's recollections of the horrific ethnic-cleansing in Bosnia during the 1990s.

The author sailing into the port of Komiza

When Paul Sr. first arrived in Santa Clara Valley, his imagination was captured. "Imagine," he told me, many years later, "There were no rocks! . . .

That's to say, no rocks had to be moved and hauled away just to farm a few square feet or plant a tree."

On my first visit to Vis, my mouth was agape to see fields as far as the eye could see, with rocks piled in the middle of each of them, often huge mounds of rocks—mounds surrounded by rock walls (forming stone pens) so the rocks could be up piled as high as possible. The rocks had come from clearing small plots of land. Literally millions of rocks had been moved by hand throughout the island.

Example of rock mounds that resulted after clearing the stone soil of Vis

John Svilich's daughter, Victoria, was a tall, stately, well-educated young woman with brunette hair and flashing black eyes, who, at the age of 14, caught the eye of Paul Andrew Mariani in the streets of Komiza. The result was a sweet, intense, and unstoppable love story that would result in their years later in the far-off land of California in 1907, in spite of a formidable obstacle: Victoria's mother. But there were even more obstacles in store for the couple before their love could triumph.

Courtship

They say people are attracted to their opposites. This cannot be more evident than in Paul and Victoria. We called Paul Mariani Sr, "Djede," which means grandfather in Croatian; I often refer to Paul Mariani, Sr., as Djede in this book, from force of habit and fond memories.

Victoria was a brilliant woman, a refined and well-educated young lady. As a young teenager she was bilingual in Croatian and Italian before she came to America; she read, wrote, and spoke both languages fluently. Paul, though enormously bright, left school at nine years old, struggled his whole life with the arts, and could hardly read or write. However, he knew how to count, which served him well in business throughout his life.

One of Djede's darkest days came when he learned that his teenage friend and the first love of his life was leaving Croatia forever at the age of 14 to join her father in America. Djede told me he cried his eyes out most of that first night. He spent the better part of the next year arguing unsuccessfully with his older brothers to convince them that he should go to Cupertino, California, in America. His family would not let him leave.

When young Paul was 16, realized he had to do something drastic. For the next twelve months he stubbornly refused to work in the family vineyard, thus foreshadowing the determination and shrewdness that would serve him so well in the future. By the time he turned 17, his brothers were so exasperated, they told Paul he wasn't any good in Croatia so he might as well go to America. His share of the family estate consisted of a third-class steerage fare to New York, $ 40 left over in cash.

Mariani ancestral home in Komiza, circa 1911

In June 2011, one hundred years later, we peered from the same windows of our family home, which has remained virtually identical for centuries.

To the New World

On Vis, Paul and his family were fishermen and vintners by trade. Upon Paul's arrival at Ellis Island in the fall of 1902, however, he found that his skills had little market value; he had virtually no education and essentially no money. But the 17-year-old was determined to make his way to the West Coast to be reunited with Victoria.

He decided he could not just show up broke in Cupertino. While in New York, he heard that fishermen were making a lot of money in the Pacific Northwest, which was closer to Victoria than where he was. He also remembered Victoria reading letters from her father describing the good fishing in that area. So, he began to do odd jobs in New York in a coconut factory for $1.50 per day to make enough money to get to Washington State. After a few months, he had saved enough to take a riverboat, then a train, to Washington. Victoria was constantly in young Paul's mind, as he longed to be reunited with his love. But near disaster was in store for him.

Being used to the calm waters of the Adriatic, Paul was not prepared for the turbulence of the seas in a little fishing boat off the Pacific Northwest. He nearly drowned during his first outing at sea. Other family members later would not be so lucky and gave their lives while fishing the same treacherous waters off the Vancouver coast in a family-group effort to pay the costs of establishing themselves as farmers in Santa Clara. Paul fortunately escaped with his life and eventually headed south to meet up with Victoria. But the homecoming for Paul was not a celebration for the Svilich family.

There were no gray areas for Great grandmother Svilich, she either liked you very much or quite the opposite. She was highly educated, speaking five languages from limited and somewhat primitive resources available on the Island of Vis. Great-grandmother Svilich made no bones about it. She was not happy about the prospect of marriage between her daughter and a 17-year-old day laborer—uneducated, a rebel, and essentially broke.

According to my father, "Grandma Svilich, while having a comfortable home and stature in the community, was unhappy and angry because she had little choice but to live in the backwaters of San Francisco." She was fit to be tied over Victoria's interest in Paul.

After all, Victoria, who had the equivalent of a high school education in Europe and an additional two years of advanced education in America, was a brilliant linguist in her own right; she was also refined and well-mannered, from the careful cultural grooming she had received from her mother.

Paul's lack of formal education was just too much for Great-grandma. Her resentment, strong will, and fierce determination continued well into the married life of her daughter with Paul [Djede.] She even had a hard time accepting any of her grandchildren subsequently from the union who appeared genetically more Mariani than Svilich.

A byproduct of Djede's mother-in-law's persistent derisions over his lack of education seeded his own realization of the importance of a formal education. Djede became determined that his own children would have both formal schooling and a higher education.

Great-grandpa John Svilich, on the other hand, got along well with everyone and made quite a reputation for himself in the Cupertino area. He had started as a day laborer and, through hard work and dedication, was becoming a substantial fruit farmer and fruit dryer, creating the foundations of our family's business in the years to come. As mentioned, it took him thirteen years to save enough money to bring his wife and two daughters from Komiza to America. He then added to the family, with several boys, three of whom survived to adulthood.[5]

Friends of the Mariani family in Komiza had preceded Djede to the West Coast; these included Doctor Kucich , who operated a company that manufactured barrels, known as cooperage works, making wine barrels from oak wood. Paul earned $16 a month. his board and room cost $14 a month. Each Saturday, Djede, taking his bicycle with him, would ride the train from San Francisco to Sunnyvale, then pedal to Cupertino, to go courting under the grim, watchful eye of Great-grandma Svilich—which meant there was always a third party present whenever he saw Victoria. Towards the end of the month, when the extra $2 after his room and board had been used up, Djede would pedal all the way from San Francisco for his one-hour visit, then find a place to stay overnight, sometimes in the barns of fellow Croatians. Very early the next morning he would get up and pedal all the way back to San Francisco in time to make it to work.

Djede, in the center, posing with other coopers 1902

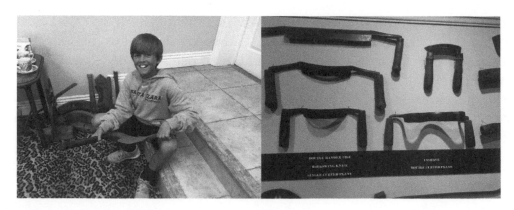

Left: My grandson Joe Wallace, holding the same cooperage tool my grandfather held in his hands 115 years earlier

Right: Cooperage tools from a century ago

One April evening, Djede was in San Francisco preparing to travel north to Washington to fish. Apparently, getting ready for the trip involved visiting friends and sharing spirits—lots of spirits. Djede never told us the exact amount he drank on the evening of April 17, 1906. Whatever it was, it was enough to keep him sound "asleep" and remain asleep at 5:12 a.m. on April 18, 1906, through the Great San Francisco Earthquake.

Djede slept through the famous earthquake. One wall of his room collapsed around him and an alarm clock lay on the floor next to him after it struck his head. Djede didn't wake up until Red Cross workers came upon him, thinking he was dead. In later years, when recounting the story, Djede omitted the revelry the night before and earnestly tells the story that a clock bonked him on the head, knocking him out as his way to explain the reason he was "unaware" of the earth shaking. The family never fully bought-in to the clock theory. Whatever the cause, he wore a scar on his forehead for the rest of his days, as a reminder for the rest of us to tease him a bit about how he got it.

Four views of San Francisco after the Great Earthquake of 1906, one also showing the fire that followed.

Djede slept through this disaster.

The whole truth of the night of April 16th and early morning of the 17th will never be known. However, Djede did have to deal with the aftermath of the quake, beginning around 8:30 a.m. There were brick-laid streets ripped open like zippers, and makeshift camps all over the city for displaced families.

Three days after the quake, while he was in a Red Cross tent camp, Djede wrote on a matchbox, "I am OK." Amazingly, the matchbox was delivered by the Red Cross two days later to Victoria in Cupertino. She trembled as she read Djede's few words, then fell to her knees and wept with joyful relief. Her sobbing was unrelenting until she was comforted by her mother.

Eighty-three years later, in 1989, the Loma Prieta earthquake struck northern California. The epicenter was near Santa Cruz, south of the San Francisco Bay Area. My brother Paul Mariani III, living in Australia, heard news flashes about the quake, complete with inaccurate claims: Associated Press bulletins reported, incorrectly, that the Golden Gate Bridge had collapsed (actually, it was a small section of the San Francisco Bay Bridge), that the "East Bay Freeway" had collapsed (this was the Nimitz Freeway), and that San Francisco and Oakland were in ruins. Paul feared the worst.

The news reported that the epicenter was south of the Bay Area, in Santa Cruz. Cupertino and the Santa Clara Valley lie between Santa Cruz and San Francisco: Paul was intimately familiar with Bay Area geography. Paul had good reason to fear the worst.

He reasoned, and agonized, that if San Francisco and Oakland were in ruins and the center of the quake was in Santa Cruz, everything between San Francisco and Santa Cruz must be devastated. And that was where virtually his entire family lived. Paul's fear was heightened as he frantically tried, without success, to call our mother and his brothers and sisters; all the lines were dead.

Immediately following the quake there was a communication blackout throughout the Bay Area, due to a combination of power failures, severed lines, and a massive communication traffic jam when too many people tried to call in to, and out of, the area at the same time. The state's entire communication system went into overload—particularly for calls from and to the Bay Area.

Paul agonized for three days in a vain attempt to contact any member of his extended family.

View of a San Francisco neighborhood after the Loma Prieta earthquake of 1989

I finally got a short fax out to him that said, "Family all OK." Paul told me later that he literally fell to his knees and wept in relief.

The San Andreas fault near San Francisco, shortly after the 1906 quake

Geological faults—the cause of earthquakes—often produce, over long periods of time, many artesian wells and springs, and water attracts people and settlements. The San Andreas Fault is no exception. Despite the geological instability of the area, made manifestly clear to us by the '06 earthquake, a broad range of Europeans and Asians continued to migrate to the San Francisco area. Over the next thirty years these immigrants included other Marianis, travelling from Vis to the region in and around Santa Clara Valley.

Djede's bicycle was actually a step up in transportation, as horses were the usual choice if you didn't want to walk. Automobiles were just being introduced into the area; by 1910 they had become the transportation of choice.

The automobile would soon become a very popular option for those who could afford it. This new-fangled contraption, with its supporting network of suppliers, mechanics, fueling stations, and the like, quickly displaced the area's carriage makers, feed stores, manure managers, and blacksmiths; not the last time the Valley would be invaded by a "disruptive technology," as it would be called one day.

Paul Mariani had found favor with John Svilich because of his hard work and honesty, but most of all, because Paul clearly loved his daughter, he finally got permission from John Svilich to marry Victoria. It is unclear whether Great-grandma Svilich ever gave explicit permission for the marriage; she may have simply accepted a fait accompli. Regardless, a year following the quake, in 1907 Djede married Victoria, the woman of his heart in 1907 at age 22 at the Mission Santa Clara.

Djede and Victoria: My grandparents' wedding picture[7]

Victoria commanded five languages (Croatian, Latin, French, English, Spanish), all self-taught or tutored by her mother. As years went by, it was clear she had different ideas regarding the traditional nuclear family and old-world class systems.

Victoria was, like her mother, a formidable force. She was an early proponent of an amendment to the U.S. constitution establishing equal rights for women [8] and became a driving force in the local women's suffrage movement. She had a very strong sense of justice, and whenever a female in the area was being treated unjustly, she was there to champion the cause of fairness and justice. She escaped any meaningful mistreatment as a result of her efforts by living in California, a progressive state. Californians didn't react as defensively as the east coast establishment; she was courageous nonetheless.

Women were often legally defenseless in America, as they remain so in many parts of the world today. Dad remembered Great-grandma Svilich's telling him about her friends and fellow suffragists jailed for picketing the White House, demanding the vote. Their sole offense had been carrying protest signs at the White House. Their story was horrific: By the end of the night, they were barely alive. Forty prison guards, wielding clubs and with their warden's blessing, had gone on a rampage against the thirty-three women.

This "Night of Terror" occurred on November 15, 1917. The warden of the Occoquan Workhouse in Virginia ordered his guards to teach a lesson to the suffragists imprisoned there because they had dared to picket Woodrow Wilson's White House for the right to vote. For weeks, the women's only water came from an open pail. Their food—all of it colorless slop, according to what, as a child, I over-heard the adults saying and later found confirmed by public records— was infested with worms. My memory of table talk by the adults during my childhood is too fuzzy for exact details, but based upon archive news sources that I consulted, the treatment of the women was indeed horrific. The guards are described as grabbing, dragging, beating, choking, slamming, pinching, twisting, and kicking the women. Some individual stories that I found I give below:

Lucy Burns: Lucy Burns was beaten, her hands were chained to the cell bars above her head, and she was left hanging for the night, bleeding and gasping for air.

Doris Lewis and Alice Cosu: Doris Lewis was hurled into a dark cell, her head was smashed against an iron bed, and she was knocked cold. Her cellmate, Alice Cosu suffered a heart attack because she thought Lewis was dead.

Alice Paul: When one of the leaders, Alice Paul, embarked on a hunger strike, she was tied to a chair, a tube was forced down her throat, and liquid was poured into her until she vomited. She was tortured like this for weeks until word was smuggled out to the press.

Grandmother had small victories in the suffragist movement, but they were victories nevertheless. She helped change the family's ancient culture of giving everything to the first-born son, replacing this tradition by giving to all her children equally and regardless of sex. Her actions, and my grandfather's open mindedness, provided an example within the local Croatian community of a new sense of equality. Even the customary naming system—a paternal-centric system—was abandoned within the local Croatian community. Although naming someone after your grandfather was regarded as a symbolic token of respect, it was also part of a caste system with privileges based on birthrights given to children, unable to know better, by virtue of who was born first or who had "inside or outside plumbing" at birth (an expression Victoria used to distinguish men from women). The strict naming tradition, she pointed out, precluded the possibility there might be another person worthier for a newborn child to be named after. The worth of someone's character was more important to give tribute to than the accident of descent.

Victoria was an early proponent of an amendment to the U.S. constitution establishing equal rights for women[9] and became a driving force in the local women's suffrage movement. She had a very strong sense of justice, and whenever a female in the area was being treated unjustly, she was there to champion the cause of fairness and justice.

When John Svilich died, Great-grandma Svilich became the sole owner of all of the Svilich family farms' considerable holdings. Great-grandma Svilich, in a moment of great irony for a champion of women's rights, bequeathed her entire estate to the Svilich boys, with a cryptic note, according to the Svilich family archives: "My daughters married successful men—they don't need the money." Victoria was enraged at this giving of the estate to the boys to the exclusion of the girls; resulting in a feud between Victoria and her Svilich relatives.

There is no doubt that it was Victoria's perspective on women rights as well that influenced Djede to divide his estate evenly among his children, breaking from the tradition of giving everything to the first-born son, who, in this case, would have been my father. The old way would have been to my immediate family's benefit. But my dad always referred to Djede's break with tradition with such reverence and respect that it made us all proud of the way the family estate was distributed after my grandfather's passing. In fact, the thought of receiving a larger share of the family inheritance never entered my mind until the writing of this family history.

The Croatian custom of naming the first-born son after the paternal grandfather was broken when my dad was born. Under the old ways, my dad would have been named Josip, but, in defiance of hallowed tradition, he was baptized Wilbur Paul Mariani (he later changed his name to Paul, Junior, a story that will be told later in this book). This was a family scandal, causing quiet whispers that continued for decades.

The Paul Mariani, Sr., family unit is a story of contrasts—nobility and refined education on one hand, illiteracy and pauperism on the other. We came from both traditions, making us both proud and humble—but mostly humble.

PART II

1900–1970's

Chapter 5

"Justice is a 'human virtue' that makes a man self-consistent and good."

Plato

Getting Started

A Sense of Justice

Santa Clara Valley was settled by a wide variety of ethnic groups: English, Chinese, Japanese, Russian, Spanish, Italians, and Yugoslavians and of course Native Americans, to name only a few. These groups settled in little clumps throughout the Valley, in rural, homogenous ghettos. The different groups had strong ethnic identities, generally seemed to get along well—except for the Serbians and Croatians. There was never a lot of trust between Serbians and Croatians, a tradition that dates back more than a thousand years. I personally did not understand the level of mistrust between some of the Balkan peoples and cultures until years later.

At the time that my grandfather arrived in Santa Clara, the Valley was only a step away from the Wild West. Indians still lived and worked at the Santa Clara Mission. Djede called the Indians, interchangeably, Ohlone or Costanoans; although they were distinct tribes, they spoke a common so-called Costanian language. Some of the Indians helped out on Djede's ranch. Djede said they spoke an odd, now extinct language, "Tamyen," spoken (according to ethnologists) exclusively by the Costanoans of Santa Clara Valley and nearby. It is strange to think that, during my short time on earth, an entire culture and language have disappeared before my eyes.

While America was giving birth to a new industrial revolution, Djede arrived, at the turn of the century, in a Cupertino still stuck in the era of "cowboys and Indians," complete with cattle ranches, ladies in carriages, and wooden sidewalks. There was an abundance of opportunity and plenty of land, but the social structure in Santa Clara Valley was defined by a combination of culture and color. The whites, blacks, yellows, browns, and reds essentially represented different cultures. The society in Santa Clara Valley at the time of my grandfather's arrival was arranged according to these labels, together with the stereotypes that went along with them.

The English who began to dominate Californian, society by sheer force of numbers, through successive waves of immigration, considered themselves "white"; Indians "red"; Hispanics (largely Spanish/Indian mixes) "brown." The Chinese and Japanese were considered "yellow." And of course, African people were called "black" or by a term formed by an English corruption for people from Nigeria. Even the U.S. government made distinctions based on skin color. Certain derogatory terms, such as "Chinks" and "Japs," were not part of the local vocabulary at the time—these are artifacts from the Second World War that were designed to dehumanize soldiers trained to kill.

At the time of Paul Mariani, Sr.'s arrival in Santa Clara Valley, Croatian, Italian, and Japanese immigrants were the working class for the dominant English. The power elite was no longer made up of local Hispanic landowners created by Spanish land grants, as in times before the Gold Rush, but rather, predominately, a ruling class of English landowners. Those with English or northern European descent held political and social power.

My Uncle Louie explained: "In Italian immigration papers, a distinction was made between 'Northern' Italians and 'Southern' Italians—stamped right on their papers." The meaning and reason for the immigration notation was to make the distinction that Southern Italians were not considered "white."

Skin color conferred social status. Even in 1950, color was a big issue in California. By 1950, our dried fruit company was one of the biggest employers in the area. Across the street from our processing plant was the Cupertino De Oro Social Club. My grandfather, Djede, was denied membership because he was not considered "all white," even though we were comparatively light-skinned Mediterranean's. We didn't readily "burn" red in the sun, but we did have a farmers tan! Rejection from membership didn't bother Djede; it was the reason behind the rejection he loathed—his heightened sense of justice was made manifest when he dissociated himself from all members of the Club.

Prior to the World War II, the Japanese American community in California was well established. The loss of dignity and property caused by their forced transfer to relocation camps cannot be understated. Scores of Japanese went to serve America in the war only to return home to families who had lost everything after being hauled off to relocation camps. Without the ability to run their businesses, they defaulted on their mortgages. Even worse, the general community turned their backs on the returning Japanese American soldiers from the 442nd Infantry Regiment in the 100th brigade by treating the Japanese Americans as if they were the enemy. Prejudices, anger, and irrational emotions ran high.

Djede said simply, "This is not right," --Djede was a man of few words. He hired all the returning ethnic Japanese-American soldiers and their family members that he could afford to employ - though there were whispers in the family that he had taken on more than he could really afford.

Djede suffered the jeers of being a traitor for hiring Japanese workers. It was only upon reflection, and when reading my dad's recollections, that I understood, thirty years later, why there were so many Japanese Americans working in our processing plant; forklift drivers called "Sarge" or "Luie," for "Sergeant" or "Lieutenant," etc. They were all part of a Japanese military contingent who had fought bravely for America. Most of these returning soldiers and their families hired by Djede ended up working their entire productive lives for the Mariani Packing Company. The loyalty and hard work and sense of family at the plant was unmistakable.

An aside: When unions tried to unionize our operation by force, using strong-arm tactics in the late 1960s, they were astonished when they were literally kicked off the premises, not by management, but spontaneously by our employees. The union organizers never came back.

As time went on, my family owed special thanks and gratitude for the loyalty and hard work of our employees, which permitted us to survive the tough decades between 1950 and 1970—the most difficult and competitive period in the dried fruit industry. Within those twenty short years, we saw seventy-eight packing companies dwindle down to nine, but we survived, largely thanks to our loyal hardworking Japanese community. We owe them a great debt.

I treasure the stories my dad told me about how Djede stood up and defended our brave solders against neighbors and so-called friends. The

Japanese community's marvelous loyalty and friendship will always hold a special place in my heart.

I have a clear memory of my father's telling me that workers who work hard will someday start buying land and found their own businesses. "Someday, David, there will be Mexican mayors."

At the time it was hard to conceive the transition from migrant workers to business owners, much less to holders of public office. But my dad proved prophetic. Today, "Rodriguez Plumbing" or "Mendez Electric" does not seem out of place; it seems even normal. San Jose sported Ron Gonzales as its mayor in 1998. Our growing community of people with Mexican or Central or South American roots, owning land and businesses and holding political office is the new normal. It's the essence of the American dream, which provides a pathway for economic, social, and political upward mobility.

Changing demographics

The profile of labor was changing; for example, from the days, early in the automobile era, when specialized mechanics drove your car for you, to later, when you just drove yourself, displacing employed drivers. (Which reminds me of my grandfather's version of parallel parking, which was to nose, head first, into a space, then get out of the car, walk to the back bumper, pick up the car with his two hands, and move the back end to the curb. He was a strong man, but cars were light in the early 1900s.)

The point is that, even at that time, many years before Santa Clara Valley became "Silicon Valley," technology was already beginning to eliminate jobs, with such things as cars you could control yourself and little labor-saving devices in the orchards, eliminating harvesting jobs. Grandfather called many of these inventions "handy"; my dad called them "clever." Later they were simply called "innovation"; then came "disruptive technologies."

Chapter 6

"Be as you wish to seem"

Socrates 399 BC

Wilbur Paul Mariani / Paul Andrew Mariani, Jr.: My Father

In 1919, Cupertino was still a sleepy backwater between San Francisco and San Jose. The population was measured by the hundreds in the hills and a few thousand in the flatlands. Most people lived on farms. But by 1919, the Great War, "the war to end all wars", was finally over and there was an outburst of joy and hope. Perhaps Wilbur Paul was a fruit of that joy and belief in the future. Wilbur Paul was a strong blonde blue-eyed boy. Father and Son adored each other.

Wilbur Paul was no joy to Victoria, however. He was born almost 13 pounds and, according to his mother, "(Giving birth to) Wilbur damn near killed me. I am not doing that again!" History shows that Wilbur Paul would be her last baby.

Besides Wilbur Paul being an energetic handful, the world around the Marianis in Cupertino was rapidly changing. For example, a little-known bank—founded in San Francisco and a source of loans for rebuilding the devastated city by the redoubtable, San Jose–born Amadeo Giannini, immediately following the '06 earthquake and fire—was beginning to prosper: The Bank of Italy as it was known at that time. Its headquarters building was constructed in 1926 in downtown San Jose. It later became known as Bank of America. Because the agricultural community was composed largely of people with Italian and Croatian roots, it was natural for the bank to acquire a large percentage of the agricultural community as customers. Within a few decades, the bank became a huge financial presence on the West Coast; Bank of America provided critical financing for local agriculture for more than a century and, later, became a major funding source for a growing number of high-tech startups in "Silicon Valley."

My father's memoir is a series of revealing stories about his life in the Valley, dictated onto an audio tape when he was 57 years old. It gives us a peek into the life and times of Santa Clara Valley before it became Silicon Valley.

Wilbur Paul Mariani was born to a ready-made family with three sisters. In this setting, it is easier to understand why, as the youngest child, and the only son, he developed the abundant capacity to absorb attention and love and affection that he was to show throughout his life—and why he had so little patience with people who disagreed with him.

The first public evidence of Wilbur Paul's impatience, over-confidence, and *un*worldly wisdom was revealed when Victoria and Paul Mariani, in 1921, wanted to take a trip of many months' duration to Europe, and in particular Yugoslavia, on their second honeymoon. As my father recalled:

"Mum and Dad had no difficulty farming out their three lovely little daughters to family and friends, but, according to Dad, not a single friend or relative would agree to take care of the spoiled little brat, Wilbur Paul Mariani, even at the tender age of two."

The result was that Paul and Victoria found it necessary to take along with them this dynamic little toddler. As the story goes, after reaching England, mother and dad and child stayed over in a posh London hotel. Just as dinner was being served, the two-year-old decided that he too should have a puff of his father's cigarette. The parents had already incurred the wrath of the headwaiter because children weren't usually allowed in the main dining room at night, and when the two-year-old started roaring because he couldn't have his smoke, Paul Sr. had a quick decision to make: smother the two-year-old, strangle the waiter, or give the little demon a puff. So, with all eyes around them disapproving the undisciplined behavior of the toddler, Paul Sr. simply held his cigarette under the table and Wilbur Paul crawled down to take his puff, then stood up with smoke coming out of his mouth, shocking the onlookers.

His mother and dad managed to survive London and travelling through France, Italy, and Yugoslavia. But they found walking the streets of Sarajevo to be another matter.

The Travelling Family of Three

My father [Wilbur Paul] remembered, this largely Muslim city in Yugoslavia was where, for the first time in his life, Wilbur Paul saw veiled female faces, and interpreted the covering up as some kind of disguise, with mischievous intent or possibly worse. For whatever the reason, it angered the little boy, who broke away from his parents and ran ahead and started kicking the poor Muslim women in the shins, berating them for hiding their faces. Mother and dad stopped this nonsense very quickly but of course were very embarrassed and apologetic to the injured veiled women. The women were puzzled because they had never seen a woman going unveiled in public, like my grandmother, Victoria Mariani.

Curiously, Wilbur Paul's first conscious recollection was not of America; it was of my great-grandma Mariani cautioning him in a very authoritative tone to be careful not to fall down the steps. These were the steep stone steps going up to the living quarters of the Mariani stone house in Komiza, which the toddler encountered on this same trip.

When the trio returned to California after being overseas for eight months, Wilbur Paul's young, now 3-year-old's English vocabulary had completely disappeared and had been replaced by a 3-year-old's Yugoslav vocabulary. When my dad met his sisters [Winifred, Mathilda and Irene] he couldn't speak a word of English to them.

Picture of my grandfather, Paul Mariani, Sr. ("Djede"), Grandma Victoria Svilich Mariani, and my father as a boy, Paul A. Mariani, Jr

My father recalls, "*With a communication barrier, frustration often led to violence. When Dad disagreed with his sisters seriously enough, the only way he knew how to communicate was violently—poor Winnie once caught a heavy crystal saltshaker in the back of her head. Irene got a (thank God) dull kitchen knife thrown at her for some unremembered injury.*

Mathilda didn't have too much to do with dad because he had usurped her territory of being the youngest in the family. It would seem like at one stage there somewhere, the whole family decided that this little animal had to be tamed.

It was during this period, at the age of 3 to 4, that I sometimes disliked my Uncle Jack, who was living with us, because of the discipline he imposed on me. He gave me small tasks—I thought small enough to be ignored. Uncle Jack thought differently. I nevertheless respected and loved him very much as I still do. It was my father that I kept very high on a pedestal and as I think back, my mum had a lot to do with that. Whereas mum and dad had their usual battles as most couples have, I suppose, but when it came down to discipline me, they had a tremendously solid front that I consciously or unconsciously found impossible to divide and conquer. I loved both my mother and father. However, I had admiration for my father, nurtured by things that I heard from friends and neighbors and relatives and the respect that people paid to him. I always felt so lucky to be Paul Mariani's son. This prompted me at age 4 to change my name from Wilbur Paul to Paul Andrew Junior.

There were many pre-school experiences that I treasure in my memory, and some of those that stick in my mind were the work experiences. It was usual in those days for all members of the family on a farm to work, particularly during

harvest time. It was simply not considered an option to do anything but work in the summertime. There were no alternatives like a summer holiday. The younger the person was, the more he felt accepted by his peers as a young adult when he joined the work force.

Early in life I learned, when I was around adults, that if I stayed put and was quiet, it would pay dividends. I learned there was a time to perform and time to keep quiet. I learned that when my father would say "show this gentleman how you can write your name" at age 4, I would laboriously print out Paul A Mariani, Jr., and explain that I had changed my name. In fact I used my self-adopted name all through school, draft boards, and marriage license. It wasn't until we had four children that I officially had to go before a court and have my name changed legally to Paul A. Mariani, Jr., in order to get a passport for overseas travel."

Childhood Illnesses

My father continued down memory lane: "*The second to the fourth grade were difficult years, because it seemed that I was down with one illness or another almost half of the time. In the second grade it was a kidney disorder called Bright's disease, which in those days was often fatal—the body had to overcome the infection by itself if it was to survive, because there were no miracle drugs in those days. I remember the tough and venerable Dr. Hall calling several doctors and specialists out to the house to consult with them, and I remember hearing parts of whispered phrases: 'hospital,' 'fatal,' and that sort of thing, which really didn't bother me as much then as I suppose it would now. I just remember feeling very, very sick and very tired, and also remember being completely turned off on malted milk, which seemed to be the only item of my diet for a period of about four months. There was no meat at all for four months. I have been a real carnivore ever since.*

I remember, night after night, my father, Jack Mariani, and John Palgrusa doing shifts around the clock, heating bricks in the old wood stove, then wrapping them in towels and bringing them to my bed every few minutes in order to keep me warm. There was no central heating or electric blankets in those days.

One incident stuck in my mind. Joe Mardesich came to visit me during this period—I remember exploding at him for no good reason at all, just that I was weak and irritable and without patience, maybe because he was up and walking about and I was stuck in bed. In any event, his older brother, John, heard my tirade and came in, and he said, 'Paul, Joe just came to see you to see how you were feeling, you shouldn't jump at him that way.' I remember being very ashamed of myself, and I tried to remember that circumstance when I am aware that people are not feeling well and they are irritable towards me. I can't say that I have developed that virtue to a fine degree—but the experience taught me a valuable lesson. After going through that spate of childhood diseases—pleurisy, mumps, scarlet fever, and I'm not sure what else—one after another in seemingly endless procession, I felt for a time like a tragic victim of an impressive parade of momentous events. But in reality, I was just a ten-year-old boy, recovering from a series of illnesses."

Chapter 7

New Family Arrivals in the United States

My father's memoirs continued:

"Jack Mariani and his family arrived in the Valley from Komiza in 1932. Amongst them was Luka (later he Americanized his name to "Louis" and was usually called "Louie" by us); he was about Dad's age and in Dad's class throughout the rest of grammar and high school. Dad recalls, "We became as close as two brothers could become." Dad and Louie enjoyed a very special relationship, beginning in childhood and continuing throughout their entire adult life."

In my father's [Paul Mariani Jr] memoir "My Life and My Dreams," Dad tenderly reminisced about his childhood, and about Louie in particular:

"Before high school, Louis and I shared our life and dreams together. Louis and I both decided university wasn't for us. Louis and I decided we could get through high school in three years. We strategized that we could take enough music units in order to gather enough units in three years to graduate. By seventh grade we had decided we were already prepared for the world, to start in the business world through farming. The plan was very specific, and we made a solemn pledge to each other—a pact.

Louie and I were as thick as thieves during our schooldays. Being in the same class at school all the way, and with both sets of our parents in agriculture, we had a great deal in common. It was during this period particularly that my physical growth and development seemed to be of a nature that I was a skinny, puny kid through age 14. I went out for football and had to stretch to make five-foot-two and a hundred and twenty pounds. even with my uniform on. Sometimes I felt like I was being used as the football!

Lou's dad wouldn't let him go out for football. This ate Lou up inside, but out of respect for his father, he never said a word about it to him or to me. However, I knew how disappointed Louie was. I could see it in his eyes. He would have been a good football player, too, because he was built compactly, tough and fast.

Lou and I played baseball together. Lou was a far more mature athlete than I would ever be. At the end of our second year in high school, Louie was taller and heavier than I was. During the next summer I grew to over six feet, so I was really strung out over a long frame, and embarrassingly uncoordinated.

I could only keep up with Louie in the world of music. In high school, we enjoyed watching college football games for free by playing in the Santa Clara University band. Hanging out with the older guys was a big deal.

It was during this period that we made "pin money" in a dance band, and on our first job, I recall our five-piece band earned twenty-five dollars for playing from seven in the evening until two a.m. That was for all five of us.

I was too young and naïve to understand why those females dressed in formals kept coming in and out of the dance hall with different partners all the time. If my mother had known we were playing in a high-class house of ill-fame, she would have pulled us all out by our ears. In those days, the Sunol district was the Chicago of San Jose.

In 1936, after three years of high school, instead of the usual four, Lou and I obtained our diplomas. Louis had no trouble convincing his dad that he would do better not going to college, and his native shrewdness, ambition, and hard work, and ability to assist Uncle Jack in keeping the family in one effective cohesive commercial effort, have borne that out. When I announced to my dad that I wasn't going to go to university either, his response lifted the roof about three feet."

Djede knew only too well the stigma he suffered from the Svilich family regarding his lack of a formal education. Dad, not knowing the reason behind Djede's emotional response, knew he should tread lightly on the subject. Dad recalled:

"I timidly pointed out that he had done very well, going to school for only three grades. Both Dad and my sister Winifred went to work on me, but to no avail. I held firm. Lou and I had made a pact.

About a week later, my dad came to me and said, "Are you ready for business?" At age sixteen I was prepared to do just that. I had already made sales trips, selling dried fruit in Los Angeles, and had flown to New York at my dad's suggestion to observe how our cherries were being sold on the auction market. Little did I know that my father had a scheme in mind.

He apparently had tipped off one of our New York brokers who represented us on the fresh fruit auction market—a man I respected tremendously—about my plan not to go to university. His name was John Slavich, Jr. So, the combined forces of Winifred, my sister, my dad, and my mother, and the crushing advice from a third party, John Svilich, Jr., were more than I could cope with. And so, "to keep the peace in the family," I agreed to go to college, like I was doing them a favor. [My father attended the University of California, Davis, 1936–1940.]

Filled with guilt from betraying my best friend, I went through one of the most difficult emotional moments of my life when I faced Lou. I had to tell him I was breaking our secret pact. This was a pivotal moment in my relationship with Lou—breaking my secret pact with him. The big lesson I learned was how Lou handled it.

Lou almost cried, which, of course, made me cry. We both sat, not looking at each other eye to eye, then with heads down for about four or five minutes. It seemed like five hours. Then Lou, after a deep breath, began to speak and said, "I understand, and wish my dad was as hard on me." Lou looked into my eyes with fire and said, "I will not make the same mistake with my children." I was amazed at the range of mental processing that had gone through Lou's head in a matter of minutes. Although he had a giant intellect, he always suffered the rest of his life, feeling he needed to prove something to make up for his lack of formal education and thick accent. He had nothing to prove to me—I knew different."

Our relationship continued over the years, and there wasn't any jam that I wouldn't help Louis out of, if he needed me. Over the years he certainly demonstrated the same feeling towards me, and I am pleased to see a great deal of this feeling of family even towards our children, who are second cousins. Whereas I realize this thing cannot be go on forever and have that same sense of obligation to close family, it is a very positive and secure feeling that I would advise you all to consider. I must caution you that it could only work if you have the attitude of what you can do for your family instead of what you get out of it. So, if you preserve that, you will preserve something beautiful and worthwhile.

The influence of the Jack Mariani family on ours wasn't limited to Lou's. Uncle Jack, Lou's father, had a powerful formative influence in my life.

Uncle Jack was our taskmaster and knew how to handle young people. For example, I can remember on occasions that, if we'd worked really well that day picking prunes, he would somehow miss seeing the occasional bad prune being thrown at a passing telephone pole while he was holding the reins of the horses on our way home. On the other hand, if we hadn't done so well that day, not a *single prune made it to its target, because he had eyes in the back of his head. (The real fun times for me were after the day's picking was over and I was allowed, on the way home, to sit on top of the full prune boxes with the big kids—my three sisters, and Jenny and Joe Popovich from across the street, and others who had helped out.)*

During harvest time, Uncle Jack would flick Lady or Baby (our two cart horses) with the reins, and they would respond to Jack's flicking as we clip-clopped on the way home to the tune of some old Slav song, then some "modern jazz"— "Bye Bye, Blackbird" was a favorite, as was "When You and I Were Seventeen," and, would you believe it, "A Wild Irish Rose"—though there wasn't an Irishman among us.

Uncle Jack also had his special ways to teach people to shape up.

Most young people can't wait to grow up, and sometimes try to do physical work their bodies are not yet qualified to handle. As an example of this, I wanted to lift boxes that were way too big for me. So: on one occasion, I went riding with Uncle Jack on the wagon, with, I believe, Lady pulling us, in the hills between Saratoga and Monte Vista to a place called Painless Parker Ranch, to pick up a load of prunes Spiro Ractovich was harvesting. In those days a load of prunes might have been 25 to 40 boxes, weighing a ton or just under. I was instructed to sit on the wagon seat and tend to the reins while the wagon was being packed, so the horses would not move prematurely. Now, I figured the horses knew far better than I when they should start or stop, and that this was a useless exercise, so I kept jumping down from the wagon to help lift the boxes. About the third or fourth time Uncle Jack told me to "get back on that seat, and stay there," the adults had evolved a plan Spiro would put into action on our next trip to the ranch.

The hills were well populated with rattlesnakes in those days, and it was no trick to find one—the trick was not having a rattler find you. On the next trip to Painless Parker Ranch, when I disobeyed again, and again jumped down from the seat to get at the boxes, I didn't know Spiro had put a coiled, but dead, rattlesnake right where I landed. That was the last time I jumped down from the seat. And I found it easier to obey orders.

Paul Jr's reflections on the Jack Mariani family are, of course, different from Djede's. Louie and Jack's family belonged to the bonding of first-generation immigrants. To this day, we enjoy fond, close family feelings that, no doubt, have their roots with our respective fathers.

However, good feelings and close relationships were not always the case when it came to my relationship with Louie Mariani."

As close as Louie and my father were, including similar their business activities (the Paul Mariani, Jr., family in fruits, the Jack Mariani family in nuts), they took different internal paths.

After re-reading my father's memoirs I realized he was a complicated mosaic of his upbringing. He was proud of his accomplishments, had a big home and lived life large, but, at the same time, was a deeply humble man. Louie was equally complicated. Like Dad, Louie was proud of his accomplishments and enormously successful financially. Unlike Dad, he thirsted for recognition yet prided himself on living in a humble home and held a poor view of people who chose to spend money to live more comfortably.

Like my dad, Louie was eccentric, but in different ways. He was a classic caricature of his times. Don Imwalle was a neighbor of ours for 20 years but never told me about his relationship with my Uncle Louie until a month before he passed away. He had been silent because that was the way Louie had wanted it. Apparently, Louie was a silent-money partner who backed many well-known real estate developers in California. One such developer was Don Imwalle. Don told me a story about the day Louie agreed to back his company, and their celebratory lunch.

"After the lunch," Don said, "the waiter was clearing the table. Louie stopped the waiter from clearing the remaining bread and asked that the cream remain."

Don ordered desert. Louie didn't. Once the deserts arrived, Louie began to dip the bread into the cream for his desert. Astonished, Don just stared. Louie, out of the corner of his mouth, said, "Son, I guess you never lived through the depression! You better not waste my money on things you don't need to develop that strip mall."

That was classic Louie. It set the tone for their relationship. Don was scared to death to ever spend any money he couldn't fully justify.

After Dad's passing, my personal real estate activity and banking activities attracted press coverage. Even though I have never called a press conference, I nonetheless had many news articles written about my and our family's business activities.

I am not sure, even to this day, why I got so much press. I speculate now that it was largely because of the recognition my father received from his accomplishments and charisma. Dad was charismatic as well as successful, and his charisma affected people all around him. He was constantly in the public eye through receiving lofty sounding awards, such as "International Businessman of the Year,"[10] etc., even though Dad never needed nor sought this recognition. And I believe I got a lot of press on his coattails

A picture of the author on the cover of *Business Journal Magazine* featuring an article about my business endeavors

Whatever the reason, Louie resented my notoriety. I heard whispers of Louie criticizing me for years, behind my back.

I think once Dad died, Louie believed he would finally get the recognition he deserved, but I was getting the press (deserved or not) instead. I think Uncle Louie was over-compensating for a poor self-image. Regardless, when folks get all wrapped up in themselves, they make very small packages. However, this is an oversimplification of Louie's character.

Louie was a very complicated man. Just before his death, he called me and asked if I would come over. He wanted to talk to me.

When I arrived, Louie asked me to take a seat.

"David," he said, "I want to apologize to you for all the things I have said about you behind your back. I was wrong to be jealous of you. It was mean to say the things I said. I needed to make this apology to you before I die…. I need to lift this burden from my heart."

We just looked at each other. I was stunned to hear this, and even more moved when tears began to flow from Louie's eyes, down his cheeks. They were tears of relief, not of sadness. They were tears of peace.

Louie's poverty of spirit was reborn and lifted up, in an instant, as a heart enriched with peace. And there I sat, in awe, for about an hour in front of a giant of man—a giant in every aspect of what it means to be a man.

Chapter 8

Dad's Early Economic Training

Dad's early economic training in "The Valley of Heart's Delight" captures a bygone era in Dad's memoirs, *"My Life and My Dreams"* Dad wrote:

> Going back in my memory—I believe I was four or five years old—I remember at the end of a day during cherry-packing season, our entire production might be 150 or 200 boxes of packed cherries, which would go on the back of an old Model-T Ford. My dad [Djede] would let me ride with him to San Jose to unload the boxes at the cold-storage plant and in refrigerated railroad cars. My big privilege was to load the back of the Model T with empty boxes, which weighed about a pound or two a piece, while Dad was taking care of getting his receipts and so forth. These were some of the real fun times I remember with Dad, teaching me Slav songs on the way into town. We would be singing at the top of our voices and having a real ball, but between songs he would always manage to interject some economic event of the day and review it on the way home, again between songs.

> As part of my early training in what I might call "the work-learning curve," I recall Uncle Jack as the taskmaster, teaching us to work quickly no matter how boring the job. His teaching was directed towards increasing our stamina, rather than allowing us to do anything where we could hurt ourselves, from heavy lifting, for example. In fact, my worst dressing-downs from both Uncle Jack and Dad were for trying to lift boxes, along with the men, before I had the muscle-power to do so.

> In later years—after Uncle Jack's family arrived and he had his own family to work with him, and I began spending more time working with my father—I also remember getting "balled out" for raising a sweat and using my back when there were laborers standing around looking for something to do. Dad's most exasperating moments were when I was trying to be a man when I was still only a boy, and pitching in hard when hired helpers were looking for something to do.

One of my earliest recollections is of Dad patiently telling me that, on one hand, labor management does not require a supervisor to raise a sweat. On the other hand, if everything is organized properly and the workers have a really good supervisor running (say) an apricot picking crew, he could set a good example, and be a pacesetter, by bringing in a bucket of fruit as quickly as any of the other pickers could. The unpardonable sin was for a supervisor to knock himself out from toil while men on payroll were "spinning their wheels"; that is, not at work.

Teaching new men how to set a ladder, without letting slower pickers fall too far behind; not allowing ripe fruit to be left behind; and not allowing green fruit to be put in the bucket, all the while picking as fast as the best of them, was sometimes a pretty good trick. Watching each step in the process, whether it was harvesting in the orchard, or each task in the packing shed, was the first step before asking how to do it differently, with fewer steps or less motion, or how to make it easier for the workers to perform. (As for that last point, Djede was a firm believer that if you took care of the workers, the workers would take care of you.)

The net result of this training was to produce young people who could move quickly with a minimum of wasted effort and get the most production and best quality of work out of our hired crew. These were lessons I pondered over and over—until, as the Jesuits say: "Drop enough rocks, and eventually it will make a mark."

My earliest recollections of training in economics were before I actually entered school, when, during cherry season, it was my job to rubber-stamp the end of each box of packed cherries. The cherries were packed in rows, according to size and variety. Each box was weighed, and the grower needed to be identified; hence the rubber stamp.

Each box of packed cherries needed to be marked with accurate information for the distributors and to follow consumer laws. This information was essential for tracking purposes, in case fruit got rejected for any reason. Hand-stamping each box with the correct information required the worker to be alert at all times. This was challenging due to the monotony of the repetition; watching one box after another coming off the packing line made the work tedious, however important. My payment for doing this was the "cull," or picked-out, cherries that could not be sold on the wholesale market because they were overripe, stemless, bird-pecked, misshapen, or whatever. In those days, there were fruit stands up and down the main highways with a limited market for the operators. They, of course, tried to buy as cheaply as they could, sort out the worst fruit, and sell the remainder retail. For the literal "fruits" of my labors, I naturally wanted to sell for as a high a price as I could. I soon learned that if I charged more than the operators were willing to pay, I would end up with unsold fruit; the fruit would soon become garbage, with no value at all. The profits from my labor under these circumstances were almost zero. Dad gave me a lot of hints on what to look for, when negotiating, on just how far you could push a buyer before he walked away. As it happened, some of these fruit-stand buyers were alcoholics, though this didn't seem to change their ability to bargain; in some cases, in fact, they were even sharper, more contentious, and more difficult to get along with after they'd had a few drinks.

After a while I learned that, instead of selling the cull at our packing shed, I could make more money by bargaining and delivering to the retail stands, after borrowing a truck and a driver from Dad at the end of each work day. This had to be done after the main truck was loaded and on its way to town, which meant that bargaining and selling were done roughly between 7 and 8 o'clock in the evening during harvest time, which, for cherries, was in early summer. This was my first lesson in the value of service. Mum didn't like me coming home that late, but Dad patiently listened to my play-by-play report on how I had gotten an extra 50 cents on a load of cherries, and he'd put a word in, here and there, to show how I could have received 75 cents if I had been a little smarter. It seemed almost too bad to grow up and graduate into selling premium picked cherries, when, in another twenty years, I might have become the best doggone cull cherry salesman in Santa Clara County.

One of the best phases of economic training that I can remember was going out with my dad [Djede] from the time I was nearly four years old through until after my college days, estimating the fresh weight of crops on orchard trees. He would show me how to pick an 'average tree,' take off a percentage for 'misses' [unusable fruit] and come up with a total tonnage in a particular farmer's orchard to be harvested."

After being shown the rudiments of estimating the tonnage of fruit on trees in an orchard by Djede, I developed into a skilled expert.

When my father was in high school, he used to keep Djede's books recording the ripe fruit coming in to our facilities. My father would make up the weight tags for the prune pickers, so we would know how much we owed them for their harvest. We paid the pickers, or harvesters, by the pound – sometimes referred to as "piece-rate. The fruit was weighed on a truck-scale. In those days, Dad used to buy, in a given year, over a thousand tons of fresh prunes from several orchards. Year after year, Dad estimated how much fruit the orchards would produce. He was consistently accurate to within 1500 pounds per one thousand-plus tons; an astonishing accuracy of 99.99 percent.

I never achieved my dad's competence on estimating prunes, but I did get very close to him on estimating fresh apricots. I guess that's because I picked more fresh apricots than I did prunes.

To further my economic training, Dad gave me almost daily commentaries on what other people were doing right or wrong, thereby helping me learn from other people's experiences as much as my own. One of Dad's cautions was to be careful how fast you move into another man's business. There are many tricks to the fruit trade; for example, there was a vast difference in drying ratios of fruit from one orchard to another only a few miles apart in Santa Clara County. A drying ratio (also called a dry-away ratio) is the difference in the weights of a quantity of fresh fruit before and after being dried. For example, if a box of fresh fruit weighed 40 pounds and the dried weight of that fruit was 10 pounds, the dry away ratio is said to be 4:1. If you paid $1 per pound for the fresh fruit, the fruit cost alone in the dried fruit form would be $4 dollars. If you purchased another 40-pound box of fruit for a $ 1 a pound but the fruit when dried weighed 16 pounds, the dry-away ratio would be 2.5: 1, which means the fruit cost with a 2.5 dry-away ratio costs only $2.50 per dried weight. The difference is a $1.50 in the cost of the dried fruit between the two boxes even though you paid the same price for the fresh fruit. If you dried thousands of tons or millions of pounds, you can make or lose a fortune overnight and never really know why[11]. Differences in dry-away ratios, from as little as 2.0.:1 to almost 4-1 in orchards within three miles of each other, were not uncommon. It was easy to understand how easy it was in those days to go broke. Newcomers would come in and get their fingers burnt in a hurry. Dad was a gutsy guy, but he didn't take crazy chances, and he emphasized often that, in business, you don't have to be very smart: "Just don't do foolish things, and you'll survive."

Chapter 9

There is nothing so delightful as the hearing, or the speaking of truth. For this reason, there is no conversation so agreeable as that of the man of integrity, who hears without any intention to betray, and speaks without any intention to deceive.

Plato

The Tickvica Family:

Prior to the formation of our family-owned dried fruit company, my grandfather entered a series of partnerships that purchased and sold fresh and dried fruit. One of the more enduring of those partnerships was with the Tikvica family. But it did not start out well.

Between 1915 and 1930, there were over a hundred small companies that packed and sold dried fruit and shipped packaged fruit all over the country. Small operators like my grandfather came up with the idea of acquiring modest amounts of fresh fruit, then drying and selling it to one of the local dried fruit companies at a profit. By drying the fruit, we added value between the fresh-fruit and finished-product prices.

During one growing season in the Valley, the year before my father was born, my grandfather, Paul Mariani, Sr., and Nick Tikvica, a very good friend and business associate, managed to borrow the money for a down payment on a crop of fresh prunes. Their idea was to buy the fruit while it was still on the trees, then harvest the fruit, dry it and sell it as a processed product to local markets.

In those days, all prunes were sun-dried, because dehydrators simply hadn't been invented yet. It seemed that Mother Nature was not going to co-operate this year by providing the usual hot, dry August and September to sun-dry the prunes. Instead, about the time a good part of the crop had been picked and laid out on drying trays, along came a freak six inches of rain within twenty-four hours, which totally destroyed the crop. So the young partnership of Nick Tikvica, Sr., and Paul Mariani, Sr., found itself without any means of repaying the loans that had been borrowed to make down payments on the crop – and of course no way to find money to pay the growers for the balance of the crops. Paul and Nick went to every one of the growers and promised to pay them for their crop if it was the last thing they did in life. The growers not only remained patient for payment, they agreed to deliver to Paul and Nick their crop the following season.

Somehow, they managed to feed their families for the rest of the year. Fortunately, the same growers they had bought from a year earlier let them buy for nothing down the following year. And, as it turned out, prices increased during the harvest, and both Nick and Dad made themselves a small fortune on the 1919 crop. The interesting thing was that, from a sad and stressful financial experience grew a friendship that was even stronger, and was to last all through the lifetimes of Paul, Sr., and Nick Tikvica, Sr. This same mutual respect and close friendship continued with their children.

"Failure is instructive. The person who really thinks learns quite as much from his failures as from his successes."
                                        John Dewey

What I would do differently

My father, Paul Mariani Jr. reflected.

"I would establish a prune-drying facility in the Sacramento Valley in addition to Healdsburg, instead of concentrating all our efforts in the Healdsburg area. That decision had seemed a good one at the time, because the prune quality out of Healdsburg was far superior to that of the Valley.

But the lesson learned is that it is always necessary to pay attention to changing markets and trends.

As time went on, the differences in quality began to narrow between Sonoma County and Sacramento Valley due to better varieties and improved farming practices. [12] Eventually Sacramento Valley became superior to the quality in Sonoma County. It seemed overnight our prune production became unprofitable in both Santa Clara because property taxes exceeded the crop value or in Healdsburg because we had inferior quality fruit.

I owned Mariani Frozen Foods, Inc., together with Anthony Gercich, who owned thirty percent. One day, out of the blue, Anthony asked me to buy out his share in the company. My mistake was not to take Anthony up on his offer—I should have bought him out, or had him buy me out, or liquidated the business right then and there. From that point forward, it was just good dollars chasing bad.

Soon after Gercich asked to be bought out, I arrived at his offices to find Gercich's office cleaned out, and his key personnel didn't report to work. Gercich was gone.

Critical to Mariani Frozen Foods were two people on the team. Anthony himself was a very confident, hardworking guy, but more than that there was Danny Cuevar, who was an outstanding mechanic and who made all the complicated processing machinery run. Both of them (among others) had left with Gercich, without any notice to me.

From the time Gercich disappeared with our key personnel, I tried to put together a mosaic of talented people, who turned out to be losers. I thought that, by my own strength, I would be able to pick up their weak spots and make up for their failings. That was probably the biggest mistake I ever made. Unless you put a team together that can fairly well operate on its own and just be guided by policy, then you don't have a team, but a bunch of losers working counterproductively. Interestingly, even though in each case, each loser may be doing his own job well, if he fails to become a part of an overall team—if he says, "I've done my job, to hell with every other department"—you have a sure formula for failure.

I was asked to list the achievements and setbacks I experienced during the period 1948 to 1968. One of the major achievements in the dried fruit business was to take a process that was developed by the University of California when I was a student there in food technology and apply it to practice. In 1949, a major growing supermarket chain wanted to have a company pack prunes in cellophane bags for them. The major dried fruit packers of the time were all equipped with carton-packing machines. They did not want to have to spend more money to buy bag-making equipment and go through the extra work of a new way of packing when they were already set up with a very substantial investment in carton lines.

Since we had no carton line, the then-second-largest supermarket chain in the country [Safeway] asked us to do this. They really nursed us along the first year, in 1949, when we packed 40,000 bags. Within five years, we were packing 5,000,000 bags per annum for this major chain and began to develop a Mariani label for our own trade. The key to this success was not only the cellophane bag. It was using a new processing of prunes in the new package. This was the first application of a soft "ready-to-eat" product in the supermarket chain trade. It's too bad we didn't register the "ready-to-eat" idea at that time, because it became a by-word in the industry – which makes me wonder right now why we don't register "fruit medley," "fruit leather," and "fruit roll" before somebody else picks up the idea. [Interestingly, thirty years later we still had not trademarked these terms. Don't ask me why!]

Getting back to the subject of selling moist dried fruit (an oxymoron at the time), "Paul, Jr.," was the talk of the town: The Mariani kid was the laughingstock of the industry for two or three years after I came out with a soft prune in a Pliofilm transparent bag. However, when I took over all the prune business of the second largest chain in the country, they were no longer laughing, and by the sixth and seventh year, all the major packers were offering prunes in transparent bags, soft prunes. My only regret is they didn't laugh at me for three or four years longer, to enable us to obtain a few other chains under our wing before the competition woke up.

Our business was too concentrated because of a couple of very large customers. It was during this period that Tierney Wilson was an institutional sales broker, with a sales office in Seattle, where he lived. I wanted Tierney to be integrated into our organization as national sales manager. He had moved down from Seattle with his family because of a sick youngster, and I told Tierney I was scared to death to have so many pounds going to one or two customers, and so I wanted to develop a domestic market under the Mariani brand. Tierney developed a team and went ahead and did just that.

In 1946 (going back a bit now), my father [Paul Mariani, Sr.] told me I should look at other areas of the world that produced dried fruit, because, though Santa Clara County, then the major producer, was a perfect place to grow fruit, its growing seasons were short, and it cost money to carry year-around inventory.

The concept of sourcing "fresh-fruit-to-dry" in a different hemisphere was thus hatched. If we grew and processed in two different hemispheres, we could get two harvests, and purchase only half as much fruit as needed to maintain a year-round inventory for the stores. So from 1949 through 1960, I studied in considerable depth all the major temperate-zone fruit growing areas of the world.

Argentina and Chile were our first choices. The growing regions of Mendoza in Argentina and the famous Colchagua Valley in Chile had *perfect Santa Clara Valley / Mediterranean climates with low labor costs. However, due to political instability, we later turned our focus to another temperate climate with a more stable political environment – Australia.*

In 1960, we began to import sample shipments from Australia. After a couple of years of modest shipments, the fruit was accepted so well that we decided to establish a growing operation in Australia and bought land in 1964.

After investigating several parcels in South Australia, I bought some land there, sight unseen, just before boarding a plane out of Perth on my way to South Africa. Edgar Sims, then our Australian contact, actually purchased the land in a joint venture. Then, for a time, the ownership was held, one-third by Edgar Sims, one-third by myself, and one-third by Matt Looney; hence the name for the joint venture, "Simarloo." Even many locals thought Simarloo was an aboriginal name.

We had been working at developing the property for a couple of years when we realized that Edgar Sims was in financial trouble. He asked me to buy him out – I believe in 1966 or '67. Subsequently, he sold twenty percent of the company to a Hong Kong company named Jardines and Matt, and I retained forty percent. We brought Jim Trowbridge (my best man at my wedding and a trusted friend) in to manage the planning and care of the fruit trees and alfalfa.[13]

After a year or two of our learning the environment down there, the trees suddenly began to grow very well. The financial picture was getting a little tight because it was taking a pile of money to develop Simarloo, and although the Hong Kong company pumped in some money through loans, the biggest loan was from the State Bank of South Australia. Matt and I came up with the balance of the needed equity. The project was beginning to show a light at the end of the tunnel when dissension in the ranks, brought about by Matt's son-in-law, provoked me to tell Matt that I wanted to sell my share, and he said that, if I was going to sell, he would too. We both sold our interest to Jardines in 1973. We sold for millions but for forty percent less than its value in dollars. My ulcer was developing because of the dissension, and it simply wasn't fun anymore. As it turned out, we came out in the black even with the discount.

The big mistake I made—and it wasn't the financial loss that concerned me so much—was the loss of a dear old friend, Matt Looney. I had given permission to his son-in-law to buy into Simarloo. The son-in-

law poisoned the mind of my friend to the point where he distrusted me. The moral to that story: never let a son-in-law come in to a deal when his main purpose is to try to impress his wealthy father-in-law, no matter what he destroys in the process.

Then, the Labour Government came into power about that time in Australia, and took most of the profit out of the fruit business via unchecked inflationary policies. About 1967, when Robern [a local Australian fruit packer] got into financial trouble, Angas Park Fruit Company, a subsidiary, went into receivership. I saw the need to have an export license if we were going to do anything in overseas marketing of any consequence from Australia , and so we needed to acquire Angas Park [which had such a license; the Australian Government had not issued any new export licenses since the 1930s]. We purchased the company out of bankruptcy and began financing its operations. Angas Park eventually developed into a major dried fruit power in South Australia and as the country's largest independent packing company.

Angas Park now processes over half the business in dried stone fruits [fruits with pits] in all of Australia. Many co-ops [agricultural cooperatives] located throughout the country shared roughly the remaining half of the dried fruit market (defined as dried apricots, peaches, pears, and nectarines). Additionally, no resale of existing export licenses ever went on the market. As a consequence, buying Angas Park turned out to be one of my better decisions.

One of my great pleasures in being associated with Angas Park was to watch a former office boy, Bert Blenkiron, who never had a job other than working for Angas Park, develop into its managing director, and a good one.

One major setback in our Australian venture was a three-year contract we negotiated with the Australian Dried Fruit Association to buy dried, cut fruits – apricots, peaches, and pears – at world market prices. In the first year of the contract, after making a few deliveries, the Association decided to renege on the contract. The second year a very small delivery was made, and the rest was reneged. The third year they would not even answer telegrams when we advised them by wire that we were accepting purchase of the contracted quantities at world prices. By 1979, this was yet to be settled in the courts. I am saddened because, had they not reneged on these contracts, our customer-supplier relationship could have developed into a major accomplishment for the Australian dried fruit industry as well as for ourselves. Fortunately, because of our financial backing of Angas Park, Angas Park delivered on all of their contracts, and our financing enabled Angas Park to purchase all we needed through this one source, instead of through an industry agreement, as had been originally intended. I believe the Dried Fruit Association was fearful of us; fearful of the potential competition we represented. Nevertheless, this was a personal setback, and, very honestly, I just don't know what we could have done differently to avoid it."

Chapter 10

The Third Generation

Mary Frances Mariani gave birth, on September 22, 1948, to a six-pound, eight-ounce premature baby she and her husband, Paul, Jr., named David William Mariani.

I was the fourth child of what would eventually be a total of seven children, including four brothers and two sisters. I was so small that my dad could still hold me in one hand when I was two years old; so small that, even as a first-grader, I played the part of the newborn baby Jesus in a nativity pageant: I sat, posing as the infant, on the lap of an eighth grader playing the Virgin Mary. So small that I repeated my role as baby Jesus the following year.

For our Christmas pageant at school I, as a first grader, played the baby in the Nativity. (The setting was on a large stage, but the scene was framed to look like a tiny picture on a wall.)

For the better part of fifteen years, Mom repeatedly told me, "The most precious things come in small packages." No doubt, Mom's taking the time to make me feel good about my size was a strategy requiring conscious repetition and reinforcement—and it worked. Perhaps it even worked too well, as it often led to unjustified self-confidence.

Meanwhile, a general spirit of innovation was occurring everywhere in the Valley. New engineering firms, CNC machines and fabrications shops began to pop up. The increased automation in every facet of life emerged like TV's, then color TV, push button telephones, and fancy gadgets in cars. There was a similar revolution in the number of agricultural inventions which laid the foundations for the attitudes of the hundreds of thousands of people who migrated to the San Francisco Bay Area after WWII. By 1970, change in the Valley had become the new normal. Anthropologically speaking, most cultures throughout history viewed change with suspicion. Just fifty years ago, someone who merely changed jobs was viewed as a suspect character. But something dramatic was happening to the culture of Santa Clara Valley. Innovation and change were being celebrated. If you didn't have a different job every five years you were often looked upon with a silent question, "What's wrong with you?"

In the recent past, failure was considered a black mark that stuck to you for the rest of your life, but not so in "Silicon Valley" in the latter half of the twentieth century. As some venture capitalist would say, "If you don't have a few skid marks on your forehead, you're not worthy of our investment capital." Failure, and learning from failure how to avoid future mistakes, became the new norm.

Though this revolution in attitudes would not happen for another generation, its roots can be found in the early twentieth century.

After World War II, in the 1940s, Santa Clara Valley's growth curve began to ramp up. I was born in 1948, so the growth and constant change in the Valley is all I have known. By 1950, rapid growth had come to be expected, and it has continued unabated ever since.

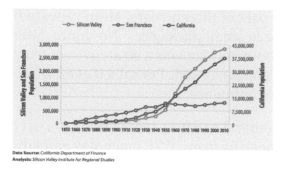

Data Source: California Department of Finance
Analysis: Silicon Valley Institute for Regional Studies

The graph above shows the population growth in Santa Clara Valley, between 1850 and 2010.

Santa Clara Valley was still a bucolic community in the 1950's. A farmer would plant a tree in an orchard and watch it grow for 6 years before he could harvest the fruit and make a living. Change was very slow. A planted orchard would remain for a quarter of a century or more until the trees died. The countryside or from the roadside seemed to look the same – year after year. The change in the size of the trees occurred so slowly they also seemed frozen in time. We knew the same neighbors who lived at the same locations for a lifetime. Suddenly everything around us began to change seemingly overnight. Orchards that had taken a decade to get to maturity were bulldozed virtually overnight, and within a month foundation were being set for commercial buildings.

A single subdivision, Rancho Riconada in Cupertino, brought a new population of people who outnumbered the entire farming community in Cupertino between 1955 -1958.

The Santa Clara Valley community was transformed with the introduction of urban developments and radically different demographics and different values. Engineers, designers and high-tech workers didn't mix well with the established agrarian community. Neither group readily understood each other: a clash of cultures.

My mother during this time was an enigma to me as she attempted to cope with our growing family and community involvement. Mom's striking features, flashing green eyes, and a ready smile made it almost impossible not to smile back at her.

Mom selflessly worked as the director of the March of Dimes. I was very proud of mom for her work in charities. But, the combination of the challenge of raising of large family and because time management was not her forte resulted in not having the time for us all.

Being a middle child, I felt lost in the shuffle. My mother's words often conflicted with her actions. Her comforting words will not be forgotten, but at times I did feel alone and forgotten.

I struggled with a series of conflicting feelings: at times, I was confident, but felt insecure and shy during quiet moments. I felt loved, yet, at the same time, abandoned. Mom would often tell me that I sometimes got lost in the shuffle. My conflicting feelings were no doubt a by-product of being a middle child.

Fortunately, my self-confidence was aided by the fact that I was discovering, in school and at play that I had been born with above-average athletic abilities. My classmates, when choosing up teams, all wanted to pick me. When I was nine years old, I got drafted into the Cupertino Crossroads baseball team, a community team for twelve-year-olds and under; later I got drafted on the regional all-star team when I broke a few homerun records; I also broke several school records in basketball and got my name with photos in the regional newspaper multiple times. I deluded myself into believing I was a big-time athlete.

I didn't yet realize that athletic talent is relative—especially relative to how big a pond you swim in. In a larger metropolitan area, I might not have "made the team" at all. Realistically considered, we were from a small rural farming community in the middle of California—at best, I was above-average, but not great. At the time, however, I thought of myself as a superstar! Upon recent reflection, I have come to realize that I was better than most players my age for the simple reason that I practiced more than most. This was a lesson that stuck with me throughout my life. Nevertheless, my delusions of athletic prowess in my later childhood years served to repair my self-esteem, which had been crushed as the result of a little incident when I was seven years old.

In 1955, the only Catholic grammar school in Santa Clara County was Saint Leo's, in downtown San Jose. We lived in Cupertino near the intersection of Steven's Creek Road and Highway 9 (today De Anza Boulevard). This intersection was the first major intersection along Highway 9 from San Francisco to Santa Cruz, feeding traffic to and from communities east and west along that part of the peninsula. It was called "The Cross Roads."

Cupertino Cross Roads, circa 1960
Courtesy of the Cupertino Historical Society

The Cupertino Store was located up until about 1960 at the corner of De Anza Boulevard and Stevens Creek Road in Cupertino, California. A trolley running from San Jose stopped here. Horses were still in common use in the 1950s, as Cali's Feed and Grain Store was across the street.

At the Cross Roads in every direction were miles upon miles of orchards except for a general store and Cali's feed and grain. These stores broke the monotony of the rural landscape and became a landmark for local travelers in that era before freeways. The name stuck even though today it is just one of many intersections. Today, the Cross Roads is hardly noticed, with hundreds, if not thousands of busy intersections in "Silicon Valley."

As mentioned in an earlier chapter, it seemed fitting that our great-grandfather had come from the "crossroads" of the Adriatic, the Island of Vis, to the crossroads of what would become Silicon Valley.

A bus line ran from the Cross Roads to downtown San Jose. We either rode the bus, or sometimes were driven, to school.

At school, for assemblies, events and lunchtime, we were sorted into two lines for each class, one for boys, one for girls. Each line was arranged from the shortest to the tallest, with the shortest first. So naturally I was always the first in the long boys line. I felt special. Everyone noticed the first in line while walking down the aisles as we entered church, for first communion and mass, and for big events like the May Day parade.

Even more important to me than the attention, I was paired with one of the prettiest, and the shortest girls in school. Then, at the end of my first-grade school year, Mom and my teacher sat me down.

Mom began to speak to me in an almost secret-like whisper, choosing her words with great care. She spoke in vague poetic and confusing euphemisms. I really didn't understand her gibberish at first. Eventually, she just asked, "It is difficult being so short?" Finally, I got it – because I was so short, the teacher and Mom had decided it was best if I repeated first grade so I would have an extra year of growth before being promoted to the next grade.

They emphasized that I was a good student and received good grades. Mindful that first grade had been easy for me, and also that I was academically lazy, my first thought was "Great! I've already done all my homework for a year in advance. I won't have to study for a whole year! . . . Play time and recess, here I come!"

My only real regret was that I would not be paired up with the prettiest girl in school anymore. But in first grade, one usually got over crushes on girls quickly. I did.

Near the beginning of my repeat year of first grade, my first big panic attack occurred during the second week of school. Mom arrived to pick us all up after school at Saint Leo's—my class had been released or gotten out late that day. As I left the school building, I saw my mother driving off with a full car of kids—but WITHOUT ME. I gaped, I ran, I cried my eyes out, screaming for Mom not to leave without me. Now alone on Race Street in San Jose, I watched the car disappear without me. But there was nothing I could do about it.

I didn't know what to do, so I began to walk, stopping and crying, then walking again, in the general direction of home. For the next five hours, this seven-year-old walked through one orchard after another heading north from San Jose. Each orchard was composed of long rows with evenly spaced trees. Row after row trees seemed endless. As the night time light grew dark these long rows of trees started to create shadows with imaginary demons lurking behind each tree. Finally, I reached the outskirts of Cupertino around nine o'clock that night.

It was about that time Mom realized I wasn't home and sent out a search party for me, including my sister, Linda, and her friend Ann Cali, and others. They found me in Cupertino, on my way home. This incident left me feeling pretty worthless. I felt that I was invisible to my own family.

The second big blow to my self-esteem stuck to my ribs for several decades. It occurred during the third week of my repeating first grade at Saint Leo's.

It happened in the playground. My kindergarten teacher came up to me in a fury, shouting at me. I was startled and struck with fear. She said, "David William Mariani, I prepared you for first grade properly. How dare you *flunk* first grade! I couldn't believe my ears." She continued her rant: "I can't believe you are repeating first grade! I am very disappointed in you." She stomped off, with an anguished, disgusted look on her face; that look of disgust haunted me for years to come. I can still see the contorted face and "stink eye" she gave me. I felt like I had been struck by lightning. More accurately, I felt like she had stomped on my heart and lungs: for a moment, I couldn't breathe.

A lump in my throat quickly followed. It hurt bad as I was hit by another kaleidoscopic rush of emotions—I didn't want the kids to see me cry, but I couldn't swallow. Questions started flashing in my head in rapid succession: "*Is the world very different from my perception of it? Did my mom and my teacher deceive me? Am I really stupid? What was the real reason I stayed back?*" In a sudden tsunami of feelings, I broke down and cried uncontrollably. As the recess bell rang, ending recess period, I panicked again, as it was time to go back into the classroom. Somehow, I managed to hold back my tears as I went into the classroom.

The pain from the lump in my throat continued. I remember just sitting in class, numb to the teacher's words. I instantly saw my classroom differently. I hated it. I wanted to be in second grade. Now I was trapped in first grade for a whole year. A year for a seven-year-old is like an eternity. A nagging question I had that persisted for years was "*What were people really saying behind my back?*"

I never told Mom about this incident. I was afraid of what she would say. I imagined her saying, "Well, David, now you know. You stayed back because you are just plain stupid." I could not risk asking a question whose answer might be so crushing. I remained silent and watched the family around me, in an attempt to distinguish what was true from what was false. I remained confused, skeptical, and quiet around home. I measured the expression of my emotions for self-protection. I knew now there was much more to this world than what the adults may say to be true. Understanding what to believe and not believe was my biggest challenge. Learning about Santa Claus that same year didn't help ease my quandary.

Home for my siblings and me was a place of both happiness and fear. It was happy because my brothers and I played constantly. We were mischievous, played practical jokes, and punched, wrestled, and teased each other constantly. The fear came because there was a period when we got spanked nearly every night—in fact there was a period of time we expected to get spanked every night.

My father, like his father, ruled his home with an iron hand. No meant no, and there was no room for talking back or stepping out of line in any way. During this dreadful period of corporal punishment, our parents had all the boys (five boys in one bunk room) put to bed at seven p.m. sharp every night. As one can imagine, putting us kids to bed at seven when we were still wide awake was a breeding ground for mischief. We invented games because we just weren't tired. Eventually, every night without fail we would make too much noise, and down the hall would come the sound of Dad marching, belt in hand. He would line us up against the wall and give us all a few whippings each. We would then cry ourselves to sleep.

One would think we'd learn. But no: each night—no matter the fact we'd been whipped just like the night before for making a racket—to bed we went, lying in silence until suddenly someone forced passing gas, and everyone burst out laughing, then, once again, down the hall would come the sound of dad's footsteps. Night after night the same pattern persisted. Eventually, Dad lined us all up before we went to bed and said, "I might as well give you a whipping now to get it over with, because otherwise I'll be back here in an hour anyway."

Both parents years later admitted: "What were we thinking, putting you all in one room, and then putting you to bed at seven p.m.? Of course, you would act up." They never admitted they were wrong to spank us as it was an accepted part of the culture at the time.

While on the subject of corporal punishment, which was the norm during those years, I think the worst psychological punishment for us was the "sucker" whippings. After some transgression (which sometimes we understood, sometimes didn't), Dad would tell us to go out to the orchard and pick out a good "sucker." (A sucker is a fast-growing basal root on a tree. They are long, skinny, and flexible when fresh, and one of them can be made into a perfect whip.). Going out to pick your own instrument of pain was more painful than the whipping itself.

We lived in an era where corporal punishment was a normal way of life—at least, it was our normal. The combination of corporal punishment and my scarring first-grade experience in school heightened my shyness. I retreated into myself and became a keen observer of life at an early age.

At some point in those early years, I convinced myself that school was just too hard for me, that it was beyond my abilities. I did not enjoy schoolwork and worked at it the least possible I could get away with. But, without effort, there is no learning, and without a command of the subjects, school soon became difficult. I began to feel stupid.

My insecurities were compounded by a genetic hearing defect affecting certain wavelengths of sound. For example, I cannot readily hear the difference between the sounds of "D's" and "T's and "N's." Sometimes I don't hear the "D" at all—the word "mind," for instance, sounds to me like "mine." I would spell the word "mind" m-i-n-e. I had to guess the spelling of many words and often guessed wrong. My brother John was a brilliant student; he was literally a nationally acclaimed writer by the age of twelve. I am just twelve months younger, and I couldn't even spell. Mom would get frustrated with the contrast of skills between John and me. She would say, "What's the matter with you? Why did you spell this word m-i-n-e?" I would say, "I don't know. The word is *mind* [which I pronounced without the 'd']." Mom kept after me, over and over again, berating me over the difference between the spelling of "mind" and "mine." All the while, all I was hearing was "mine" and "mine." Mom was about ready to scream, as she knew I was academically lazy and naturally assumed my inability to spell certain words was a product of lack of effort. Now she thought I didn't get it because I was being stubborn. It never occurred to me or to Mom that I did not hear like everyone else. I just concluded I was dumb. I went to bed crying many nights after late-night spelling-correction sessions with Mom.

School for me was rapidly becoming a self-fulfilling prophecy—I concluded now that school was difficult for me because I was dumb. It was a perfect storm of academic laziness, a low self-image, and low self-confidence. I began to hate school. My view of school and my view of myself were reflected in my earning below-average grades in English and spelling. Any test is difficult if you don't know the answers; I often didn't know the answers because I didn't study. I somehow missed that simple connection—I attributed my failure at tests as a result of my being stupid, not of my being lazy. Every day I would see my previous first-grade classmates in second grade, the class where I should have been. It was a constant reminder that I was a failure. For the first time, I felt very small.

Sports were my savior. In grade school, from playground games like red rover to kickball, I was always one of the first picked on a team. Often I was the captain and did the choosing.

For second grade, in 1956, I was transferred from Saint Leo's to another grammar school, Saint Joseph's of Cupertino, near the Cross Roads. This was a measure of relief as no one in my new school knew I had stayed back a grade; I was just an ordinary second grader. Much to my chagrin, I was still the shortest in my class. That extra year hadn't bought much in terms of extra height. Throughout that year I obsessed anxiously that I would be kept back in second grade at my new school because I was too small. When admitted to third grade, I was relieved my days of staying back in school were over.

Interestingly, how I have long remembered my childhood schooling, and my low sense of self-worth that resulted, did not jive with reality. In 1980, while cleaning old files from my mom's storage area, I was stunned when I came across a complete record of my grammar school report cards—all together in one stack (Mom was a pack rat and saved items with little regard to their value). Finding my report card records was a moment when for once I was grateful Mom had saved everything from our childhood. My grades were almost all A's, spiced with a few B's. I was flabbergasted by the difference between the reality of my academic record and my obsessive childhood perception of myself, in this case as a failure in school—the abyss between my perception and reality was astonishing. I suspect this is the same for most young kids growing up and trying to understand the world around them. The lesson: like athleticism, IQ is relative. Being average in a household of very bright parents and siblings can distort one's perspective about oneself and the world around him.

The Valley Begins to Rapidly Change

My older brothers and my sister continued at Saint Leo's, each day taking the bus. At Saint Joseph's, I missed the daily bus rides from Cupertino to San Jose. Both sides of the road were planted with orchards until you reached the outskirts of the city. The orchards, in blossom during springtime, were breathtaking; the splash of vibrant colors and fragrance, for thousands of acres as far as the eye could see, was overwhelming. That scene is no doubt one reason why Santa Clara was known as "The Valley of Heart's Delight."

One day, during a family trip to San Jose for shopping, we saw a big orchard being bulldozed. The trees were being ripped from the ground and heaped into a huge pile; it was like an arboretum holocaust. A week later a fire was set, and all the uprooted trees, with leaves still green, were burned, leaving a great empty space where, a few weeks before, there had been acres on acres of flourishing trees.

Blossom Scene in the Santa Clara Valley of California

You are most cordially urged to visit "The Valley of Heart's Delight"
For detailed information, contact the San Jose Chamber of Commerce
Address—Santa Clara County, California

Flyer for "The Valley of Heart's Delight" Booklet

What followed was even more puzzling. Earth-moving equipment, cement trucks, and workers came flooding in and started building. We couldn't imagine why anyone would build, especially on such scale, in the middle of an orchard in the middle of nowhere. We were witnessing the building, in 1955, of our first regional retail shopping center. Someone was spending an ungodly amount of money to build it. We figured they must know something we didn't. It seemed beyond the reach of ordinary mortals, and of myself in particular, to ever understand how someone could (a) have that much money and (b) know enough to be brave enough to make a multimillion-dollar investment in something that would require a vast number of customers to justify it. The shopping center still exists: it's the present-day Westfield Mall.

We were accustomed to small, standalone retail stores, not big shopping complexes. The Cross Roads in Cupertino comprised, on one corner, Cali's Feed and Grain store and, on the opposite corner, the Cupertino Store (our local general store; originally the "Home Union" country store), which carried most of the things you might need around the home. The latter was a classic western-style store, complete with wooden sidewalks in front, like the ones you can see in old western movies today. It was operated by a branch of the Regnart family, also early immigrants to Santa Clara, dating back to the 1800s. (See Appendix IV for historic photos of the Cross Roads.)

The 1950s in Cupertino was a time when you got your windshield cleaned, your oil checked, and your gas pumped, without asking, all for free, every time you stopped by a gas station. And you didn't pay for air in your tires. And you got trading stamps (called Green Stamps) to boot. At the Cupertino Store at the Cross Roads, there were laundry detergents with free glasses, dishes, or towels hidden inside the box. Stuff from the store came without safety caps and hermetic seals, because no one had yet tried to poison a perfect stranger via a commodity purchase.

My grandfather built a family gathering center – a place for the whole family to meet during holidays and other festivities. As our family business grew, it was decided that we needed to modernize with computers. In the early 1960's we installed an IBM punch card computer. Punch card computers were used before silicon-based computers. The computers and storage of punch cards took up the entire room. The punch cards were fed by hand into the fancy Systems 7 IBM computer. It made such a racket; the operators often wore ear plugs. Today our smart phones have literally tens of thousands of times the memory and computer power.

With a sense of wonderment, I can drive down De Anza Boulevard from the Cross Roads, which is now Cupertino Town Center, to Apple's headquarter's campus, located right in the middle of where our oldest orchards once flourished.

For me, school was now only three miles away from home rather than twenty, which it had been in San Jose. Mom often forgot to pick me up at school, so Dad had one of his salesmen take me home on most days. When the sales guy was out of town, I would just wait at the country store for my older brother to arrive at the Cross Roads from Saint Leo's, then the two of us would wait for Mom to take us home. This gave my brother and me some idle time. And idle hands and active minds lead to mischief.

In fact we were guilty of so much mischief while hanging around the store that the management complained to Mom. We were, apparently, a public nuisance and the vagrancy laws were invoked against us. Rather than Mom's solving the problem by picking us up on time, she solved the problem by instructing us to start walking home as soon as I was picked up by my brother and she would pick us both up between the Cross Roads and home. As months went by, we began to get closer and closer to home before Mom picked us up. Eventually she stopped picking us up most of the time, and we walked all the way home.

This pattern of neglect or forgetfulness was our norm. It was Mom being Mom.

We made the best of it during the three-mile walk home. We invented little games: whoever spotted a discarded Lucky Strikes cigarette package on the road first, or stepped on it first, was entitled to hit the arm of the closest brother or sister as hard as they could. I have no idea why we thought this was so funny, but we laughed all the way home. It apparently didn't take much to amuse us. After a time, we had memorized the exact location of every Lucky Strike package we had ever noted along the way. It made the time go by faster.

One December day in 1958, when I was a ten-year-old in fifth grade. I had basketball practice scheduled for a Saturday morning between 9:30 and 10:30. After practice I sat on the curb at Saint Joseph's, waiting for Mom to pick me up. All the rest of the kids either had parents waiting for them or were soon picked up. By four o'clock, when I was still sitting alone on the curb, a nun, a priest, and a custodian had come out at different times to see if I was O.K. "No problem," I told them. "Mom said she'd be late to pick me up." I lied. Finally, when it got dark at 5:30, I began crying. It was a moonless night and pitch dark at 8:15 when Mom finally showed up. I was dry-eyed. I was cried out.

Mom said, "Sorry I'm a little late, dear." That was all she had to say on the entire way home. Little did I realize until many years later that Mom had begun to show signs of reduced mental capacity during the prime of her life, manifested by confusion, repeating stories of the day endlessly, then beginning all over again with the same stories, and finally losing track of time altogether. Leaving a little boy alone on the side of the road for ten hours (with three hours in the dark) was just a symptom of her mental confusion. It was later explained to me by our doctor that extraordinarily bright people could cover up Alzheimer-type symptoms for decades. Mom was extraordinarily bright. My heart healed when I learned that we were dealing with a medical condition rather than a lack of love.

During this time, Dad was busy empire-building, establishing business interests all over the world. He worked at our dried fruit company during the day and our frozen food company in the evening. When not directly managing two companies at the same by working double shifts, he traveled on business. He was, for the most part, an absent father.

To help fix the growing confusion in our house, while he was on a trade mission to Central America and Chile, Dad arranged for visas for a couple from Panama to help out at home. In that era, domestic helpers were commonly referred to as servants. In modern parlance, they were live-in, full-time domestic help. Louise did the chores in the house, cleaning, washing, and cooking. Her husband, Ira, chauffeured us to and from school.

Ira was always on time, but we dreaded his arrival. Our showing up in a stretch limousine with a chauffeur, complete with hat and uniform, did not make us the most popular kids at our small agricultural community school. Regardless, the limo led to jealousies, resentment, and taunting.

We eventually solved our "chauffeur" problem by having Ira drop us off four or five blocks from school. We walked the rest of the way to school. When Dad discovered, years later, that Ira didn't drive us all the way to school because we were ashamed of being driven to school by a chauffeur, he roared, "Since when is it shameful to ride in a Cadillac with a driver in America?" It was difficult to explain the problem of petty jeoulously in a rural community. Dad simply didn't understand why youngsters would be taunting us.

The fact that there was a need to explain this to Dad told me he was a bit out of touch with day-to-day life, despite the fact he was so in tune with his workers at the processing plant. Dad was a bundle of contradictions

While we were growing up, our classmates often ridiculed and chided us, saying things like "Your dad sits around all day with his feet on the desk, raking in money." We were branded as the "rich kids." We didn't feel rich; we felt rather the opposite— sometimes poor in spirit.

Another reason we didn't feel rich was because there was the perception that rich kids didn't work, or shouldn't have to. But Dad made his kids work hard. We were given the hardest and dirtiest jobs in the fields and in the plant. Dad was committed to instilling a strong work ethic in all of us. We saw Louise and Ira as workers along with us as a result of Dad's drilling into us the value of hard work and insisting that we respect the dignity of workers, no matter what their work was, and that we be proud of doing our work well, no matter how small.

And Dad led by example. As mentioned, he worked two jobs, coming home late at night, every night. We had twice the chores of other neighboring kids, including feeding the horses and cows on our ranch on Bubb Road (now Rainbow Avenue in Cupertino) and working in the orchards all summer. We never went on summer vacations because summer was our busiest time of the work year—it was harvest time. We worked long exhausting hours during the summer harvest while our non-farmer classmates living in tract homes played all summer, without a care in the world. If we didn't work in the field just as fast as the *Brasaros* (guest workers from Mexico), we were denied lunch. Dad used to say, "We need to work harder and faster than our hired hands—to lead by example."

Additionally, we didn't feel rich due to Dad's obsession to save money and what you might call Dad's Eleventh Commandment, which he added to the original ten: "Thou Shalt Not Spend Money Unless Absolutely Necessary."

Dad often said, "We don't make money—we save it." What he meant was that, to be competitive, operations needed to "run lean," by continually scrimping and saving whenever possible. While our classmates continued to take digs at us for being "rich kids," we watched our pennies, worked hard, and felt poor. Looking back, I can see I was a bit confused by the mixed messages of how the community perceived us and how I felt internally. However it looks on the outside, inside it never looks quite the same.

In the 1940s, northern Santa Clara County, including Cupertino, Los Altos, Mountain View, and Sunnyvale, had few homes. The homes were either very modest or, a few, very grand. The area was mostly farmland, scattered with a few wonderful, old circa-1800 homesteads, or more utilitarian housing. Los Altos was mostly orchards, with a few mansions. Toward the north, beginning at Atherton and Hillsborough, San Francisco socialites had built mansions, often used as summer homes—and with good reason. As Mark Twain is supposed to have said, "The coldest winter I ever spent was a summer in San Francisco." Also, wonderful estates in the area, such as the Hamilton and Dawson estates, had been built in the 1930s by out-of-state tycoons wishing to escape the humid summers of the eastern states.

However, between the farmhouses of Santa Clara and the summer mansions, virtually nothing had been built. Even shortly after the Korean War, there were mostly orchards and pastures and fields.

In the early 1950s, a new type of development began, which seemed to appear almost overnight, by traditional building standards. These "developments," also called "subdivisions" and "tract homes," began to litter the land in small pockets among the orchards.

After World War II, waves of servicemen returned from overseas through San Francisco and Oakland (main points of re-entry for many demobilizing after the Pacific war). I overheard my parents and relatives talk about how these servicemen and women marveled at the near-perfect climate of Santa Clara Valley, and many wanted to stay. Cheap little houses started being built—hundreds at a time. A few years later (in the early 1960s), I remember my grandfather's debating with my dad about an orchard Dad wanted to buy. My grandfather wanted to buy a different property. Dad argued that the apricot orchard he wanted to purchase produced better fruit with higher production than the orchard Djede preferred. The debate ended when Djede, in his strong Croatian accent, said, "Buddy, this is a great place to grow 'zee' apricots, and a great place to grow 'zee' babies . . . and zee babies are going to vin (win). Zat is why I vaunt to buy zee orchard where there are zee cross streets and lots of traffic." Djede, with his third-grade education, intuitively understood that one day we would stop raising trees and cultivating the soil and begin cultivating clients and raising buildings.

Photos of my father on the cover of the *Palo Alto Times*. (Courtesy of *Palo Alto Times*)

The above newspaper article featuring father and son, Paul A. Mariani, Sr., and Paul A. Mariani, Jr., It highlighted the respectful dynamics between an extraordinary team throughout a span of time that ushered in the past of Santa Clara Valley and the present Silicon Valley. Our packing was a typical Santa Clara Valley scene.

Speaking of tract homes, back in the 1940s my Dad retold on many occasions how he caught hell from Djede for buying one of those ready-made tract homes. Dad apparently purchased one, in 1945, for $3,625. Djede repeatedly made the point, "I built a perfectly good home two years earlier for $2,500. Why are you so stupid to pay so much for a production-house?" The Montgomery Ward Catalogue was advertising a Christmas sale, houses shipped complete. Assembly required! (We complain today about assembling a toy. That's nothing compared to the '30s and '40s.) Djede also accused Dad of being too lazy to build his own house; questioning whether Dad considered building his own home beneath him, as he, Djede, had done, right there in Cupertino. Today, few locals would consider building their own home.

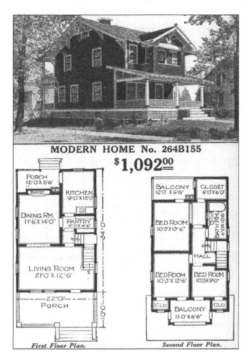

Notice for a typical three-bedroom home for sale— less than $1,100.00— about the time of World War II.

In Djede's trademark style, he always finished his criticisms with a bit of sage wisdom: "If you buy a prune orchard, you will eventually be able to afford a home. If you buy a home first, you will never be able to own a prune orchard." Ever since Dad caught hell from my grandfather, he had become very sensitive to home costs. So it became a game for Dad to build a nice home for less than $2,500. (What a difference between 1940s Santa Clara Valley and twenty-first century Silicon Valley, when [at the time of this writing: 2017] the average cost for a home is over $1,000,000!)

Dad sold his tract home for a $150 profit and used the proceeds to purchase a nineteen-acre orchard planted in prunes. The orchard, in Cupertino, cost $3,150. Dad had no money left for a house, so he moved in with Djede and lived there, rent free, for a year until he got his first prune crop.

From the net proceeds he received from that crop, Dad then began to build one of the most bizarre homes ever seen in Cupertino.

At the end of the Second World War, the military had a program of selling surplus assets that gave registered farmers first priority to buy at auctions, before the general public. From his first year's income from the orchard, Dad purchased several surplus pre-fab housing units made for temporary housing for the army, with thin, single-thickness (that is, uninsulated) walls. Dad placed the units in the middle of our nineteen-acre orchard.

Over the years, as our family grew, Dad bought more of the old-army temporary housing units, cleverly linking them to form a horseshoe. The inside of the horseshoe shape formed a patio, which was eventually enclosed with sliding glass doors along the open side and a flat roof on top. It became our living room.

Our kludged farmhouse had four front doors. Visitors had no idea which "front door" to knock on when announcing their presence. From the outside, the house looked essentially like a maze, but on the inside, it was amazingly cozy. Nothing inside it was new, but it didn't matter if you kicked a hole in a wall; with a little plywood and paint, the place looked almost new.

For water we had a redwood barrel tank set atop a 45-foot tower. A windmill pumped water from the water table up to the storage tank; the height of the tower provided the pressure for our household use. For every foot of lift or falling water, you get about 0.43 lbs. of pressure. Our water tank/windmill combination thus gave us about 20 pounds of pressure (psi) in the house, without using a lick of electricity. Today we would be seen as innovative, "green," living "off the grid," using renewable resources. At the time, it was just the standard way you provided water to a house.

No childhood home, at that time, was complete without a tree fort. Since prune trees have poor structure, my brothers and I constructed a fort between the timbers of the water tower. The views from the foothills of Cupertino elevated on our water tower are memories that are hard to forget. As far as we could see were the tree tops of one orchard after another.

The assembly, into a single house for his family, of prefab army housing units that cost Dad less than $1,500 in total gave him bragging rights with his father. Dad more than once chided my grandfather that he had built a bigger home for less money than the home built by Djede. His bragging rights were at the expense of our living in one of the strangest homes one could ever imagine.

My father, forever a master of contrasts, would arrive, in his chauffeur-driven limousine, to a ho me constructed, essentially, from kludged-together Quonset huts.

Chapter 11

The amount of eccentricity in a society has generally been proportional to the amount of genius, mental vigor, and moral courage it contained. That so few now dare to be eccentric marks the chief danger of the time.

John Stuart Mill

Dad the Eccentric:

Helicopters Save Our Cherry Crop

Though Dad was a brilliant man, it was his magnetic personality that was responsible for much of his success—as well as for some of his folly. He seemed to have the ability to fill up any room he was in—he'd simply walk in and everyone would be drawn to him. But his magnetism camouflaged his eccentricities. He would do things that were anything but normal but seemed normal because he did them with such confidence and flair.

By 1950, the time-honored culture that celebrated doing the same thing over and over again, of being consistent and frowning on new and seemingly hare-brained ideas—on change of any kind—was itself changing, and just at the right time for my father. He had some good ideas, and some that were not so good. The combination of these cultural changes in the Valley with Dad's brilliant mind, magnetic personality, and confident ways allowed him to accomplish some amazing things. It also ushered him into his share of trouble.

Dad was an interesting study in contrasts. Our crazy home in Cupertino, contrasted with full-time live-in help and a limousine with a full-time driver, is just one example. Dad at one moment in time might refuse to spend money on a new delivery truck, but when the rains came one May during cherry-picking season, he was not afraid to open his wallet and spend whatever it took to save his crop. Dad was facing a complete loss of his crop because rain causes ripe cherries to split.[14] So Dad conceived an audacious plan.

Within hours of the start of the rainfall, he convinced the National Guard and Heller helicopter to have a small flotilla of helicopters hover above our cherry orchards in Cupertino and Sunnyvale, the wind from the horizontal propellers shaking the water from the trees to prevent the crop from being ruined.

Using helicopters to shake the rain from cherry orchards was not exactly a standard, accepted practice by farmers in the U.S.: today if helicopters were seen hovering for hours in stationary locations over Sunnyvale and Cupertino, people would immediately assume they were security helicopters protecting an important personage, such as the President of the United States.

The result of Dad's brilliant idea, however, was that we were the only California growers with undamaged cherries for sale that year - a farmer's dream. Usually any crop with high prices is a result of low crop-yields or crop failures, whereas low prices are usually associated with large crop yields. Getting both a large crop and high prices was a bonanza: we earned more money on those cherries in one year than our cumulative cherry based earnings from the previous ten years of selling cherries. Thinking "outside the box" sometimes works and sometimes doesn't. This time it worked. Today, using helicopters to dry off the cherries following a rain has become standard practice in California.

Dad pointing to a map showing the location of our cherry orchards, just before the helicopters went up

Government helicopters hovering over our orchards to save the crop

By the end of the 1950s, the Bracero Program was coming to an end. The Bracero Program issued guest-worker visas for Mexican nationals to work short term in the fields of California and other states.[15] The program functioned well from the farmer's point of view. The guest workers came to the U.S. during the harvest months and afterward went back home to their families. Farmers needed field workers, the field workers needed jobs, money flowed to impoverished families back in Mexico, and families remained united. We were a law-abiding society; everyone involved was following the law.

Unfortunately (or fortunately, depending upon one's perspective), after the Bracero Program was terminated and the guest worker program discontinued, without anything to take its place, the flow of migrant workers stopped for a time.

Immediately following the end of the Bracero program, the Valley, with thousands of acres of orchards to harvest, faced significant shortages of field workers. Many of the crops weren't harvested and so they spoiled. Facing a crisis, dad again flew into action.

Few people today will remember the days when, the Valley was inundated with migrant Arab farm workers. Several trade associations pressured Washington to allow working visas for farm workers from the Middle East to fill the labor gap. The politicians who killed the Bracero Program were only too eager to avoid a looming political disaster by sponsoring large-scale immigration from the Middle East. The influx of these migrants felt like an invasion due to the sheer number of middle eastern new arrivals. It was a cultural shock on many levels, but religion was a non-issue. The middle easterners were drawn to California for the same push and pull dynamics that brought the first Croatians to California.

There were three major Arab migrations into the United States, beginning in the 1800's. In the mid-1960s, a third wave of Arab immigration began coinciding with the abolition of the Bracero program. According to _American Demographics_ by El-Badry, more than 75 percent of foreign-born Arab Americans identified in the 1990 census immigrated after 1964. This influx resulted in part from the passage of the Immigration Act of 1965 which abolished the quota system and its bias against non-European immigration.

The third wave included many unskilled and semi-skilled laborers. These immigrants often fled political instability and wars engulfing their home countries. They included Lebanese Shiites from southern Lebanon, Palestinians from the Israeli-occupied West Bank, and Iraqis of all political persuasions. But many professionals from these and other countries like Syria, Egypt, and Jordan, and unskilled workers from Yemen also emigrated in search of better economic opportunities. Had conditions been more hospitable in their home countries, it is doubtful that many of these immigrants would have left their native countries.

As a young teenager, the contrast in cultures between the Mexican and the Arab workers was striking. The Mexicans were a quiet bunch. They quietly listened to harvesting instructions, followed the rules, and processed correct harvesting procedures carefully; they worked hard, got paid, and left. In contrast, the Arabs were a wild bunch. They came into the fields exuberantly, singing or talking loudly, a mile a minute. They were a happy and playful group, but uncontrolled and with too much energy, if there is such a thing. In contrast with the Mexican farm workers, the Arabs were hyperactive, careless and rough with the trees. After the Arabs finished harvesting an orchard, the orchard looked like giant locusts came through destroying much in their path—tree branches and fruitwood were often broken, affecting next year's crop. Ladders and boxes were strewn haphazardly, fruit boxes broken, and tree props taken. The orchard looked more like a war zone than a tranquil, post-harvest orchard. It took several years to train the Arabs, but, by that time, the preferred Mexican laborers, often entering the country illegally, were becoming more plentiful. The Arab clans began to assimilate rapidly into other professions. The Arab influx into Cupertino was soon to be a forgotten chapter in the Valley's agricultural heritage.

As mentioned, the Mexican (and also Central American) workers eventually came back for seasonal work, though this time illegally. During the 1960s, immigration agents were everywhere, making raids on packinghouses and fields, with workers often running for their lives. As farmers, we needed the labor, the laborers needed the work, and law enforcement officers were just doing their job.

Most of the farmers were honest, "salt of the earth" types. Most farmers, facing the prospect of financial ruin, generally wouldn't hire a returning Mexican laborer without proper identification in the form of a valid Social Security number. Because of this widespread ethos within the farming community, overnight, a robust industry in fake IDs and Social Security cards emerged, providing the new Mexican arrivals with documentation to get work.

For the farmers, a pragmatic approach of not looking too closely at their workers' documentation was the rule of the day.

It was an odd contradiction to grow up in a strong law-and-order culture that seemed to "look the other way" when we hired people who were likely here illegally, then watched our crews disappear when the sirens came blaring onto our properties during raids by federal agents.

By the late 1960s the dangers of crossing back and forth over the borders had increased, and migrant workers began to stay, wiring money back home. The social price was high, however, as this development separated many families for decades at a time.

Mexican border smugglers, called *"Coyotajes,"* exploited their own countrymen who just wanted a better life for their families. Mexico was a poor country. The peasant class could earn two years' worth income in a few months working in the USA. The unscrupulous *Coyotajes* contracted at exorbitant rate with migrant families in smuggling operations at with their own countrymen.

Behind our packing plant in the heart of Cupertino, we had a camp for our workers. The labor camps reflected the cultural mores of Mexicans from rural villages and were made up largely of Native Americans from northern and central Mexico. Many of these workers were accustomed to dirt floors—and at least some of the Indians, if given a choice, actually preferred earthen floors. We are aware of this, but the government was not, and we had more than one write-up by government inspectors on public health issues in the camp mostly because of the dirt floors.

In response, we built wooden floors in the camp's living quarters. However, some of our workers then just pulled up the wooden floors and used the wood for cooking on an open fire rather than using the stoves we had provided. One year in particular—1962—we had an especially difficult time keeping our wooden floors intact. We were fined repeatedly by the health department for unsanitary conditions; they even took pictures of the camp's dirt floors that ended up in the newspapers.

Mechanization and automation provided a merciful end to the camps because machines largely replaced the harvest crews. By 1965, our little labor camp was like a ghost town—a silent reminder of a bygone era for stone fruit farmers.

The changing labor force showed that an increasingly expensive and unreliable labor force needed to be replaced by machinery—but how? It is said that necessity is the mother of invention. Innovation and automation came upon us seemingly overnight.

Giant Earthworms

Innovative new ideas were the fuel that got my father out of bed every day. Upon arriving home from Australia in the 1960s, Dad excitedly related to us his discovery of giant earthworms in Australia. (No, I am not making this up!) However, this story begins much earlier.

Dad made a deal with Nestlé's coffee division to dump processed coffee grounds onto property we owned in Ripon, California. The property was in two tiers divided by a fifty-foot-high bluff: the upper bluff section was planted with almond trees; the lower thirty acres banked up against the American River. The lower section was subject to occasional flooding and so remained unused, open ground; useless for our business, until we struck a deal with Nestlé to dump onto it all of the waste coffee grounds [16] from their Ripon instant-coffee processing plant over a twenty-year period.

Dad didn't realize how many trucks would be dumping on the site—soon, roughly fifteen trucks a day started dumping coffee-grounds onto the property. That would mean (after doing volumetric calculations) that, unless we found a use for the grounds, within twelve years we would have them piled up thirty feet high across thirty acres.

"Not a problem," said Dad when the long-term problem was pointed out to him. He figured that all this wonderful organic material on our property should be worth something if he was clever enough to find a use for coffee-ground waste. Upon research, it turned out that coffee grounds are a good fertilizer. Another interesting feature is that coffee grounds generate a tremendous amount of heat when they decompose. In fact, the grounds on our property decomposed so hot that they burned the new growth of sprouting weeds.

A deal with the State of California to buy the grounds for the state highway system, to help control weeds and fertilize soil, was approved by the Department of Transportation.

The plan was to spread the coffee grounds two inches deep along the highway landscaping throughout the state. Tests confirmed that the coffee grounds conditioned and organically fertilized the soil, helped retain water, and controlled weeds. The big bonus for the state that, ironically, killed the deal was the coffee grounds' weed-control features. Then acting-Governor Edmund Brown (Sr) intervened. While he acknowledged that the deal would save the state millions of dollars, it would also put too many state highway maintenance workers out of work.

Dad was disgusted. The product was too good! The kind of thinking that led to blocking this deal would, he feared, someday bankrupt the state of California. However, his fear was overshadowed by the angst of realizing that, every day, another fifteen trucks were dumping coffee grounds onto our Ripon property. Alarmed at watching the thirty acres filling up, he searched for alternative uses.

Dad discovered that, in the northern part of Australia, there lived giant earthworms that grow to nearly ten feet. The giant Gippsland earthworm is so big that one can hear it as it moves through the ground. Dad's idea was to import these giants and have them consume the coffee grounds. These worms loved to eat coffee grounds. The worms also had a by-product, worm castings - *giant* worm castings. At the time, earthworm castings were known to be "the perfect fertilizer," with just the right balance of NPK and PH. [17]As a result, worm castings have become so valuable that they are sold, even today, by the ounce. Giddy visions of grandeur turned into despair after several attempts to quarantine the giants for export to California failed: they couldn't survive outside their native environment in Australia.

A typical giant Australian worm

Two more views of the giant worms

But despair was soon replaced by fear. Now ten years into a twenty-year contract, with an ever-rising mountain of coffee grounds, anxiety rose even higher, without the benefit of knowing what was in store for us.

The massive decomposing hill of coffee grounds, having risen to nearly thirty feet, now began to heat up. Spontaneous combustion followed. Fires began flaring up monthly.

After more than twenty fire-department responses over a two-year period, and facing massive fines for air pollution along with mounting fire-department bills, Mother Nature was good enough to provide for a solution; a great flood. And dry coffee grounds float!

The American River jumped its banks and lifted up the entire contents of the coffee grounds, and the entire thirty-story mass floated on down the river. It was quite a sight. Thank God for Dad there was no EPA yet, no Endangered Species Act, or fish and game concerns, and thank God Nestlé released us from our contract under *force majeure* provisions.[18]

No matter how much we worried or how hard we worked to solve the coffee grounds dilemma, sometimes in life, the problem solves itself.

Chapter 12

Pal the Babysitter

In the middle of "Silicon Valley," circa 1958, our Cupertino homestead also included a handful of cows, three dozen cats to keep the barnyard mice away, and fourteen horses. Santa Clara at that time was still horse country. My brothers and sisters and I participated in horse parades into the middle of town and rode sometimes in horse-drawn buggies for special events. Our neighbors also had horses—some thirty of them—which they kept at a horse-boarding facility called "The K-5 Ranch."

The K-5 was a popular place for the locals. The community congregated there to ride or board horses, take riding lessons, and sing and dance at the square-dance hall located there, and on the weekends the ranch was filled with local farmers and cowboys.

In the central area of Cupertino (the Cross Roads) stood Saint Joseph's church and school, where I went to grammar school as described earlier. Saint Joseph's sponsored a fundraising event each year, called "The Indian Summer Fall Festival," held over a three-day weekend, that attracted visitors throughout the entire Valley and beyond. The festival had Ferris wheels, cotton candy, and rides in diminutive trains. Horse rides were included in the festivities.

My family volunteered our horses for the horse-riding concession. With the help of our farmhands, we set up a riding rink on the church grounds. The make-shift rink was made up of poles of eucalyptus wood wired together, and a hitching post set in concrete in a fifty-gallon barrel. The posts and rails were removable after the festival for reuse the following year.

"Pal" was the name of one of our horses; I was assigned to lead Pal around the rink. She was always the favorite horse at the horse-riding booth and later became famous, as far as a horse that isn't a racehorse can be famous. She was an unusual horse for many reasons, including ones I could never guess.

The ride began when we walked the horse up against a platform, about the height of a horse's back, where the excited youngster would climb on. My brothers and I got the boring job of walking the horses around the rink twice while the youngster held the saddle horn for dear life. After two trips around the rink, we returned to the platform for dismounting. Rides were five cents each. It was boring walking around and around the rink for eight to ten hours a day, but I felt important. As a ten-year-old, I was being given responsibilities. I had grown up with horses and been responsible for taking care of them—feeding them twice daily, making sure their water trough was filled, shoveling manure, etc.—so, for me, horses were fun but no big deal. To my surprise, there was always a line of kids waiting for a horse ride, for a chance just to get on the back of a horse. This was in fact a sign that Santa Clara Valley was changing from the farm country it had been for several generations, becoming gentrified, as most of the kids attending the festival were living in subdivisions, with tiny yards and no livestock.

My brothers and I watched over the horses during the three-day festivals, sleeping in the open field on church property adjacent to the horse rink within the festival grounds. Leaving kids from eight to fourteen years old alone to sleep with the horses was perfectly natural at the time.

The early changes to the landscape around Cupertino during the 1950s and '60s seemed only on the surface. But other, deeper changes were also occurring. Increasing population density eventually made the rural life less safe, and community values and perspectives began to change. Fences between houses began to appear. The new population wave were families largely employed with technology companies and support services rather than with the farming community. They tended to keep to themselves and the overwhelming spirit of neighbors helping neighbors began to rapidly disappear.

Now back to the story why we called our favorite horse "Pal the Babysitter."

My siblings and I often rode in local parades on Pal's back—all four of us at the same time—and as a result she was dubbed by some local wag "Pal the Babysitter." The nickname stuck for good when a feature written for *Western Horseman* (a monthly magazine with nation-wide distribution) described Pal's unusual intelligence and disposition.

Photo in *Western Horseman* of

"Pal, the Babysitting Horse." From left to right: brothers Paul and John, the author in the middle, sister Linda and brother Mark in the front.

Everyone wanted to ride Pal. She was particularly gentle with little kids. If one of us were slipping to one side, she would lean down to one side, to straighten us back up. No wonder she was a favorite horse to ride at the fall festival.

At times we abused Pal's good nature. When playing with her on wet spring grass, we'd grab her tail. Other horses, in similar circumstances, would just buck or try to kick us—for good reason. But not Pal; instead, she would do a slow gallop as she towed us around by her tail.

During the summer, when other kids might be water skiing, it was harvest time for us—we had no time for summer vacations, so riding behind Pal and sliding on the slick wet grass was the closest we came to real water skiing.

Amazingly, Pal would go wherever we wanted her to go—with a light tap of a switch we carried, from one side of her hind quarters to the other, to give her clues which direction to run in an open field off Bubb Road.

Sister Linda on Pal, brother Paul and the author on the roof, and brother John on the saw horse

Besides Pal's marvelous temperament, she was astonishingly bright. She could open any standard corral gate at will unless it was padlocked. She was truly an amazing horse.

Horses have a distinct social order. There is always one dominant matriarch of the herd. The matriarchs provide order and discipline within the herd. "Pal," of course, was the matriarch in our herd of horses. But during one winter, Pal's life changed forever. I was twelve years old. I remember vividly that fateful day.

Shortly after the festival that year, my parents took a trip to South America for a month. Because each summer the family was kept busy with agribusiness and harvesting chores, vacations were taken in winter instead, and each year, during their vacation trip, Mom and Dad would take one of us kids with them, in rotation.

Sometimes Mom and Dad would leave for two to three months at a time. Our aunt Mathilda was usually the designated babysitter while they were away, but during this particular trip, during the winter of 1958, my seventeen-year-old sister Linda was in charge.

Daily life continued as usual—feeding the horses and doing other chores—until the second week, with our parents already in Argentina, when our favorite horse, "Pal the Babysitter," went down.

Linda took the call from a neighbor who saw Pal lying on the ground with all the other horses surrounding her. Another neighbor called and said, "Pal was running in the pasture, leading the herd, when another horse, 'Trinket,' nudged her right into a tree stump. I think she might have broken her leg by the way she went down." It turned out the injury was serious. Linda called the vet, neighbors from all over heard the news, and a crowd began to arrive. I sat on a fallen tree log and saw a bone sticking out of Pal's leg above her kneecap. That day I learned what a compound fracture meant. After overhearing the vet say, "Her leg is broken, we will have to put her down [a euphemism for shooting the horse]," all of us kids started crying, in unison. My brother Paul said, "Pal is part of our family. You can't just put her down. It's like putting down a member of the family!" Linda followed: "Paul's right, you can't put her down. Isn't there something you can do?"

It was no contest as the veterinarian stared at six sobbing kids. "Well," he said slowly, "theoretically, it's possible to reset the leg, if there is not too much bone damage. But horses don't do well lying down. She needs to be upright, but at the same time, she can't have any weight on her leg, splinted or not." Essentially, Pal needed to be in traction. Further, there were no guarantees she would even come out of the anesthesia she would need to take; it was a cold night, and she might go into shock.

Faced with six sobbing, pleading kids, the vet hesitated.

"Let's do this," a collective voice was saying. "Let's make it happen."

"Wait a minute, do what?" said the vet. "I've never set a horse's leg in my life."

Linda stared at him and said, "Well then, this will be your first."

Our neighbor's horse farm, the K-5 Ranch, had a big barn and heavy rafters. The Kenoyer boys (our K-5 neighbors) were handy and very creative; they said, "If you sedate Pal, we can get her next door by sliding her onto a lowboy trailer. If she survives surgery, we'll need to rig up a sling that will hold her upright with the weight off her feet while she recovers."

It was getting dark and getting cold. A mad rush for time was on: making preparations, creating an operating floor in the open field, with a huge bonfire to keep Pal warm to prevent shock on an unusually cold night. It wasn't until three that morning that we heard Pal had come out of the operation alive, and the leg was successfully reset.

The Kenoyer boys worked throughout the night rigging up a sling for Pal in one of their barns. They reasoned that they needed to get her into the sling while sedated so she wouldn't fight getting into the harness.

Remarkably, by the early morning hours Pal was suspended in a K-5 ranch barn—safe and sound.

We bolted out of bed in the morning and ran across the twenty acres of prune trees separating the two ranches to see Pal. She looked tired but safe, suspended from the rafters with her leg in a splint.

Our joy was short-lived. Three days later, Pal figured how to escape from her sling and flipped out of it, shattering her leg bone in many pieces. But we remained determined to save her, so a similar scene followed as we reasoned with the vet: "You can't put Pal down, she's a member of the family."

"The leg can't be saved, it's too badly damaged," the vet said, assuming that would be the clincher. "The only other option is to amputate."

"Well then," said Linda, "we'll cut the leg off."

The poor vet, again faced with a crowd of red-eyed, whimpering kids, said, "Well, I hear it's possible for dogs to get along with three legs. I suppose it's possible a horse can, too."

Pal still sedated after her amputation

Pal's leg was amputated. The next risk was if she couldn't figure out how to stand or walk on three legs. If not, she would soon die. On the second morning after the amputation, as we watched with neighborhood friends and family around a bonfire, Pal, in a very weak condition, finally struggled to her feet. She was made famous in yet another feature story in *Western Horseman*; this time the title was "A Second Chance for Pal."

A Second Chance for Pal

The second article about Pal in a national magazine (*Western Horseman*), describing the events that led up to her amputation

Pal lived for twenty more years. The cost of the operation was never discussed, and my parents never second-guessed our decision.

The author at age 12, with Pal, now with only three leg.

There were long sleepy days when we were neither harvesting crops nor in school. When I was eleven, to fill my extra time, I started researching photography. I was fascinated by the chemical reactions on the film, by negatives, and by how light and exposure and focal points worked. With some coaching by an old photographer I befriended, I rigged up my own dark room, with red light attachments and enlargement equipment made with a proper lens mounted inside a coffee can: amazingly, it worked. The problem was that no one took me seriously as a photographer. No one wanted to have his or her picture taken by an eleven-year-old amateur. So, at twelve, with few options, I ended up taking what are now called "selfies." I promise you that these "selfies" were not out of narcissism. More challenging in those days, were the mechanics of taking a photograph of yourself. It proved to be tricky.

I found an old Brownie that had a short-spring delay trigger. By placing the camera precariously on a wood stump or something like it, I got some pictures that have survived all these years and that capture, in the background, a bit of Silicon Valley in its infancy.

The author, at twelve, with dog, Lika (top), and cat, Snowball - "selfies" in 1959.

Mariani Estate: Villa Maria

Villa Maria

Our rural life in Cupertino was about to change dramatically.

Shortly after Pal's amputation, Dad told us we might be moving to a nice home in Los Altos, which was already an upscale area at the edge of the Valley. However, he had some conditions: "It's difficult for us to afford to buy this home, so we won't have a budget to maintain the grounds. Therefore, as a condition of our moving into this nicer home, all you kids must agree, without complaint, to maintain the outdoor landscaping."

We jumped at the chance of moving out of our maze of quonset-huts called home. We figured Dad's conditions couldn't possibly be more work than doing all of the farm chores at our Cupertino ranch home, so everything seemed fine to us. After all, as Dad said, "How difficult can it be to mow a few lawns?" And he continued: "You must swear to take care of the entire yard without ever complaining, or I am not buying the house." We readily agreed to the terms of our new home. Of course, we hadn't yet seen the house or the grounds.

After visiting Villa Maria for the first time, we realized this would be no ordinary home. It was the Hamilton Mansion, built in 1930: a magnificent home, about a quarter of an acre under one roof, Moorish architecture built by craftsmen from all over the world. Regrettably, the main residence included five-and-a-half acres of meticulously cared for landscaped gardens. Once we moved in, these gardens became our responsibility to maintain! When we complained under our breath about the amount of work we had to do, Dad would simply say, "A deal is a deal."

Although we worked hard in the yard, we also played and laughed and made up all sorts of games in our new home and grew very attached to it. Years later, after Dad passed away, I purchased the Villa Maria from Dad's estate and raised my own family there; thus, it stayed in the family for a total of forty years. During the twenty years raising my children at Villa Maria, we employed three full-time gardeners to take care of the grounds. They were kept constantly busy every day. In retrospect, I can see Dad had made a pretty good property-maintenance deal with us.

Chile

About a year after we moved into Villa Maria, it was my turn to travel with Mom and Dad on their winter vacation. It was a trip to South America, in 1961. I was in seventh grade.

What Dad called "vacations" were really business trips. He loved his work so much that he often declared, "Work is my vacation." It seemed natural that local businessmen would entertain us at every stop in South America. Mom and I would sightsee while Dad spent his time in business meetings. On this "vacation," while Mom and Dad first traveled alone to New York, I traveled directly to South America, separately from my parents, but accompanied by Dad's senior food scientist, Dr. d'Alquaz, Philippine-born, though Spanish was his mother tongue. Our first stop was Brazil. Then we went to Argentina to meet up with my parents. I remember having a queasy feeling while buying "death insurance" for the flight. ("Flight safety" was considered something of an oxymoron in those days.)

Argentina's capital, Buenos Aires, excited me, filled me with a sense of wonder, and seeded in me a hunger to learn the perspectives of other cultures. The language, architecture, and fine foods, all had a distinct European flavor – Since I had not yet visited Europe, I didn't recognize the European based culture – I just saw the city's architecture, art, museums with wonderment from young eyes. Fortunately, at most social events everyone spoke English with charming accents, so I had no trouble communicating.

At one point, Dad decided we should all travel, a few days earlier than planned, to Santiago, Chile. Dr. d'Alquaz explained to me that it was dangerous to stay in Argentina, as the national elections were the next day; apparently, military coups were the country's national sport.

A series of coups had made the country's political environment unstable since the Peron coup in 1955, which had been followed, in 1958, by the "Revolución Libertadora," which brought in the unstable government of Frondizi, who also lost power in a military coup to the Peronist José Guido. As we left for the airport, I could see military men at every street corner carrying machine guns. I asked Dad why a certain marble building had so many pockmarks in it. Dad explained that a soldier had emptied his clip into the wall to scare people. Well, it worked—it scared me.

Flying over the mighty, majestic, snowcapped and glacier-filled crevices of the Andes was an unforgettable thrill—though flying in heavy turbulence in a state-of-the-art propeller plane of the time made me ill. Anyway, I was glad when we landed in Santiago, with a thump and two bounces down the runway—it would not be my last adventure at this airport.

We met with Dad's local fruit-growing partner in Chile, Alejandro. (His last name escapes me.) I didn't fully understand why we were even growing fruit in Chile until a decade later. At that time, businessmen and foreign investors in Chile were concerned about the growing influence of Marxism in the country. Looking back from today, those years are often referred to as the "pre-Allende" period.

Salvador Allende, a Marxist / radical socialist, was gaining in popularity. He had run for president in 1958, and would run again the following year, in 1962. The long pre-Allende era was gripped with the fear that, if Allende were elected, the country would be conquered by Marxist principles, as had happened recently in Cuba after the overturning of Fulgencio Batista by Fidel Castro; Allende was finally elected in 1970. The pre-Allende government was concerned with the flight of capital as a result of this fear. In 1962, the Chilean government enacted many restrictions on taking currency out of the country: you could only take money out of the country if you resided in Chile. Since Dad, for estate-planning purposes, had our families' agribusiness interests owned by us kids through a children's trust, the political situation in Chile created a bit of a problem. Dad wanted to sell the company's ranches in Chile, but how would he be able to get the proceeds from the sales back to the U.S.? He and Alejandro were stumped. As a twelve-year-old, overhearing a discussion about the dilemma over dinner one evening, I offered a solution.

Impetuously and frankly with little thought I asked, "How about if I stay behind and go to school for a year or two until all the ranches are sold?" I said.

Dinner in Chile 1961

Far left Maryfrances Mariani (my mother)Fourth from the right, Paul Mariani Jr and second on the right David Mariani

The conversation came to a dead stop—a handful of people around the table stared at each other in silence. My mother finally broke the silence by saying, "Are you sure you'd be willing to do that? You'd be away from home for a very long time." My first thought was what an adventure this would be. My second was that I'd be getting out of doing the gardening at Villa Maria. "Sure," I said. "I don't mind."

That night Mom and Dad grilled me again about whether I was sure I was O.K. with staying in Chile for so long. I was genuinely fascinated by Chile's culture; I kept saying "yes," without understanding how homesick I would become over the weeks and months that followed.

The next day, after the decision was made for me to stay in Santiago with a local family, I suddenly felt very important. Within a week, a power of attorney was executed and recorded, school and residency permits were obtained, interviews were had with prospective families for me to live with, and I took an entrance exam and was accepted into a local school, *San Jorge Collegio*.

A Chilean family was found for me to stay with, in their modest home. They had two older girls and a boy my age. The mother was the head of the household; the father was a heart doctor who practiced at a ski resort and, strangely, never visited. I never met him.

As I watched the plane take off, carrying Mom and Dad and Dr. d'Alquaz back to the U.S., I suddenly thought, *"What did I just do?"* and felt very alone. I looked up at my dad's business partner, Alejandro, who reassured me: "Don't worry, we'll check in on you with your Chilean family host to make sure you're O.K." The nice man was true to his word and a comfort to me—until tragedy struck. But I will never know the answer to the question I asked myself of "What did I just do" and whatever happened to Alejandro.

I stayed homesick for the better part of a year. I was young, but I learned about a new culture, a new language, and made new friends. It burned into me a different perspective   Chilean's had for America. The experience gave a different perspective of myself and my identity. In later years, this international perspective served me well and constantly reminded me how separated I felt from many Americans who had only a single, parochial view of the world. However, as I write this story, I take a step back and wonder, "What were my parents thinking, leaving behind their twelve-year–old, with the prospect of a Marxist regime about to come to power in Chile, and the very real possibility of widespread political violence?"

I learned much later that investing in the fruit business in Chile was my dad's attempt to solve one the dried fruit industry's fundamental problems, the high cost of carrying inventory throughout the year. A fresh fruit season last a few weeks – it was the only time to buy the fruit to dry; yet the inventory needed to supply grocery stores was year-round.

Logistically, Dad needed to purchase in advance about sixteen to seventeen months of fruit to supply grocery stores uninterrupted supply of dried fruit year-round.

The solution was to access supply from the Southern Hemisphere who enjoyed opposite seasons. [Height of apricot season in California was June and in the Southern hemisphere it was Christmas day]. We only needed to purchase and inventory half the amount of fruit to supply our customers year-round.

Dad reasoned, it cost about 30 cents a pound to inventory fruit for 12 months and it only cost ten cents a pound to ship the fruit from the Southern Hemisphere. When dealing with tens of millions of pounds, these savings quickly added up.

So my dad began investing in growing, processing, and shipping stone fruits (apricots, cherries, peaches, prunes, and the like) from Chile in the late 1950s in order to take advantage of these circumstances.

It was through this activity in international trade and commerce that he was introduced to families who managed large trading companies and agribusiness concerns in Chile. And I ended up, at the age of twelve, spending almost a year in Chile just as the political situation started heating up.

While I was living in Chile in 1961, Alejandro took me for road trips, and along the way we visited the homes of some of the older families in Chile who were involved with international commerce. One such family, the Duncons, raised a massive number of sheep—literally in the millions—with operations, I believe, primarily in southern Chile.

The Duncons were connected with a company called *"Compania Explotadora de la Isla de Pascua"* (*CEDIP*), owned by the famous trading company, William-Balfour. *CEDIP* had leased, in effect, all of Easter Island for the better part of the twentieth century for sheep grazing.

My dad always told me that no one learns anything while the lips are moving, so I listened to the adults talk. They talked around the dinner table about how the Easter Island lease had been unjustly taken away from them to enable the establishment of a Chilean naval base. (The lease cancellation had taken place around 1953.) In 1960, I was too young to understand the cultural devastation that resulted from European-type settlements and the intense use of land that results from a sheep operation. I was also too young to understand how the commercial operations had displaced and largely destroyed the island's unique culture. So, without understanding the broader perspective and cultural significance to Easter Island, I sympathized with the Duncons for losing their lease. The cultural decline, of course, had begun centuries earlier.

I was not too young, however, to marvel at Easter Island's artifacts.

I had a chance to examine the island's Rongorongo tablets, which are made of *toromiro*, a type of tropical hardwood. The tablets are inscribed with minute symbols in irregular, angled rows, which are believed to state either the prevailing myths of the island people or their origins or belief systems. The tablets looked like long rectangular paddles, three to four feet long. There is no Rosetta Stone for the Easter Island people to enable a translation of these tablets. They remain a mystery even today.

The most amazing Easter Island artifact for me, which I will never forget for the rest of my life, was not the famous fifty- to a hundred-ton Moai heads on the island, which I knew from pictures, but a rather simple musical instrument, a rectangular wooden box that appeared to be a solid piece of wood. It was ornately carved with various symbols. Along the top were three deeply carved slits across the width of the box.

Astonishingly, when you waved your hand over the top of the box, without touching the box, music began to play. It sounded to me (when I tried it) like a low hum riffing up and down like a slow funeral march. Imagine playing a musical instrument without ever touching it! No one knew how it worked.

The only theory proffered was that the waving of the hand created an air current that vibrated reeds inside the box. Sound would only emanate when the hand moved back and forth just above the top of the box. Because the box appeared to be a single block of wood, and because the slits were narrow (less than a quarter inch wide), it was difficult to conceive how anyone could have gutted the interior of the box and inserted reeds. The slits were cut at a steep angle, preventing a line-of-sight examination of the box's interior. I always wondered if the box might really have been made from two pieces joined tightly together, with the joints camouflaged by the ornate carvings—though neither I, nor anyone else, could see any telltale signs of a joint. It was even more a piece of art than a music box.

Allende lost the election, and we sold our properties, but the political turmoil in the country was evident to everyone. Chile had a small middle class, and a very small class of the very wealthy, making socialism appealing to the masses. Social unrest and violence, fomented (some believed) by the Soviets, began to erupt.

I began to feel very alone when Alejandro stopped coming to visit me. I tried to call Alejandro but my Chilean host would not allow it. This made me angry. Despite all attempts to hide what happened to Alejandro, they resolved the standoff on calling Alejandro by finally blurted it out, "Alejandro had been shot in the head by one of his workers, for no known reason." I was numb from shock. Fortunately, by the time the secret of his murder leaked out, it was time for me to go home.

En route to the airport, it started to snow—a very wet, heavy snow. This was extremely unusual for Santiago. My host family's mother said, "I have never seen it snow before, look how heavy it is coming down!" We could hardly see more than a few paces ahead of us on our way to the airport. In a city where it almost never snows, there was no snow removal equipment to clear the roads or airports. We heard on the radio that the airport might close because of the heavy storm.

I got on the Pan American flight home—Flight 46—back to the good old U.S.A.; headed for California via a connecting flight at Miami. We rolled onto the taxiway, waiting for permission to take off. The pilot announced that permission had been granted. We rolled into position; the engines began to roar, when suddenly all of the runway lights went dark.

The entire Santiago region had blacked out.

The rare, devastating, wet snow (wet snow being very heavy) had broken power lines and thus knocked out all forms of communications throughout the entire region. We taxied back to the terminal and de-planed. There was no communication with the outside world for the following five days; the airport was closed for four.

Meanwhile, back home, Dad's New York business associate, Bill Burke, an elderly diminutive soft soul, had been sent to Miami to meet me at customs, to ensure I would get from the international terminal to the domestic terminal, where I would take a flight back to California. Mr. Burke waited patiently for my plane to arrive, but of course it never did. He didn't know my plane had never taken off from Santiago. Alarmed, he called Dad. Dad called the airlines, who confirmed that the plane had been given permission to take off in Santiago, but that was all they knew, since all communications with Chile were out. About fifteen hours later, the plane was officially listed as missing. Dad's constant barrage of questions, which included a call to the president of Pan American from one Congressman Gubser (a friend of Dad's), finally produced a speculative answer that Dad did not want to hear. A top official from Pan Am had confided to him that they suspected the plane had crashed in the snowstorm. I was, of course, completely unaware of the sobbing and gnashing of teeth back home. Bill Burke camped out at the Miami airport, waiting for any word or instructions from Dad.

On the fourth day, I arrived in Miami via the same carrier but with a different flight number, as we had to stop in Peru for fuel; due to persistent heavy weather conditions, we couldn't take off with a full load of fuel from Santiago.

Bill was told that there was a little boy in customs who had just arrived from Peru. They didn't have the flight manifest but offered to escort him into a holding area to see if it was me. Seeing this grown man break down in tears as he fell to his knees and hugged me for the longest time frightened me. I didn't know what all the fuss was about. We thought everyone knew that our plane had never taken off. After Bill explained to me the situation, I said, "We need to call Mom and Dad." I cleared customs, and Bill went straight to the pay phone. There were no cell phones in those days. Bill didn't have enough change for a long distance call. I spotted a currency exchange booth and hustled over to exchange my Chilean escudos for dollars. Bill finally got the long distance call through to home. (It was 8 a.m. in Miami and 5 a.m. in Cupertino.) Bill's chin was still trembling when he got though. All he said was, "I got your boy." That is when I heard Mom's screaming through the phone receiver in the background— screams of relief over the phone. I felt so bad that everyone was so worried, but I also felt very loved at the same time and couldn't wait to get back to my family and Villa Maria.

Chapter 13

Santa Clara Valley Comes of Age

We all knew about the Military base, Moffett Field, that housed dirigibles during WWII. The giant hanger was hard to miss as it stuck out like a sore thumb in rural Santa Clara Valley. Upon my arrival back home in 1962, I saw that Santa Clara Valley had changed beyond military bases. There were more cars on the road, more housing developments and regional malls were being constructed. How could our rural farm community have been transformed so quickly?

It was annoying that housing developments were being built right up against our orchards. Imagine: people were complaining about us, with the noise of our tractors and spray rigs. "Hey, we were here first," was our attitude. "We didn't tell you to move here."

We had an old army Jeep from an army surplus auction, with shrapnel still imbedded in its sides, that I drove to our ranches around Sunnyvale and Cupertino.[19] We could get to most of the ranches traveling through the orchards, off road. The Jeep had a high wheelbase and four-wheel drive, which kept me from getting hung up on levees or in muddy ground.

One of my jobs during cherry season was to chase kids out of the orchards. Local mothers would send their kids out to pick our cherries—from our point of view, this was trespassing and stealing. By the mid-1960s, property taxes began to soar because they were indexed against its new commercial value rather than its agricultural revenue value. We were having trouble just paying our property taxes from our net fruit proceeds, and these kids were stealing our fruit. Many of the old farmers in those days, using shotguns with rock salt and a light load, would shoot at the kids, to scare them off. I would just chase them out using the army Jeep. It got to the point where, as they heard the old Jeep coming, I could see them scattering before I got into the orchard.

A typical Cupertino scene, in 1960, of prune picking before the invention of picking machines

Before the machines, crews of prune pickers, each bearing a stick and a hook, would shake each branch of a given tree individually until all of the ripened prunes on the branch had fallen to the ground. Then another army of workers, toiling on their hands and knees, would put the prunes into buckets, then pour the prunes from the buckets into "lug" boxes, two buckets per box.

My brother and I were experienced prune pickers. We were grateful to be promoted to the job of "swamping boxes"; this meant carrying the fifty-five-pound lug boxes on our shoulders to a flatbed truck for transport to the dehydrators.

Bucket after bucket of prunes were poured into the lug boxes, [two buckets per box] These boxes needed to be hand loaded onto flatbed trucks called "bobtails", for reasons unknown for transport to the processing plant. The process of loading the boxes onto our flatbed trucks was called "swamping", for reasons again unknown. I was called a "swamper." We "swamped"—easily a thousand boxes per day per person. By sunset we were exhausted, but grateful we were not on our hands and knees, picking prunes.

The prune business was also changing. Labor was becoming expensive, so automated prune-picking machines were invested in and prune-processing dippers were invented. We had fewer workers, but only a small number of people knew how to run these specialized machines. So, during prune season, I, now fifteen years old, worked hundred-hour weeks, operating these machines.

With the advent of a picking machine, only sporadic prunes were left on the ground after the machines went through the orchards. There were too few "dropped" prunes to make it pay to hire someone (at piece rate)[20] to pick them, so the job defaulted to us boys.

Machines shaking prunes onto canvas sheets that deflected the falling prunes onto a conveyor belt (above), with the conveyor moving the prunes into bins (below)

I don't know for certain who was "the last prune picker," but my guess is I may likely have been the last person to pick prunes from the ground. My oldest brother had been promoted to driving trucks by that time, brother John was always hiding under trees or under empty boxes to avoid work, and brothers Mark and Rick were too young to be out in the fields when automatic prune-tree pickers were introduced. So, I think I might have that dubious title of "the last prune picker."

It was about this time I recall my father and grandfather's anxious conversations over a proposed minimum wage. In the 1950's it was a $ 1.00 per hour – now in 1963, the national minimum wage was proposed to be $1.25. The dinner table chatter was about how, figuratively speaking, the sky was falling, in with a spirited debate whether or not we were going to survive with such high wages imposed on us by Washington. This discussion in retrospect sounds pretty silly with our economy adjusting to nearly $ 15 an hour today.

But change was in the air everywhere. In the early 1960s the Santa Clara Valley had been riddled with "cutting sheds." These sheds were makeshift shade houses set up during harvest time; small armies of people had work stations where they cut apricots in half and lay them onto drying trays to be smoked and then dried in the sun.

Now machines were cutting apricots and peaches in the dry yards; a forklift with one driver could clear a field of full lug boxes on pallets from the orchards within an hour, replacing a full gang of "swampers" loading trucks as a standard practice just a few short years before.

We changed to using bins, rather than the small lug boxes, to fill and carry fruit. Forklifts had side-sliding forks to carry the bins, so the drivers didn't need to be skilled. Also, the process of washing prunes was no longer done by hand. Hydraulic lifts tipped the bins into big vats of water to wash them, then placed the prunes automatically onto trays for drying. Within five years, with new, automated technology, a handful of workers replaced hundreds of people to work the ranch and process the fruit.

During the 1960s and '70s, the Valley was an odd mixture of a rural artifacts of an agrarian community and the new economy driven by high tech and innovations. Fairchild, the first big semiconductor company in the area, was talked about over our dinner table. Then we learned that some guy named David Packard had started a small electronics company in the Valley; it was more important to us that Packard grew apricots.[21] We also learned from David that high tech was more than a passing spasm within the Valley. Something fundamentally had changed in the valley.

Part III

Chapter 14

Danger takes Form

Boarding School and High School:

After returning home from Chile, I learned that boarding school was being planned for me. It was Dad's idea to send all of us kids to The Abbey School, a heralded international all boys finishing school in Canon City, Colorado. We suspected it was Mom's way of coping, shipping each of us out of the house when we turned fourteen. Regardless of the reasons, we were shipped off to boarding school for ten months of each year, coming home to work the fields during harvest time, often out of the bay area [Sonoma County].

Thus, my two older brothers had, by age fourteen, essentially, moved out of the house. I guess the thinking was that I would be able to do so as well. So, our most formative years were spent during the fall and winter months at the Abbey School, with summers in Healdsburg or at our other ranches to work the harvests with my grandfather and my smiling grandmother close behind, lending support by providing our meals, etc. From my perspective, as a result of my time in Chile, I was more or less out of our family house by age twelve.

Dad believed in nurturing self-reliance at an early age: beginning with our freshman year in high school, Dad put money into the saving accounts of us kids every September in an amount sufficient to pay our direct living expenses for the year (September 1 through August 31). Our discretionary spending money came from money we earned working in the summer. We were not exactly on our own, because included in our September deposit was a budget for our own expenses at the boarding school, including tuition, books, and clothes. This was Dad's way of pushing us to grow up, take responsibility for ourselves, and learn at an early age how to manage money, the value of hard work, and the value of a dollar.

The summer before leaving for boarding school, I developed a painful boil-like inflammation on my derrière. As a self-conscious fourteen-year-old, I was mortified. Avoiding embarrassment, I decided to "wish away" whatever was causing the pain, so I endured the pain for about a month to avoid a physical inspection by another human being. Finally, I gave up my modesty and told Dad. I felt like fainting when he told me to bend over for "inspection." Fear came over me when Dad exclaimed, "Holy Mother of Mercy, we need to get you to a hospital right now." On the way to the hospital, I hoped it was not going to be a nurse who "inspected" my posterior. Sure enough, not only was the nurse female, but attractive, which somehow added to my embarrassment.

The diagnosis was an advanced case of a festering fistula that had broken through my colon to my buttock, close to the rectum. The passageway of eaten-away flesh from the infection was large enough to require an operation if the cavity was not able to heal through constant flushing of the infected area with sterilization fluids. The latter would mean sitting on a bucket of hot water with sterilization salts for fifteen minutes every hour for two months. I was determined to avoid another "inspection" of my backside by the nurse or anybody else, so I opted to try self-healing rather than endure the operation. Although I was fastidious about the sterilization and washing routine for the entire summer, the self-healing didn't work.

It was one week before I was supposed to board a plane for the boarding school in Colorado when the doctor said, "Your fistula isn't healing. We'll need to operate." The operation was successful, with the help of thirty-six stitches sewn up inside my body. Sore, with great difficulty sitting on the airplane, I was off to school.

The first week at the Abbey was great. Everyone knew my older brother, John, who was the senior-class president. I was voted president of my class—on the heels of John's enormous popularity (I suspected), since I was new to the school. The school was located on the grounds of a functioning Benedictine Abbey. The Benedictines are a Catholic religious order of priests, brothers, and nuns under the authority of an abbot rather than the local bishop. Consequently, the Benedictines of the Abbey School were an autonomous and self-sufficient community growing food for the school and selling produce to the community to pay for expenses. The entire school was staffed by the resident priests, brothers, and nuns. The religious lived by strict rules, with rigid routines, and they expected the students to follow strict rules and rigid routines as well.

One routine was that, at exactly 5:00 p.m. each day, the church tower bell would ring twice. That was the signal that, precisely fifteen minutes later, when another bell rang, all students were to be in their rooms to get washed up for dinner. At precisely 5:30, yet another bell would ring for everyone to go to the dining hall.

After the 5:15 bell, the floor priest would check each room so that all students would be accounted for each day. The consequences of not being in your room at the appointed time were different types of punishment and work details. Canon City was best known for housing the state prison; the local joke was the Abbey School was the other prison.

For the first week of school, I was hyper-diligent and got to my room a full ten minutes before the 5:15 bell rang. On the sixth day of school, I remember casually leaning on the door jamb of my room, talking with a fellow student across the hall when the bell rang. He jumped back from his door jamb into his room; surprised by his action, I, unfortunately, peeked out into the hall. That was when I first heard Father Allen scream my name. Father Allen was a lean wearing a constant sour expression. I could not understand what was happening, because I was clearly in my room, albeit with my head sticking out.

With his hands behind his back, Gestapo style, Father Allen just kept screaming, in a frenzy, over and over again, "Mariani! Come down here right now!" I knew I was in my room, so I couldn't imagine why he was so angry. I walked up to him, frightened by the uncontrolled rage on his face. Father Allen bellowed, "I could see your head down the hallway sticking out. You were not all the way in your room. Now turn around." I did so, not knowing that behind his back was a solid wooden paddle, about four feet long. He swung with all his might, hitting me squarely on my posterior, rupturing sixteen stitches, I am told. I don't remember much other than a sharp excruciating pain as I began hemorrhaging on the floor. I remember my head spinning with pain and seeing the blood pooling around me, then I passed out.

Two doctors and a nurse greeted me with worried looks when I woke up two days later, as they had kept me heavily sedated. With an IV in my arm and multiple units of blood transfusions and painkillers in my system, I felt fine. I was told I would be well enough to go back to my room and resume school in a few days. When I returned to my room, I picked up, on the door to my room, a three-week detention notice for violating school rules about being in my room at the proper time. It was galling to me: *"For not fully being in my room at 5:15."* I was flabbergasted. The idea of being away at school no longer seemed so appealing. My brother John, in a comforting way, tried to explain, regarding the detention, that rules were rules.

The next day, after classes, feeling annoyed and resentful, I reported to my first day of three weeks of detention with a chip on my shoulder. One "detention day" equaled, for each day, two hours of hard work. On the first detention day, I was assigned to report to a gardener in the flower garden inside the Abbey walls. (Well, it was better than plowing the fields, another common detention chore.) An old gardener in well-worn clothes handed me, without a word, some tools to work the ground. Silently, I got to work. After about five minutes, he said, with a warm smile and a twinkle in his eye, "I think the nuns will be taking the pastries out of the oven about now. Let's see if we can get some sweets. Don't tell anyone."

I immediately responded, "Sure." I wasn't going to complain. We proceeded via the back way behind the kitchens, which were off limits to students. We sat together on a bench, ate pastries hot from the oven, and talked on a variety of subjects for the rest of my two hours of detention. I mostly ate. The donuts were terrific.

Quietly going to the back of the kitchen became a ritual for us each day. Ten minutes of work followed by an hour and fifty minutes of great pastries and good company. The gardener was soft-spoken, with kind eyes, and an engaging conversationalist. Finally, after about a week, he asked me about Father Allen and what had happened. He listened but didn't say a word. He asked how I felt about Father Allen and the Abbey School. I didn't like either Father Allen or the school and felt I could tell him the truth. He asked a series of questions over the following weeks about the school routine and which teachers I liked and which I didn't like; which teachers seemed prepared and which ones were only going through the motions of teaching. The old guy had a knack for asking a few questions and listening to me go on and on. I felt he really listened. In an odd way, I felt better about the Abbey once I had fully served my detention period. The opportunity to talk through my anger proved beneficial.

About a month later, in October, was the Feast of All Souls. The local bishop and the abbot himself would be present at the mass. The bishop, ceremoniously parading in with his staff in hand, was followed by the abbot, who rode on a platform carried by the brothers of the Abbey. My eyes fell first on the abbot's richly ornamented ceremonial gowns, then my eyes met the abbot's. Our eyes actually met! I was staring into the eyes of my gardener friend.

I seldom saw Father Allen for the rest of the year. When we did run into each other, Father Allen seemed circumspect. In fact, he never said another word to me for the rest of the year.

The following school year, I badly wanted to be home and go to school locally. Though my parents still wanted me in boarding school, I managed to convince them to let me stay home and go to a local school, Saint Francis High School, in Mountain View.

From the Valley of Heart's Delight to Silicon Valley

In Santa Clara Valley, with more tract homes and more cars and more people, net in-migration was the new norm. The Valley was changing before my eyes.

For as long as I could remember, Santa Clara had been known as "The Valley of Heart's Delight." The Valley was so famous for its agriculture that Santa Clara had become an adjective meaning "quality" all over the world. A "Santa Clara prune" was a common expression. It carried great pride for us locals because it meant "best quality" in the fruit industry worldwide. By the late 1960s I began to hear—though infrequently at first-people refer to Santa Clara Valley as "Silicon Valley." I thought it was a clever play on words but never dreamed it would stick. It actually annoyed me a bit . . . it was like outsiders today referring to San Francisco as "Frisco": it was grating for the locals.

Whether they called it "Santa Clara Valley" or "Silicon Valley," it was good to be back home to finish my high school years at Saint Francis. The school had only 400 students, with only one classroom wing completed, and was surrounded by orchards. By the year 2000 it had become a sprawling campus with football, soccer, and baseball fields replacing the surrounding orchards, and hosted 1400 students.

My entering Saint Francis began a new tradition for the Mariani family. My younger brothers and younger sister followed my lead—no more boarding schools. From 1963 to 2003, for forty straight years, Saint Francis hosted at least one or more Mariani family members as students.

Saint Francis had a very active sports program. After my athletic successes in grammar school, I went out for the football team, expecting not only to make the team but to become a great football player. I had these expectations even though I was only 4'11." The word "delusional" comes to mind. After being literally knocked unconscious during my first practice, I heard the coach who walked me to the infirmary and tell me, "I love your heart for the game, son. You come back out when you grow six inches." I protested, and said, in my concussion fog, "But, coach, the season start in two weeks, I can't grow that fast." The coach gently repeated his comment three more times before I finally got it: I was being cut from the team.

The sobering reality sank in that perhaps I was not a gifted athlete or gifted but just too short.

Mom picked me up from school that day. I couldn't talk because I had a lump in my throat. I wasn't going to cry in front of my mother. I just couldn't talk. She didn't notice I was upset. As we pulled into our driveway, she was furious and sarcastic. "Since you see fit not to say a word to your mother on the way home, or thank her for picking you up from school, you can walk home from now on." It was the last day she picked me up at school. Since home was nearly five miles away from school, I learned the art of hitchhiking.

Since I was too small to play football, I concluded I must be too small for basketball, so didn't even bother trying out for the team. After some thought, I realized the only two sports not dependent on size to be successful were wrestling (classed by weight) and tennis. Wrestling against someone else's sweaty body didn't appeal to me, but Saint Francis, as a new school, had no tennis program.

That summer I took lessons at John Gardiner's famed Tennis Ranch in Carmel Valley. It was a concentrated, three-week program to learn to play, and play well. About the same time, I finally got a growing spurt to average height, which made me a bit uncoordinated for the first time in my life. Learning tennis was difficult, but because Dad had taught me the value of hard work, I practiced hard, and, at the end of the three weeks, was awarded "most improved player." It was really no secret how I did this. Most of the kids slept in until the camp reveille bell rang, but I would get up two hours earlier (at five a.m.) to practice hitting and serving. I also practiced after dinner, while everyone else was goofing off. It just takes work—effort and practice—to improve at a skill.

The following summer Dad wouldn't let me attend the camp, as the prune harvest was early that year, but by then I had caught the tennis bug, and one of my tennis buddies, Steve Stefanki and I played tennis every chance we got.

By that September, we had convinced our math dean, Mr. Johnson, who had never played tennis in his life, to be our "moderator" and coach. We raised money from our unfortunate parents for uniforms and league fees, and got permission to use the tennis courts in Mountain View's parks and recreation facility to practice and host matches. We were all set for the following year.

Throughout the rest of our high school years, we earned varsity letters: Steve and I alternated as # 1 and # 2. We battled each other to be top dog, and practiced with each other well into the night, under lights, every chance we got. Later, I became the youngest registered tennis pro and taught for several years at the Los Altos Country Club, and Steve eventually became the U.S. Olympic coach in 1984. I was moderately successful because I practiced for hours on end. Steve and his two younger brothers, John and Larry, were the ones with true natural talent. Mr. Johnson continued coaching tennis, and eventually retired from tennis coaching with the most wins in the CCS (Central Coast Section) league's history.

My years at Saint Francis were also the last time I would live at Villa Maria until many years later. Consistent with the deal we kids had made with Dad, my weekends, were consumed by working the Villa's grounds.

Although Dad's business was global in scope, our family never seemed to have much money. We lived in what seemed to be a dichotomy; we resided in a mansion but scrimped and saved every penny. In our household, spending even ten cents that was not utilitarian was a near-sin. Only years later, when I was the CFO of Dad's global empire, did I understand, at least in part, why.

Like most Catholic schools, Saint Francis always had some kind of fundraiser going on. For example, we were required to sell chocolate candy bars as a regular part of our school duties. The school would distribute several boxes to each student. At the end of two weeks, we had to return the boxes we didn't sell, together with the money from the sales.

I was accountable for every bar, or I had to pay the school from my own meager allowance. As a product of our environment of scrimping and saving money, I was developing a mild fear of not having enough money.

Early one morning, I caught a younger brother stealing from my inventory of candy bars for his personal consumption. I got angry at him and started shouting. My mother came down from her bedroom and started to scream at me for disturbing her. Then, unexpectedly from a mother who never swore, she shouted, "You son of a bitch!" (she apparently never saw the irony in that statement) and started violently kicking me in the my private parts. In shock, and enraged that she would do such a thing, I grabbed her and held her tightly up against the kitchen wall and started screaming myself, warning her never to do that again. (I'm not sure, but I might have used a few choice words myself.) The ruckus, regrettably, woke my dad.

My father, not having a clue about what had just happened, came barreling down the hall after me just as I was leaving the house for school—his first closed-fisted blow to my head I didn't see coming. Unfortunately, it did not knock me out. The beating was unforgettable. Eventually, I scrambled to my feet and out a side-door to escape. Dad, forever the authoritarian, began yelling at me not to return home until I apologized to Mom. I was not about to apologize, so I did not return for many weeks, remaining incommunicado and staying at different friends' homes on different nights. There was no communication—just silence from both sides.

Dad managed to get a message to me via the school principal's office that he wanted to talk. After a long rehearsed written speech, he read to me about how the Bible teaches that I must "honor thy father and thy mother," I remained silent. Finally, I said I would apologize for not honoring my father and mother according to God's will, but I would not apologize for what Mom provoked me into doing or to Mom for what happened. It amazed me that Dad did not follow with an apology for his own actions, or that Mom did not apologize for her behavior. They did a great deal to dishonor to themselves which hurt more than the beating I endured.

With my youngest sister and two younger brothers too young to do any meaningful work, and my two older brothers and oldest sister no longer living at Villa Maria, the lion's share of the yard upkeep fell on my shoulders. I was okay with that. From my perspective, it was an accepted part of life and family obligations. For that reason, Dad finally relented and gave me some relief. He brought in a worker from our factory, named Dusan, to do more than just the heavy trimming of the trees. I was grateful that, during my senior year in high school, the yard work burden thus dropped dramatically. I noted that Dad would often have long conversations with Dusan, in the gardens. Dad had a great admiration for the dignity of work and admired people who worked hard. Dusan's work ethic made him, in Dad's eyes, an equal. They were genuine friends. You could see it in their eyes, by their smiles and warm hugs when they greeted each other.

The contrast of Dad talking one moment with Dusan as an equal, then later in the afternoon greeting and entertaining royalty or heads of state will always burn in my memory. It profoundly formed my own value system. It became the moral prism through which I saw the world. Dad remained an enigma, exhibiting a complex combination of, on the one hand, pride, arrogance, even hubris, and, on the other hand, a genuine, gentle, soft humility.

Danger in the Seminary

Mom and Dad were devout Catholics. Mom, a convert, outwardly expressed her faith in part by acquiring religious artifacts. As a result, Villa Maria slowly turned into what looked to some people like a monastery or part of a mini version of the Vatican Museum; the Villa even had a chapel, including an altar, priest's vestments, bejeweled chalices, a solid-gold monstrance—the works.

Dad expressed his faith by being a "doer." Few of Dad's business associates knew that Dad spent at least fifty percent of his time during the last third of his business career traveling the world, establishing new chapters of the Serra Club. The members of this club are pious men dedicated to helping establish religious vocations all over the world. I am unsure of the exact number, but I believe Dad established clubs in more than seventy-five countries. Dad likened it to the work of Father Junipero Serra (canonized in 2015), who set up missions all over California. As a consequence of Dad's missionary activity, we had a string of clergy as houseguests in Villa Maria. Some stayed longer than others, some for months at a time. Some were remarkable men; some of our guests, unknown to my parents, were deeply flawed human beings.

Religion, and in particular our faith, Roman Catholic, was a dominant part of my upbringing. My brother John joined the Christian Brothers in 1966, and in 1967 I entered Saint Patrick's Seminary, intending to become a diocesan priest after I graduated from high school.

My awareness that Dad was helping establish vocations for Holy Mother Church, combined with my natural desire to please him, was, no doubt, a powerful subconscious influence on my decision to become a priest. My passion was to be a missionary, but I was conflicted whether to become a Maryknoll missionary or diocesan priest. On the advice of a Maryknoll priest, who pointed out that, unlike Maryknoll fathers, a diocesan priest did not have to take a vow of poverty, I made a practical decision to become a diocesan priest.

My vocation was based, simply, on my reverence for the Almighty and an understanding that I felt best inside when I was doing something for someone else. I experienced spikes of happiness in receiving from others, but those feelings were fleeting. My toys received at Christmas gave me great joy, but one that lasted scarcely a week.

One experience I had of the profound joy of giving left on me an especially deep and lasting impression.

It was winter, and I was driving with my buddies toward Lake Tahoe in the Sierra Nevada, for a few days of skiing. En route, we hit a bitter cold front and a heavy snow storm and stopped the car to put on our snow chains. We got them on in record time, for us. Meanwhile other cars on the road had also stopped and their drivers were laboriously adding chains, leaving the road relatively, if temporarily, free of traffic. Our speed with the snow chains had the added advantage that, by getting back on the road before the other cars, we'd have the road free for the next few miles and be able (we figured) to avoid heavy traffic ahead.

As we began pulling out onto the road and driving past the other cars, I saw an elderly gentleman with hands bloodied from unsuccessfully struggling to put chains on his tires. I was driving; I took a long look at the man struggling, then screeched on the brakes, saying, "Guys, let's jump out and help this guy with his chains." We put his snow chains on as we watched the cars moving back onto the road until the traffic jammed, as we had predicted, to a slow crawl. We had missed our window to get ahead of the traffic.

After we finished, the man's deep blue eyes—his wife freezing inside the car—began to fog with tears of appreciation, combined with a big hug and many thank you's. He insisted on getting our mailing addresses. He was a pistachio grower in Fresno, as I learned later.

It was the look in his eyes and knowing we had done a good thing when we really were tempted to just blow by him, that warmed my heart. So, giving was better than receiving. However, in this case giving led to receiving; every year, for fourteen years after the incident alongside that snowy road, until he passed away, the man we had helped sent me a box of pistachios.

So, what better walk in life is there than to devote your whole life to giving—giving to others? The priesthood, in theory, is a lifetime of such giving. I reasoned that not all priests were like Father Allen. And so, after much reflection, I became convinced that the priesthood was for me. I had many girls who were friends, as well as girlfriends, in high school. I still had to become mentally reconciled to the fact that my decision meant I would never know a woman and have a family.

My priestly ambition was, however, short lived.

Seminary life closed me off from the world. No newspapers, no magazines, no TV. The only outside contact was tightly controlled by a priest who wielded absolute control. This was censorship and mind-control through the control of information. My first two years of college seminary (which I entered as a college freshman) took place on the same campus as the seminary high school. I watched from our side of the campus the high school side of the complex, and wondered about the wisdom of these young kids (some as young as fourteen) experiencing such a narrow life experience. It might be too strong to call it "mind-control by information control," but those were the thoughts in my head at the time. "At such an early age, how can one make informed decisions?" I wondered about the similarity of the seminary experience in those days to the tactics of a cult.

When I entered the seminary's college, I noticed that most of my classmates had also attended the seminary's high school; only a handful of us entered as college freshman students with a normal high school experience. I was worried.

I admired one guy in my class, named Jack, who had done two tours of duty in Vietnam. He was seven or eight years older than me and "worldly," judging from some of his stories. He was a man's man and clearly heterosexual. He made his "warrior to priest" decision after seeing firsthand how chaplains had given peace of mind to his soldiers: "This guy [the chaplain] was a rock. This guy was solid." Jack was one of the few who got up for daily mass with me at 6:30 a.m. It was the only time mass attendance was optional.

Each seminarian got assigned to a priest, who became his spiritual advisor. My advisor also taught Greek. It was the last year that a seminarian needed to learn Greek, so I saw the class as pointless and seldom attended—a big mistake. My advisor brought me in on my first spiritual consultation and informed me, without ever having spoken to me (including during class), "I think you are too obsessed with materialism and fashion. We know about your family's mansion close by. You need more humility." I thought to myself, "*If this guy only knew that my family always teases me about my* lack *of attention to fashion, and that Villa Maria is just our home— that's all. This guy has no idea who I am as a person.*" My respect for this priest dropped, and my respect for him continued to drop during the upcoming months. My spiritual advisor also was extremely effeminate, but I didn't read much into my observations at the time.

The seminary began an experimental program that allowed visitors for one hour on Saturdays, from three to four p.m., before dinner and vespers. One Saturday, my spiritual advisor saw Jack with several of his Vietnam buddies, who were visiting, drinking a couple of beers in the seminary parking lot. Alcohol was, of course, forbidden, since most of us were underage. Jack was thirty years old and just having a brew with his buddies. He was expelled from the seminary. He was devastated. We talked, and I concluded the church had lost a good man.

I first believed Jack's expulsion was about alcohol. Little did I realize it was about something far more disturbing. I would soon find out the real reason.

Over the next three weeks, a girl who was a friend of mine came to visit each Saturday. Although we had dated at one time, we were still good friends. My spiritual advisor brought me in after visiting hours were over and asked, "We noticed you have a female visitor coming to see you on your Saturday visitation periods." I said, "Yes."

"We are concerned. Are you not serious about becoming a priest? Do you not realize that you must take a vow of celibacy?"

I retorted, "Yes, I know. Celibate is a vow not to marry; it does not mean to renounce women."

"But why would you put yourself in the near occasion of sin?"

Astonished, I said, "I think God wishes us to be ministers to all of God's people, not just half. Talking and engaging in a friendly manner with women I would think was healthy. I don't agree that it is putting me in the near occasion of sin."

The next question flabbergasted me even more. "Do you like women? By that I mean, are you attracted to women?"

I said, "Of course. Aren't you?" By the look on his face, I knew I knew something was not right. I said to myself, "*Oh, now I get it.*" My spiritual advisor turned stone cold and just stared at me. In an effort to take the pressure off me, I started pulling at straws and said, "Is that why Jack got kicked out of the seminary—because he's heterosexual?"

"Officially, Jack was dismissed because he drank alcohol on the premises."

"Oh, come on—one beer is enough to turn away a vocation, a vocation given by God?"

"I said that *officially* Jack was dismissed because of the beer incident. You can read whatever you want into my statement."

After that session with my spiritual advisor, I was on red alert.

The very next day I saw two seminarians who had exaggerated feminine mannerisms duck into one of the priest's rooms—the room of my spiritual advisor. Still in denial, I blocked out the indicators of all the parties and reasoned, "They must both be confessors to the priest, since it's strictly forbidden for anyone to be in anyone else's room—including the priest's rooms." I began to notice special privileges given to these seminarians. I now had a nagging worry.

That night I wrote a letter to my dad, which Mom gave back to me thirty years later. If Mom had not kept the letter along with Dad's things, I would have forgotten what I wrote. Regrettably, the letter proved prophetic, portending a disaster in the making. The letter was dated December 16, 1967:

Dear Dad,

Seminary life gives me a bird's eye view of what it is like to live life as a priest. I am living with them and observe their daily routines. I find the life of the clergy is subject to the same distractions of everyday life inside the priesthood as outside the priesthood; petty jealousies, bureaucracies, politics, the chores of managing assets and facilities consume their day. It surprises me how little time they have to actually pray, or minister directly to people in need, or time to perform charitable works. The question I have to ask myself is whether I would be more effective outside or inside the church system. As an independent outside the system, it would allow me to get involved in any project I want, without layers of administration and approvals and politics.

More importantly, there is something very wrong with the Sulpicians. [NOTE: Sulpicians are a community of diocesan priests supporting, guiding, and teaching priests and future priests; my spiritual advisor was a Sulpician.] It is my conclusion, too many of them may be homosexuals. This may seem outrageous, but from what I am witnessing, I think I am right. I see a filtering process going on that is systematically weeding out solid vocations of heterosexual men and rewarding those with homosexual tendencies. Our future recruits into the priesthood could be disproportionately made up of homosexuals, and perhaps pedophiles. Don't get me wrong. I am not saying all homosexuals are pedophiles, nor is there's anything wrong with celibate homosexuals.

However, I am becoming more and more convinced that many of the seminarians are being abused by the Sulpicians and may become abusers. This can't be good.

Also, Dad, I am beginning to have issues with the whole idea of celibacy. Saint Peter and Saint Paul were married. Eastern Orthodox priests can marry. All-male communities are very inviting to individuals who are attracted to men. I am very concerned that, in the next twenty to twenty-five years, there are going to be abuses and scandals, with the hierarchy turning a blind eye because they are also of like kind. I think there are bad things going on with young boys now in the seminary. I have no proof. But circumstantially, it is pretty obvious to me what is going on. I think the Church will get a black eye over pedophilia within its ranks over the next twenty to twenty-five years.

It pains me, Dad, to see you work so hard for vocations only to have the best and the brightest run out of the seminary because the teaching order is sick.

I have decided that I need to get out of here. I know how much you want to have priests in the family. However, I hope you will support me in this decision.

Love, David

Dad supported me, and I never regretted my decision to leave the seminary.

Guatemalan Armed Rebels

During the summer of 1968, I attended a talk in nearby Menlo Park by a missionary priest, Father Alvarez, that turned out to be a fundraiser for the needs of his mission. At about the same time I met Father Humberto Almazan.

Father Humberto Almazan had an "actor to altar" career. He had an actors good looks to go along with his persona. In 1950, Humberto met and married his French wife Ginette, a war orphan who had suffered from malnutrition during the German occupation of France. Although the doctors warned against it, Ginette became pregnant, and the young couple spent months of idyllic happiness in anticipation of the birth of their child. In the eighth month, complications set in. Ginette died in childbirth and the baby, a boy, was born dead.

Shattered, Humberto buried himself in his work, finishing his studies and traveling to Italy for a film with Ingrid Bergman. By the age of thirty-five, Humberto Almazan had had performed in twenty-one movies and thirty plays and attained his goal of becoming a famous actor. His career had taken him to

France, Italy, and England, and he had performed with a number of well-known stars, including Sophia Loren and Anna Magnani.

In 1955 he won the "Ariel"—the Mexican equivalent of the Oscar. He became a star on Mexican television, and his name a household word in that country.

On top of the world, Humberto found it a lonely place. Father Humberto's story was beginning to sound familiar to me, after all the many success stories I had heard in Silicon Valley. Remembering the love and happiness he had shared with his wife, he felt that if he could find a way to love and share his life with others, he could be happy again. So he left the life of glamour and became a priest.

In 1969, during one of his visits to Villa Maria, Father Almazan briefed us on the Indonesian government's desire to begin promoting Bali as a tourist destination. However, the island's leprosy stood in the way of tourist dollars and riches. The government was exercising a form of genocide by isolating the natives with leprosy in colonies by the sea, then putting them on starvation diets to "kill off the problem." He recommended that I visit and work at a leper colony in Mexico to gain experience prior to any decision to go to Indonesia to help establish a clinic there.

In the meanwhile, while attending a meeting with Father Alvarez, he described his biggest needs was a way to communicate with the far reaches of his ministry. He explained that many of his parishioners lived high in the mountains, where there were no reliable telecommunications. They were unable to attend mass – but they wanted to listen to his services. In Silicon Valley Father Alvarez had found the sophisticated equipment he needed: a frequency-hopping, dual-band-secured radio transmission and reception system. The secured radio signals would enable Father Alvarez to hear confessions from his isolated parishioners high in the mountains. He explained further that a car had been donated to his mission. He was looking for a volunteer to drive this car down to the mission in southern Mexico, along with the communications equipment.

It just so happened the mission was on the road to the leper colony in Chiapas that Father Humberto Almazan had told me about earlier. I wanted to visit the leper colony firsthand and find out if there was anything, I might be able to do to help. This would be my ticket. Or so I imagined.

I raised my hand to volunteer. A girl in the crowd, named Karen, also volunteered. The priest questioned her if she really wanted to go. She said, "I would never go alone, but I would with someone else. I've never seen Mexico. I think it would be a fun adventure."

I was thinking, *"Either work the harvest season for the family in July or drive down to southern Mexico with a pretty girl."* It seemed a no-brainer.

It didn't take me long to reconfirm with Father Alvarez that I would drive the car to his mission. Father Alvarez stayed overnight at Villa Maria. The next day he gave me directions where to pick up the car in a couple of weeks.

The trip was supposed to take six days, then I would fly home. I finally returned, almost two months later, through the intervention of a congressman in Washington, D.C., and a few white lies. I didn't expect the trip to be one of the most frightening episodes of my life. I should have stayed home and cut apricots.

My brother Paul dropped me off at the Menlo Park residence, where I was shown an old, rusty, vintage 1952 Dodge coupé. With some relief, I found the car started right up, and the tires looked new. The donor of the car explained that Father Alvarez had loaded the trunk with the equipment while the donor was out on an errand. Father had also left a note: "I have an emergency and need to go back to Mexico immediately." His note continued: "Make sure you deliver the car with the equipment in ten days. Address: Alvarez Mission, La Trinitaria, Mexico. Everyone in town will know Father Alvarez. Just ask and they will tell you where to go. The import taxes on the equipment are three times the cost of the equipment. We cannot afford it. So keep the equipment in the drop floor of the trunk." I thought it strange at the time that I wasn't given a more specific address, but thought nothing of the fact we were being asked to smuggle equipment into Mexico.

Armed with no address beyond the name of the town—with an old car, a car key, a few medical supplies and blankets, a trunk with a drop floor inside which were hidden communication devices, and a cryptic note to deliver the car and equipment within ten days without fail—I naively began preparing for the trip. As I reflect back, one word comes to mind: stupidity. As they say, "Love is blind, and trust in the clergy can be equally blinding." By not exercising reasonable skepticism, I reasoned that everything was okay.

I picked up Karen at the train station two days later, with a full tank of gas, a credit card with a $500 limit, $200 in cash, and eight gallons of drinking water, since most Mexican water was not potable for visitors at the time. We put blankets over the bottom of the trunk, then loaded, on top of the blankets, our suitcases, water, and medical supplies. Another little detail I was unaware of was that there was a twice-value duty tax on any American-made car being brought into the country. The importance of this little fact became very apparent to us soon.

The first part of the trip was uneventful. We stayed in a little roadside motel in Chula Vista, where I discovered Karen had brought with her only $63 dollars. We ended up sharing a motel room. It was awkward for me, but she seemed to prefer it. (I was fresh out of the seminary and had no clue she was interested in me.) On the second day we crossed the border, after a brief inspection and both our passports were stamped. My passport as the driver of the car was stamped twice: one stamp was the entry stamp and the other, in red, said "con automóvil," which meant I had entered Mexico "with a car." After traveling south for about three hours, well into the state of Sonora, we came upon a checkpoint on the only road through the area. This time we were thoroughly inspected. We had to take everything out of the trunk, at gun point. As I removed the blanket from the trunk, I began to panic that they would discover the drop floor. I thought my heart was going to stop, and bile floated into my throat. They did a quick look, then ordered us to re-load the trunk.

We climbed back into the car; elated, I exclaimed to Karen, "We're home free!" I admitted to her that I had been pretty stupid to bring this equipment into Mexico. We laughed that it was all over and looked forward to smooth sailing down to southern Mexico.

Soon, with no air conditioning, the desert heat of Sonora became stifling. We drank a lot of water; Karen wilted and began to strip down to bare essentials. It was really hot, not erotic—believe me.

By early evening the car began to run rough and overheat, and we stopped at a gas station. We were low on water, and the oil was almost empty. We put several quarts of oil in the car and filled the radiator. Every time we needed fuel, it seemed we had to add water and oil; eventually, every time we saw a gas station we stopped to put in oil and re-filled the radiator. The cost of oil was killing me. So we slept in the car to save money.

I was praying the car would hold together for the rest of the trip, and that Karen would stop complaining about the heat. Unexpectedly, when we entered Chihuahua, there was another checkpoint; there were further checkpoints in Durango, Zacatecas, Mexico City, Puebla, and Oaxaca. Each time my palm-sweats got worse. As we neared the Guatemalan border, the checkpoints became more serious, with tapping of the floorboards and inspections of the car's undercarriage.

While traveling through the mountains of Oaxaca and into Chiapas, I experienced a series of events I will never forget. We were climbing a mountain road heading for the summit, in the middle of nowhere, when the car began to overheat. We pulled to the road side and filled the radiator with the rest of our drinking water and hoped to make it to the summit. We hadn't seen a town or a car for over an hour. Hopefully, if we made the summit, there would be a town close by. When we reached the summit, the motor temperature needle was on red and the car was smoking, but there was no town in sight. Then we began going downhill. The road went down for as far as I could see. I turned the engine off before it blew.

Amazingly, we just kept coasting and coasting for mile after mile. As we made a turn in the road, there was another long stretch of road ahead of us, all downhill. In the distance we could see two figures on the roadside. As we got closer, we saw they were two Indians, one chasing the other with a machete in hand and catching up quickly. As we passed them, Karen said, "That looks bad." As I looked in the rear mirror and Karen turned back to look, the machete was swung and beheaded the victim. Shocked, Karen screamed. The combination of witnessing a beheading in broad daylight on the side of a public road and Karen screaming put chills down my back. I kept saying to myself, "*Did we just see what I think we saw?*" Karen continual screaming confirmed that we had seen exactly what I thought we had. Between driving an unreliable car, having little cash, smuggling goods into the country, now witnessing a beheading, our paranoia and stress levels skyrocketed. Meanwhile, the car kept coasting downhill. Seeing another human beings head chopped off left an enduring nightmarish memory; unfortunately, it would not be the last beheading.

For another fifteen minutes or so, we just kept coasting, but the road was now rolling up and down; we had to let the car go fast enough to make the next rise but not too fast to get out of control. Finally, there was a sign for a little pueblo, and we turned off the road and coasted into town. The second building on the right-hand side of the road in the tiny town had a sign reading "*Taller de Radiadores.*" "Oh my God," I exclaimed, in disbelief. "A radiator shop! Are you kidding me?" We literally coasted to a stop in front of a repair shop. It was like a silly coincidence in a corny movie. The old mechanic turned out to be very good and found that our radiator had a hole in it and plugged it up, then found some oil to refill our tank. Fortunately, we didn't have an oil leak; the valves were old, and we were just burning a lot of oil.

About three hours later, we were back on the road—and not looking back. We wanted to be as far away as possible from that bit of local scenery. Our next stop was the leper colony in the mountains near Chiapas. We found the colony: I was shocked by its squalor and filthy conditions. The dull eyes, with no hope in them, of very sick people with untreated, pustulating wounds wrapped in gray, moldy rags will burn in my memory forever. The disfigurement from the disease was horrifying. My first impression was that a catastrophe had taken place and I was looking at the survivors. My spirit writhed. I felt defiled by my own health and the money in my pockets. I felt lacerated with guilt—guilt which then flamed into anger: *What kind of government or system allowed this kind of suffering?* I left the leper colony only hours later, because I realized there was nothing at that moment I could do; if I were ever going to help, I needed to be prepared. I needed a plan.

After leaving the leper colony, we traveled further south along the sultry jungle roads. The surrounding areas became more primitive. The natives looked more Indian, the roads got worse, towns got smaller, and infrastructure seemed not to exist. We kept driving.

Finally, we limped into the outskirts of La Trinitaria—the town where we were supposed to find Father Alvarez's mission—one early evening around five o'clock, with the car sputtering badly and the clutch beginning to fail. We were excited and proud that we had accomplished our mission. Naively, we looked forward to some praise and appreciation from Father Alvarez.

The praise would have to wait because we couldn't find Father's mission. After asking several people in town for directions to the mission, we were finally directed to Father Alvarez's residence. However, there was something ominous in the eyes of the lady who gave us directions. I saw fear in her eyes when I mentioned Father Alvarez. Fear was not an emotion I expected to get when mentioning the name of a Catholic priest.

Guatemala was in the throes of a brutal civil war, and we were very close to the border with that country. We followed directions and parked and went on foot to a small building that didn't look like any mission I had ever imagined. We looked through one window and could see nothing, until someone opened an inside door leading to interior courtyards. Karen quietly cried out, in a hoarse whisper, "Oh, God, they are going to kill us."

There were about thirty heavily armed rebels in one of the courtyards. Then, still looking through the window, I saw Father Alvarez with a machine gun flung over his back and a radio device of the same brand as the one inside our trunk; he was barking out instructions. I instantly realized we had just smuggled, through seven checkpoints, contraband radio equipment to enable the rebels to communicate in the mountains. They were making raids into Guatemala, then hiding out in the border mountains of Mexico to prevent counterattacks by the Guatemalan military.

One of the rebels spotted us peering through the window. Father Alvarez came flying out moments later. He did not greet us. Rather he was furious that we had arrived early. He angrily said, "I am very busy right now. Go to Hotel San Jorge in town and get a good night's rest. I will come by to see you in the morning and pick up the car. Thank you for doing God's work." We turned and left.

I reasoned with Karen, "We know too much. They are not going to just let us leave now. We're pawns in a bigger game. I agree with you. I think they may kill us." Karen echoed my thoughts: "There's not a chance I am going to just go to sleep tonight in this town. We got to get out of here."

Instead of heading to the hotel, we went directly to the bus station. There was a bus heading north (heading north was all we cared about) in forty-five minutes. We purchased two tickets, then drove the car to the hotel and abandoned it there. We took a broken-down old taxi back to the bus station and, at 7:15 p.m, headed north on the bus.

We sat, side by side; I could feel Karen shaking, and she could feel me shaking. Karen began to cry. "All I wanted was to have an adventure. I never traveled outside of San Mateo County before." She babbled on, "I thought it would be fun. But I'm terrified, David. Once they know we split, they're going to come after us."

We went from one bus route to another, taking an unlikely route from city to city in case we were followed. We didn't care what bus we took so long as we kept moving north. Paranoia added to the drama. Sleepless for days, hungry and dehydrated and imagining spies following us and hit men on every corner, we finally arrived in Mexico City.

A friend I had met at a summer camp in the Santa Cruz mountains a year earlier —Sally Stojkovich—I knew was visiting her parents, who lived in Mexico City. I found her parent's name in the phone book at the Mexico City bus depot.

I called and explained our situation. Sally's parents were gracious and took us in until we could get a flight back to the U.S. the next day. I broke my last $20 bill to pay for a taxi to an upscale part of town where the Stojkovich's lived. We must have been quite a sight: hungry, tired, and dirty, smelling from not having showered in days in the summer heat. Our exhaustion was, I think, more caused by the fear of being followed than by the hectic trip back north. I rang the doorbell, at the same time looking around to see if anyone was watching us. We were consumed in paranoia.

We were warmly welcomed. After a good shower, and a hearty meal, and a call to my parents, we made plans to leave Mexico the next day. Dad was not amused that Karen had no money for a ticket, but he wired money through Western Union for plane tickets for both of us.

At the airport ticket counter, we showed our passports when we purchased our tickets. Karen's ticket was processed normally, and she was off in a few hours, flying back home safely on Dad's nickel, never to be heard from again. I was detained for attempting to leave the country without the car I had brought into the country!

They released me with the instructions that I could not leave the country unless I got an exit stamp "con automóvil," to counter the "con automóvil" on my entry stamp. The regulation was designed to prevent anyone from bringing a car into the country without paying the twice-value duty, mentioned earlier, and leaving it in the country indefinitely. I explained that it was not my car; it was a gift to a priest and I didn't have it anymore.

Defeated, I returned to the Stojkovichs' home. Unflinchingly, the family opened their home to me with gracious hospitality. Mr. Stojkovich made a few calls. I called Dad. I was directed to one security office, then bounced from one bureaucracy to another. I sat for hours, then for days, all the while looking over my shoulder for some goon who might shoot me. I had never experienced a sense of overwhelming threat before. I froze in fear without knowing what to do next. A sense of threat can induce the most fanciful imagined dangers and blinding fear. It occurred to me that paranoia is simply an unjustifiable fear in the face of a given threat. But I also knew that what I was indeed terrified and believed the threat was very real.

I went to the U.S. embassy in Mexico City. They treated me like white trash, and some low-life bureaucrat stiffly informed me that the issue was a matter for the Mexican government. I found myself back at the Mexican immigration and customs office. Clearly, they were not going to let me leave the country without the car. During one of my visits to the customs office, I learned, from an unsavory clerk, the meaning of the Spanish words "soborno" and "mordido"; apparently, low-paying clerks take bribes as a customary way to help support their families. I told Dad I thought I'd be able to get an exit stamp if I gave a "soborno." Dad said, no, we were going to get this done legally. "It can also be a trap," he added, "and an excuse to arrest you."

Meanwhile, Dad had flown into action. He called the local bishop in Mexico to determine if Father Alvarez was a real priest or an imposter to raise money in the U.S. to fund the rebels. Astonishingly, Dad learned that Father Alvarez was a real priest and, to our collective dismay, the bishop was fully aware of Father Alvarez's activity. The explanation was that, between the Mexican and Guatemalan governments, in cooperation with the bishop, it had been decided to let Father Alvarez continue his rebel support under the bishop's umbrella. This way they could keep track of his whereabouts and general activity. It was confirmed that he was a dangerous man in the company of dangerous men. This heightened my paranoia-induced hallucinations of seeing gunmen behind every tree whenever I went outside.

Anxiety ran through my veins until, from time to time, I would start shaking uncontrollably. Three weeks later, during this living nightmare, Dad got hold of Charlie Gubser, our congressman in Washington. This got the attention of the U.S. embassy, which suddenly discovered the resources to determine the law and our options. There was an obscure Mexican law, discovered by Gubser's research assistant, that allowed me to exit Mexico under a special provision for family emergencies. My dad faked a heart attack as the cover story for the family emergency, and I was soon safely back home.

Soon after my return from Mexico, we had more visiting clergy at Vila Maria. Father Keagan was an independently wealthy priest stationed in San Francisco. He was grotesquely overweight, and it gave him an almost cherub-like baby face. I remember him walking in, taking little baby steps, in his silk slippers.

There was something not right about this man. I hated it that he could easily charm my parents. He would take one of my younger brothers out for excursions alone with him, and I idly wondered if these excursions might be planned opportunities to abuse him. Several years later my suspicions about the moral compass of Father Keegan proved correct: he was later the subject of multiple suits for child molestation in San Francisco. Soon afterward he mysteriously disappeared. In what would eventually become a familiar story and pattern, it appears that Archbishop Joseph T. McGucken decided it was time to reassign Father Keegan to another diocese—a diocese conveniently out of the country.

Approximately ten years later, Father Keegan was finally located, serving as the pastor of an all-boys orphanage in Mexico.

In retrospect, there seemed to be circling vultures of child abusing priests hovering around our family and my brothers. Surrounded by the most despicable of human beings like Father Keegan, Father Clark, Father Pritchart, and Father Phil McCrillis certainly tests one's faith. Miraculously, my brothers and I ducked danger and avoid lasting harm. With regret, my premonitions while in the seminary were being validated.

The days of first communion—when I reverently received Holy Communion with a feeling of fear and awe that I was actually "eating the body of Jesus"—were long gone, and I began to wonder if everything a priest said was actually true. I buried such thoughts because faith was a gift from God. I wanted to believe, and I did believe, and felt a warm comfort that somehow was due to my being blessed personally by God. I would not permit my thoughts to go beyond those that were compelling and comforting. But I knew, down deep, that my faith was based more on hope than on conviction. I was hoping the afterlife was true.

During the fall of 1969, fresh out of the seminary and glad to be back from the Mexico rebel nightmare, I entered Santa Clara University as a sophomore.

It was a surreal time, with the Vietnam War and peace demonstrations and protests, drugs and free love in the Haight Ashbury in San Francisco, and the killings on campus at Kent State. "Sensitivity sessions" were the rage, and LSD and marijuana were everywhere. Santa Clara was a comparatively tame campus in the Bay Area, but it also reflected the times. My roommate grew pot in our dorm room, motorcycles literally roared up and down the dorm halls at night, and the atmosphere of the time seemed to be permeated with pot smoke, long hair, beads, and political and social anger.

To me, fresh out of a sheltered seminary, the rebellious social unrest seemed crazy. Although I was horrified by the social and human tragedy unfolding in Southeast Asia, my intellectual opposition to the war was on constitutional grounds. Without a declaration of war by Congress, I saw the executive branch, by sending our youth to a killing zone, as over-reaching its authority and acting illegally. I believed it was a dangerous power grab by the executive branch. History proved I was more right than wrong. Subsequently, the dangerous precedents set in the 1960s became the gateway to the Serbian war, the two Gulf wars (including the invasion and occupation of Iraq in 2003), and the war in Afghanistan, Yamen and Syria. These conflicts were all engagements in war, regardless of what words are used to describe them. They were all conducted without a declaration of war by Congress, though it gave tacit approval by funding the engagements.

My father, with his right-wing tendencies, feared I might become a revolutionary. He listened to enough of my ramblings about the stupidity of the "domino theory" that he decided to do some research. Dad, a maverick, was not content to read what the papers had to say about the subject. His way to study the issue was to go to Vietnam in the middle of the War!

Shortly after I entered Santa Clara, Dad, and my youngest brother Rick decided to visit my brother Paul (known as Paul III). Paul served as a First Lieutenant on the front lines in Vietnam. It seemed reasonable to me at the time, like a typical "Dad thing to do." Wanting to go to Vietnam during the height of the War and going is a different matter.

So how did Dad go to the frontlines with his young son, Richard in the middle of a war? The combination of my father's irresistible charisma together with his good friends with Congressman Gubser, and Governor Ronald Reagan. The four-day visit was all set with the Military brass highly annoyed to be ordered to escort civilians through a war zone.

As the story goes, Dad and Rick immediately knew something was wrong upon their arrival on a military transport plane landed at the Camp Phu Loi Military base. Helicopters were the safest way to transport Dad and Rick to Paul's encampment. A helicopter was supposed to be waiting for Dad and Rick as they deplaned. Upon arrival, there was no helicopter waiting for them.

Because they were civilians, they were not allowed to leave the tarmac unescorted. They stood on the tarmac in sweltering Vietnam heat in three-piece suits and spit-shined shoes. Minutes became hours. After three on the tarmac with heat waves rippling up in the air and sweat dripping down their temples, they no longer worried about their six pieces of luggage and ruining their three-piece suits from sweat. Anxiety, fear, and safety crept into their thoughts. Finally, they spotted a jeep traveling at high speed onto the tarmac. In the Jeep, with his driver, was First Lieutenant Paul Mariani III.

It was unnerving to learn that their safest way to Paul's encampment was by helicopter which was shot down and exploded on their way to pick Dad and Rick up. Now they had to travel to Paul's encampment on treacherous roads in their little Jeep.

Paul stacked the luggage around the perimeter of the Jeep, successfully giving Dad and Rick a false sense of security. Dad and Rick jammed in the middle of the Jeep and readied themselves for a dangerous three-hour drive through the jungle.

Before they left the compound a plane in one of the hangars exploded. The Jeep swerved off to the side of the road.

Dad and Rick were ordered to dive under the Jeep for cover. Paul threw his personal 9 mm gun to dad with the instruction, "if he saw anyone that didn't look like him, shoot." Dad and Rick dove under the Jeep and sliding smoothly in the muck and mud. Rick, during moments of paralyzing fear, Rick oddly remembers his shoes getting muddy. Our minds, I suppose, redirect our thoughts us away from the terror at hand when needed.

Although Dad was a life-long right-wing Republican, he was not a typical "hawk." He often said about War, "I don't think I could ever kill another human being, even if faced with my mortality." However, while Dad lay prone under the Jeep, he knew if he saw anything move, he was shooting.

Paul and his driver were off to scout the area with M-16 rifles in hand. After it was determined the mortar was a "one-off" munitions launch, they quickly re-boarded the Jeep and continued the journey; seemingly, with a clarity of purpose.

Paul commanded an encampment deep in the jungles providing vital supplies to troops. Upon the arrival of Paul's supply camp, the bunkers, ditches, and defensives structures were all stark reminders to Dad and Rick that they were deep in the war zone. Paul's men, along with most of the men they met while coming and going from the camp, generally had very low morale.

The next evening the Viet Cong attacked with mortar shells and started overrunning the camp. Paul again threw Dad a 9mm pistol, and they all jumped into a trench. With bullets flying in all directions, my father admitted later, with chagrin, "In the heat of battle, of kill or be killed, a strange surge of testosterone kicked in. Again, there is no question; if a human body had come flying over the protective mound, I would have fired my weapon". They decided to cut short their 4-day visit and leave the next morning. [22]

Dad was strangely silent about the War after he came home. My brother Paul brooded about his experiences in the War for the rest of his life.

To me, at Santa Clara, Vietnam had seemed far away. Dad's trip made the conflict personal; it now seemed like a conflict close to home.

Despite the distractions of the war protests during my years at Santa Clara, I could see that the Valley was continuing to change rapidly. I saw many new buildings rising along El Camino Real and Steven's Creek Road. Most of the buildings had nice landscaping and so-called low rises. – one to two stories. The predominant building type built at this time were called R & D buildings – usually tilt up building with lots of glass windows. The idea of dense developments and the expense of building two-story office buildings created many questions in my mind. The first question was, "Who is constructing these buildings?" My next questions were, "Who will be occupying those buildings, where will the companies and people be coming from, and why?" I already was missing my orchards and the miles upon miles of fruit blossoms in spring time.

In Santa Clara University, I would have nothing to do with so-called "campus life." I went to one beer party that was nothing but a long drinking binge. I thought it was stupid as I watched students getting progressively drunk. Looking back, I suppose I was a boring straight arrow; it appeared to my classmates that I looked down on drinking and using drugs. In reality, I just didn't see the appeal of drinking too much and throwing up. I wanted to get on with my life, and drugs and alcohol got in the way. I attended classes in the morning and worked as a watchman at night. My college life was not typical: my focus was to learn enough to get out of school and save as much money as possible so I could be on my own by the time I was twenty. It had been drummed into our heads all our lives to stand on our own and make our own way—a message that resonated more for some of my brothers than others.

Anyway, each day I attended class until about mid-day, practiced tennis for the tennis team, then slept for six hours prior to reporting for my job as night-watchman at our frozen food processing plant in Santa Clara. The work shift was eight p.m. to eight a.m. The job required that I walk through the buildings each hour. I needed to punch a time clock registered around the four corners of the building to prove I was on the job and watching the facility. I studied between rounds. It was a lonely time for me, but I couldn't relate to the other students on many levels. My only extracurricular activity was playing on the Santa Clara tennis team. My attraction to the team, besides my love of the game, was their dedication to hard work and focus. In retrospect, I was obsessively serious about life—perhaps too serious—and missed out on what should have been a formative and playful time that others seemed to treasure in later years.

Spending time as a night-watchman at our facility afforded me the opportunity to think about the plant in full operation during the season, and to contemplate everything I had learned and had yet to learn.

During the 1960s and early 1970s industrial safety was still poorly understood. The ongoing American industrial revolution since the nineteenth century had been a marvelous boom to the country's standard of living. But it was also the advent of mayhem in the workplace through industrial accidents. Slogans that are common today—such as "Safety is our number-one priority"— were not even concepts until the mid-1970s in most factories.

We grew up with the notion that "accidents just happened." They were a part of life. They were the result of bad luck. Thinking rarely went beyond that, to ask, "Why did *this* accident happen? Could it have been prevented?" This was particularly true if a solution cost money that you might or might not have at the time.

One night at our frozen food processing plant in the mid-1960s, I was on duty as a supervisor over hundreds of people, even though I was only seventeen at the time. At our plant we had a long line of peach-pitting machines[23], with women stationed at each machine; a moving conveyor belt carrying peaches passed by each station for the ladies to feed into the pitter.

The pitter had a rotating arm with a hand-like cup at the end, with a razor-sharp, knife-like blade in the middle of the cup. The pitting arm moved toward the woman at the station for her to feed peaches, one by one, into the cup. The arm returned to the center of the pitting machine with the peach in the cup, and a chain-driven stamping mechanism sliced the peach in half and removed the pit.

These machines were horrifically dangerous, with minimal safety instructions. One night, while I was on duty, a young girl was reaching across her body for a missed peach, when the pitting arm caught her elbow and pulled her into the machine. By the time an emergency stop was tripped, her arm and elbow had been pulled in and out of the pitter several times. She was a bloody, pulverized mess. I drove her to the emergency room at the hospital, sick to my stomach, my heart racing from the horror of it all. There she remained for over five months of reconstructive repairs.

I went back to work, but nothing changed (aside from my being emotionally scarred from the experience). At one point, I walked past perhaps fifty open sprockets and chains, without safety guards. The sprockets and motors drove the movement of the processing line. Our senior mechanic didn't like the guards because it took too much time to remove them when chains jumped from the sprocket teeth and had to be put back onto the sprockets, like the chains on a bicycle.

It was obvious to me that the open sprockets were a disaster waiting to happen. Our senior mechanic, Yosh—somewhat paradoxically, given his stated dislike for securing the sprockets with the guards when he himself was not in any danger—shared with me his fears, in fact nightmares, that someday someone would unknowingly hit the power back on while he was still working on the sprockets and chain adjustments in the processing line; without the safety guards, his fingers might easily be amputated. This fear became an obsession that was beginning to become a phobia, in my judgment, until one day there was another horrible accident.

While working on replacing a motor and putting the chain back on the sprockets two elevations below the top processing line, Yosh first heard the roar of the power going on as the lines of conveyors began moving. There was a splatter and a scream and blood in his face as he quickly looked down and saw seven fingers bouncing off his chest. He looked at his hands and saw no fingers. Yosh was hallucinating; though he momentarily saw no fingers on his hands, the fingers bouncing off his chest (as well as the scream and blood) had come from someone else working on a motor above him as the fingers fell through a labyrinth of pulleys, chains, and support structures. Yosh's fears had materialized, for someone else. He was never quite the same again. He increasingly became moody and paranoid.

Yet, despite these disasters, the idea of safety kill switches and guards to prevent cloth and body parts from getting caught in moving production-line machinery never entered our minds.

Probably the most disturbing industrial accident scene I witnessed occurred while on location in Australia, at our Simarloo ranch in South

Australia. It was harvest time, so I was there to help coordinate the harvest with Dad's longtime friend Jim Trowbridge.

We had farmed several thousand acres with alfalfa prior to planting the virgin ground with fruit trees. Alfalfa is a leguminous plant; at the tips of its root structure, it produces nitrogen. These natural nitrogen-fixing plants add natural fertilizers to the land, which would be needed by the fruit trees that would soon follow.

We purchased a large cubing machine—a "cuber"—which, hauled behind a dump truck, harvested, chopped and compressed the alfalfa into small cubes, then spat out the cubes into the truck. (The compressed alfalfa was later shipped to China and the U.S., where it was used for animal feed and, at the time, cat litter.)

The big dump truck that pulled the cubing machine was housed in a small barn about half a mile from our headquarters. We sent a young, seventeen-year-old boy down to the barn to pick up the truck and hook it up to the cuber for harvesting that day. Not long afterward, Jim and I, at the ranch headquarters, could see the truck driving randomly in circles out in the field. We jumped into a Jeep to see what was going on. Our working theory was that the kid was screwing around.

Upon reaching the truck, we could see him in the truck, headless. I am not sure why my body reacted this way, but I began to just shake from the gruesome scene. After recovering our composure, we called the police and ambulance. I'm not sure why we called the ambulance; it was not like there was a rush to get to the hospital. We, along with the police, began to reconstruct what had probably happened. After finding the boy's head back in the barn, we concluded that, while he was slowly driving the truck out of the barn, he must have opened the driver-side door and stuck his head out in order to get a better look behind him, to make sure he didn't sideswipe the truck on the side of the barn. He apparently drove the truck door against the wall of the barn, pinning his head out the door while the door slowly closed as it was being crushed along the side of the barn while the truck moved forward. The low compound gear of the truck did the rest. . . . The poor youngster's feet were pulled off the pedals, and the truck slowly moved out of the barn and down into field.

Revisiting these horrific experiences is a glimpse, and a reminder, of a bygone era. Industrial accidents were common before the arrival of Occupational Safety and Health Administration, or OSHA. When OSHA was created, it was met with "don't tell us what to do" resistance by the industry, including myself. Even though I had seen plenty of accidents in my short number of years working, OSHA was viewed as an unwelcome governmental intrusion into our lives.

Our work camps had dirt floors (as described earlier) and overloaded extension cords for electricity distributions to outhouses for personal needs. Water came from a common sink fed by an unfiltered well.

While working in our forklift repair shop one summer, I learned to pour dirty crankcase oil down a drainpipe that was just a hole in the ground—as virtually all ranchers did at the time; it never dawned on me where the oil went. All of these practices seemed normal (though they are no longer legally acceptable, by OSHA or EPA standards).

Disposing of used engine oil can be a problem. Solution: Dig a hole in the ground with a posthole digger and fill it with fine gravel. Then pour in the oil. It will be absorbed into the ground before your next change. Cover the spot with soil.

166 POPULAR SCIENCE JANUARY 1963

A recommendation from Popular Science Magazine, circa 1963

At the same time, not far from our ranches, "clean rooms," designed to be almost sterilely clean environments for the manufacture of semiconductors, were being built, practically under our noses.

In retrospect, the benefits of OSHA went beyond providing safety standards. OSHA created uniform requirements for factories so they would all conform to the same standards of safety and at the same time. Prior to this, anyone spending serious money on safety would be put at a competitive disadvantage against those who didn't. Food-safety and employee-safety programs cost a lot of money. Retrofitting with such features as safety switches, sprocket guards, stainless-steel food surfaces, or accommodating high-temperature sterilization processes, safety instructions, and the like, all cost money—a lot of money. It broke many companies that simply didn't have the capital to comply. The ones able to survive the higher standards and associated costs had the benefit of competing with each other on a level playing field. They then learned that, in the long run, companies with high safety records actually saved money.

For me, as a teenager in the 1960s, industrial accidents were how the world worked—it was simply a fact of life. Looking back at it with modern eyes, I have to ask myself how stupid can stupid be.

Chapter 15

College, Marriage, and My Early Career

1969–1979

"Mother Goose" and Arlene

Back to Santa Clara: I wanted a real job, a job during the day. I wanted to drop out of school so I could work full time. Dad didn't think my dropping out of school was a very good idea.

I applied to the University of San Francisco's night-school program about a month before the end of the 1970 school year at Santa Clara.

A few days after my application to USF, Sister Costello, Sacred Heart nun, affectionately known as "Mother Goose," asked me to help her out at a barbeque she was hosting for the Santa Clara University boys' baseball team. She was a local legend, bigger-than-life type personality and someone you just didn't say no to.

I sat in my car while waiting at the mission for Mother Goose to pick me up. About fifteen feet away, sitting on the lawn, was a coed reading a book. We both sat facing each other but not really looking at each other. I found her attractive and thought I might have seen her before on campus. Mother Goose arrived, and I got out of my car to meet her. The mystery coed came to greet Mother Goose at the same time. Apparently, we were both waiting for her. Mother Goose introduced us, and said a name I didn't quite catch, and off we went to the barbecue.

The barbecue was successful, even though the prevailing wind pushed smoke into my eyes while I worked the grill. I was surprised when the girl I had met with Mother Goose came forward with a complete plate of food and handed it to me. "Everyone else has eaten except for you," she said. "I'm the queen of barbecues at home, so I'll give you a break."

Hungry, I gave her little protest. After I ate, I took over again at the barbecue. I didn't see her again, other than from a distance, while she socialized with friends.

A few days later, I called Mother Goose and said, "What was that girl's name again you introduced me to?"

She answered. "Joanne, or Jan, Morey."

Those names didn't sound right.

"No, I don't think that's it."

"Oh, I think I introduced you to her sister, Arlene."

That name rang a bell: that was the name Mother Goose had used when introducing her to me.

"Arlene! That's it! O.K., thanks."

This conversation, in the near exact order, went on for three more days. For some reason, Arlene's name flowed in one ear and out the other. Once I got her name firmly nailed down, I got up enough nerve to track down what dorm she lived in. I paid her a visit.

I had been so impressed with Arlene at the barbeque. Her pure act of selflessness stuck in my brain, her giving, when the rest of the students seemed self-absorbed at the party. The rest were just in "party mode." While I'm sure there were many thoughtful people in attendance, it was Arlene's thoughtfulness that made her different in my eyes. I wanted to get to know this unusual person.

We had our first date. It turned out to be helping me host a Serra Club party at Villa Maria for my dad. Three of the four "help" didn't show up for the event. Arlene worked for four straight hours along with me. By evening's end, with both of us exhausted, I brought her straight back to the dorms for the night. She said, "I had a great time, thank you" and kissed me on the cheek. I secretly thought we had romantic magic, and at the same time I feared she wouldn't go out with me again. We had a second date, then a third.

I had no way of knowing that a seemingly insignificant moment at a barbeque highlighted by a pure random act of kindness would become a pivotal moment in my life. I had no way of knowing that someday she would give us five beautiful daughters and be married to me for over forty-eight years and counting, as of the time of this writing. Arlene is still my precious bride and the love of my life.

While I tried to make sense of the changing world around me in Silicon Valley, there were a couple of visiting priests at Villa Maria during this time who caught my interest. Getting acquainted with them led me down an unexpected journey

The following summer I would leave Arlene to travel halfway around the world, but she was constantly as close as ever in my mind and heart.

Father Oprandi was a six-foot four blonde Argentinean missionary with aqua blue eyes serving on the island of Bali. He stuck out like a sour thumb. He was however a solid priest with a committed mission. He stayed with us at Villa Maria while fund raising in the U.S. I understood the unspoken truth about Bali: at that time (1969), Bali had the highest concentration of leprosy per capita in the world.

Now, with some exposure to the disease, I said, "Somebody has to do something about this." Father Almazan agreed with me, but declared, "I don't know where to start."

I was already getting an idea—in fact, a whole series of ideas.

On a "real date" (which meant, in those pre-feminist days, that I bought dinner), I told Arlene that I was going away to Indonesia to work in a leper colony. Arlene, though surprised and concerned at the same time, was immediately supportive.

Arlene and I travelled with my mom to Bali two decades later. We avoided all the usual tourist traps and traveled up a valley to a little village outside Denpasar, the island's capital. We walked into a little clinic. To the right was a small faded, yellowed picture of the guy who had helped build the clinic twenty-five years earlier. I was staring at myself.

It was while I stared at myself on that wall in a clinic in Bali that I began to understand the importance and value of ignoring your fears and using your passionate conviction "to actually do something." My story working with the infected natives began in 1970.

The fear of getting leprosy was only fleeting; It was quickly pushed aside by the need to do something about the atrocity of the Balinese genocide of its own people, which is what the government's policy toward the natives with leprosy of Bali amounted to.

A common symptom of leprosy are complications associated with reduced blood circulation. Sores don't heal, resulting in chronic open wounds.

While our visiting priest lamented and anguished over the plight of the infected natives, I sat back and asked a series of questions. "How would we treat those who are already infected?" Then I said to myself, "*It's equally important to understand how to prevent leprosy.*"

This led me to the next question, "What causes leprosy?" Then a tougher question came: "Why is leprosy so prevalent in Bali?" If I could answer the last question, I knew it would be the ultimate answer, because it would, in essence, solve the root of the problem. Astonishingly, no one was asking the most important question.

I immediately began researching how leprosy should be treated and what drugs were needed. I also researched the cause. Sulfa drugs and other medications were standard treatments. Leprosy is a chronic infectious disease caused by *Mycobacterium leprae*, identified by G. H. A. Hansen in 1873: also known as Hansen's disease, it is a chronic infectious disease primarily affecting the skin, peripheral nerves, upper respiratory tract, and eyes. From various notes while In Bali, I learned that the causative agent is an acid-fast bacterium, *Mycobacterium leprae*, first identified in 1873 by the Norwegian physician, Gerhard Henrik Armauer Hansen.

Father Oprandi, the local missionary priest in Denpasar, Bali, told me how leprosy had been historically considered a divine curse for sin in the Old Testament and a karma in Buddhism. The term leprosy originates from the

Latin word *lepros*, meaning defilement. I believe the fact that leprosy has been deemed an incurable disease, causing severe deformities and disabilities, has resulted in severe stigmatization. This has resulted in double suffering by victims, both from the disease itself and from public discrimination. Although the disease is well documented since antiquity, leprosy currently remains endemic in some developing parts of the world.

The diagnosis of leprosy is mainly based on clinical signs and symptoms of the disease. Most leprosy health workers, with the required, generally brief, training, easily observe and recognize these features.

Through our family business interests in Australia, I networked with doctors and pharmaceutical distributors there. My pitch to doctors was to donate thirty days, every other year, to man a clinic in a village outside Bali's capital, Denpasar (a clinic that, at the time, existed only in my own mind).

Denpasar was chosen because the village was a hotspot for tuberculosis and leprosy. The village also had Catholic missionary church and complex of other buildings that gave me a home base. The local priest, Father Oprandi, was a friend of Father Almazan, who made the introductions. Father Oprandi also had land available in the village for a clinic.

After six months of receiving many noes and some yeses from Doctors in Australia, I managed to get twenty-four doctors on rotation for our Denpasar clinic. The next stop was to get distributors to donate dated drugs—drugs that could not be sold by law but were still viable. My pitch was that the shipping costs to Denpasar would be less than costs for warehousing and disposal. Bingo! It worked. So now I had the doctors and the medicine—but no clinic. I was twenty years old. What was I doing? Was I insane?

Upon arrival in the little village, an hour's drive outside of Denpasar via Jakarta, I traveled by Jeep with Father Oprandi and Father Almazan. It was quite a contrast from Jakarta's ballet of traffic fury—a ballistic dance of cars and buses, trucks, bicycles, and carts, scooters and people, going their own ways with mysterious efficiency.

Now on the exotic island of Bali, there were sounds of people rather than honks of cars, and sweet smells of perfumes rather than diesel smoke, and a not-unpleasant mix of voices rising up everywhere like an unfamiliar music.

I was first struck by the beauty of Bali. Then, as a twenty-year-old and full of hormones, I couldn't but notice the Balinese women walking along the roadsides wearing waste-high sarongs—all were topless. After about twenty minutes of my eyes wondering from side to side, together with a few double takes, the novelty of topless women wore off. My lasting memory of these beautiful, half-clad women was not sexual; it was of their soulful spirits and authentic elegance. Work began immediately. We walked miles by foot along the waterfront, packing food and medicine for the leper colonies to avoid the armed guards who guarded the colonies from the interior—guards who were in mortal fear of actually entering the leper colonies and being infected. Over the following weeks and months, we treated the patients and learned the customs of the people. We spent our days either arranging for food or delivering food to the inhabitance inside the leper colony or treating their open wounds with either sulfur compound, or cleaning, sterilizing and/or wrapping open sores. Our long-term project was to build a clinic in the local village to eliminate the need for leper colonizes through education, and local treatment.

The Balinese are incredible artists, in songs, "batik" designs, sculptures, and paintings. One man infected with the disease, as a token of appreciation for our work, carved a Balinese dancer for me in beautiful equatorial wood. Two days after he had finished the sculpture, rodents ate off most of his fingers during the night. Leprosy constricts blood flow to the extremities, which causes disfigurement and loss of nerve function. He couldn't feel the rodents feeding on his fingers, but he could feel the art in the use of his hands to create a treasure I adorn in my home to this day. It was his last work of art. He gave it to me in tears.

Shown here is the author treating a leper.
Nerve damage in the extremities is also common.

It was while visiting the colonies and working on building the clinic that I pinpointed the reason for so much leprosy in Bali. The leper bacterium is common all over the world. The reason leprosy is not so widespread is because a person needs to be in a condition of weakened health before the leper bacteria can take hold. A healthy person can normally fight off the bacteria.

In Bali at that time, sixty percent of the population was suffering from tuberculosis. Additionally, the amazing terraces and canal network throughout the island were also sources of disease, because many, if not all, of the canals were interconnected. It was common for people to relieve themselves in a village canal that was used a few hundred yards downstream for drinking and cooking.

In these days before the Peace Corps and United Nations aid organizations, and before NGOs grew active in the area, it became clear to me that we needed to treat the afflicted in Bali. We participated in creating an educational campaign to prevent leprosy and TB. We constructed a latrine system separate from the canal water for community uses such as drinking and cooking, to prevent the spread of disease. Our clinic addressed all of these issues, besides being a place under one roof to have babies, instead of having them often in a rice paddy—I know, because I assisted in delivering a baby three weeks after I arrived.

This happened suddenly. I was waiting for Father Oprandi to come back from town, and no one else was at the parish compound when a young girl (I doubt if she was more than17 or 18 years old) came into the courtyard, walking in obvious distress. I showed her a little room with a cot to lie down on. It was obvious from the size of her stomach, which appeared to be having contractions, that she was about to have a baby. I was about to bolt to find someone to assist, when she grabbed my arm in an effort to prevent me from leaving. Although we did not speak a common language, the combination of hope and anxiety in her eyes told me to stay. Mercifully, the baby arrived quickly, about twenty minutes later. The amazing miracle of life in my twenty years old hands burns in my memory to this day, over fifty years later.

After suffering from scurvy, dehydration, exhaustion, and a scorpion bite, I found my time building a clinic and treating the natives with leprosy was rapidly coming to an end. I wrote often to my friend, Arlene, who was becoming more than a friend. Her thoughtful letters of encouragement constantly reminded me of her loving spirit. She was becoming a soul mate—a treasured soulmate, with her understanding and caring gift to me. I thought of her while I shivered with fever from the scorpion's venom. I thought about her gentle kindness: "I know you are doing good work, but keep safe. I worry for you. The days seem so long. I can't wait for your return. I miss you. Love, Arlene."

Her words comforted me and warmed my soul. I wanted to go home and see her; to see her tender smile and the glint in her eye. I began to ache for her, at the center of my chest, but the work here was not finished. I found myself love-struck in the middle of the jungle, six thousand miles from home.

At one point, I discovered that we were $6,000 short of the money needed to complete the clinic. So I went to the Bali Hotel and called my dad. At that time the Bali was the only hotel on the entire island and government-owned, though built to Western standards. I explained the problem to Dad and asked him if he would donate the money to complete my dream. He said no.

I was furious and hung up.

Later, I managed to beg, borrow, and scrape together enough to finish the clinic. It was a grueling, dispiriting time, and—though not in the way I hoped it would be, because of several compromises—in the end it was completed and operates to this day, more than forty years later.

After the clinic was finished, I traveled through Japan and met with family business associates, staying in their family home. Strangely for me, the home was made largely of paper in a central residential area of Tokyo. The energy and commerce was a stark contrast with life in Bali.

A month or so later, I arrived home. I did the mature thing and gave my father the silent treatment for about three weeks. Dad finally asked me to join him in the library for a chat. Dad said, "Are you not curious why I said no to your project?" I said, "Well, that is one question I am curious about. Tell me why you said no." I was still seething.

"I watched you through this whole process of working the leper colony and clinic," Dad responded. "You're a resourceful person. You should go into business."

I railed at him: "I am more interested in helping other people than being a predator and screwing people and helping myself."

My dad did not react for several minutes. "Is it your idea that businesses screw people?"

"Absolutely," I said.

Dad then asked, "Have you ever witnessed our company being a predator and screwing people?"

"Well, no."

Dad went on to explain that sometimes companies are deceitful and dishonest, but that, in the vast majority of small businesses, people are honest and hard-working. My quick answer of "Absolutely" began to sound misguided to me.

Dad continued: "The magic of free enterprise is that, if we do our work well, we creatively figure out how to create better goods and services for our community. Because of constant competition, the creative process is constantly wringing out waste and creating new products and new jobs. If we are really good at being cleverly creative, and watch our costs, the community is rewarded with better products, at lower costs, and jobs are created, and we are rewarded with a profit. A profit is nothing more than a score card that measures how hard you work and how creative you are. The profits are simply an enabler to continue to be a positive influence on your community beyond the amounts needed for nonessential sustenance.

"Son, it's easier to make money than it is to raise money. If you put your skills to work in business, you'll be able to fund not one hospital but a hundred hospitals. You won't need to beg for funds; you can just fund it yourself. You see, son, the real meaning of business and making a profit is *why* you do it. If it is to just to increase profits for yourself, it is a selfish enterprise. If you do it to enable you to do good work for others, then your entire life experience is a labor of love for others. David, I said no to you as a wakeup call. I don't want you to think you can just call people up and get money whenever you want. Consider redirecting your passion for all the right reasons into business."

This was a seminal moment in my life. I returned to school with a new set of eyes….seeing the world in a completely different way.

As I drove back and forth from Santa Clara to Villa Maria, the Valley was becoming a stranger to me. Things called "industrial parks" were beginning to pop up. However, I had a new set of curiosities. I could not understand who had the money to buy the land and incur the holding costs for so many years, and invest millions and millions of dollars in roads, utilities, and offsite improvements on a speculative bet that companies might want to buy land or construct buildings as long as a decade later. It was a big mystery to me who made these "industrial parks" and how they were possible. I was determined to figure out how the world worked in our own backyard in Silicon Valley.

I learned that large industrial parks were developed and financed by giant insurance companies or multinational corporations, because, generally speaking, only they, in the private sector, had the financial resources to develop such speculative ventures that, from start to finish, could take decades to develop and produce positive cash flow and a profit. This made sense to me, since I didn't know ordinary people or mere mortals with that kind of money. Even with my farmer mentality, which was comfortable with long investment horizons, I didn't know anyone with the long-term investment time requirement for developing an industrial park. Yet such parks were being developed throughout the Valley.

I pondered what was happening to my dear Valley of Heart's Delight.

I grew up in a world that defined money as coming from the productivity of land. With a robust crop, more money was circulated within our community. It was essentially a closed loop, an economic microcosm. Nature provided an abundance of fruit, the people in the Valley cultivated and harvested it, and the world outside purchased it; any profits stayed at home for reinvestment. Then a new phenomenon of money flow and patterns began to emerge. Money was now coming from outside the Valley, independent (at least for a time) of what was being produced there. Money was pouring in to fund new companies (so-called "startups"). Where was all the money coming from, I wondered?

I didn't anticipate I would get my answer from Cupertino apricot growers during morning breakfast breaks in our company break room.

At our packing plant we had a break room or coffee shop of sorts. Called variously our break room, coffee shop or coffee room that was open to the local public, it was a simple wooden building with creaky floors that seemed to be made of highly polished, oiled wood. In actuality, the patina resulted from the fruit oils on people's shoes. The rubbed-and-oiled look came from the heavy, daily foot traffic of hundreds of workers filing through our onsite coffee room over the decades. The floors were also grooved with wear, from the queuing-up line for our famous "10 cent" breakfast, which consisted of bad coffee and delicious, hot, fresh out of the fryer donuts.

Our onsite coffee shop was the poor man's Starbucks. It served as a place for hundreds of our employees' mid-morning and afternoon coffee breaks. The coffee room was also a regional community commons for townsfolk from Mountain View, Sunnyvale, Santa Clara, and Monte Vista. The local farmers from these areas gathered every morning. Sometimes as many as thirty locals would come by to chat and get caught up on the events of the day, the quality of the bloom, or whatever was the topic or rumor du jour. It was our form of social media.

I often marveled and wondered why people, every day, without fail, came flooding into our old break-room with its worn wooden steps and rough-sawn, planked timber on the building sidings, floors, and ceiling. It was far from elegant, but I suppose long on character. The sweet smell of sugar and fresh donuts was a compelling draw. But it was more than the aroma of freshly baked pastries that drew people in. There was energy in that room. There was always a certain excitement in the air as the community at large from converged at the Mariani Coffee house or break-room. The exchange of community information about the weather, the crops, who had died and who'd been born, and whose crazy kid was sniffing glue again were all discussed at the Mariani's break room. Gossip reigned eternal. The morning ritual was like a gathering of the local tribe. This morning ritual gave everyone a sense of community at a time when the community was radically changing before our eyes.

The break-room discussions purportedly solved all the world's problems. My elders, whom I looked up to, were always sure (though often wrong) with their declarative proclamations on social values and political perspectives through the prism of the mores of the times. Listening to my elders carefully as they sermonized on a broad range of topics helped to form my value system and the way I viewed the world around me.

I remember listening carefully about water rights. "I bought the Doyle ranch because it had senior water rights. I paid a premium for the property because of the water—and I will be damned if some politician is going to take it away from me." I heard this in the context of a push by the county government to require our wells to be registered. The fear was that, "if the farmers allowed the county to force them to register their wells, then next thing you know they will begin to require us to monitor the damn wells. Mark our words, slowly but surely, the county will begin to impose drilling restrictions, pumping restrictions, regulations. And to support all this bureaucracy, they will begin to tax us on our own water. The next thing you know, they will try to take our water rights away from us . . . water rights we paid good money for."

At the time I thought their arguments were preposterous. It was inconceivable to me that the simple act of allowing the county to register our wells would lead to taxing us for using our own water. But a few decades later, the old farm wisdom seemed prophetic.

I suppose many of the old timers in the 1950s remembered the argument that had been made a few decades earlier, in 1913. Congress finally passed the 16th amendment, making an income tax constitutional, with a 1% tax rate. The fear was that, if Congress were empowered to levy a tax, even at 1%, what would stop Congress from changing the rate later to, say, 2% or 3%? The argument that won the day was, "If Congress raised the rates to 3%, we would have another American revolution!"

During the early '50s and '60s, we didn't understand the concept of salt-water intrusion, or underground water migration, or subsidence due to over pumping beyond sustainable re-charging rates in connection with water usage and well-pumping. In order to live in a sustainable world, monitoring well and pumping output data is needed. Monitoring costs money, and taxes are needed to support it. Little of these issues were on the minds of we farmers, beyond the idea that "we paid good money for our water rights; don't mess with us."

Our coffee room could hold perhaps seventy-five to a hundred people. Everyone sat in the same place, day after day. It was an unspoken rule, or perhaps we were just creatures of habit. The executives sat at a long series of tables—altogether about fifty feet in length—that ran down the center of the room. Employees and truck drivers and the like sat at tables along the perimeter tables. When my dad or Djede, or the city mayor, would come and sit down in what was usually someone else's place, it created a silent stir . . . everyone adjusting where they should sit.

A Cupertino pioneer and farmer, Pete Carmada, came by the break room every day for forty-five years for breakfast at 9:30 a.m. One day Peter came in late—it was one of those days when someone was sitting in his place—and went into one of his classic tirades. We all laughed and reasoned with him that, since he'd been late for breakfast, he'd lost his place.

Pete had just come back from doing some tractor work for a guy who owned an apricot orchard in Los Altos. I wondered who was farming apricots in Los Altos Hills, which was a high-rent district in those days. Lots were going for $25,000 an acre, which was respectable money then. Pete said, "Oh, it's some guy by the name of Packard. He's got a small forty-acre piece up on the hill with cots [apricots]. I charged him twenty bucks less than my quote because I was able to disc [24] a little faster than I thought. I thought discing up and down the hilly ground was going to take longer."

This guy Packard had seemed flabbergasted because Pete charged him less than his quote. It was the beginning of a long friendship. The simple farmer spent hours and hours with a national figure and international statesman.

As mentioned earlier, we knew Dave first as an apricot grower, and I learned only years later that he was the founder of Hewlett Packard. More importantly, it was the relationship Pete had with Dave, coupled with Pete's marvelous story-telling ability, that gave me an insight into what was driving many of the changes in Silicon Valley.

One afternoon (sometime in the mid-1970s), Pete called me to ask if I would drop off a spare trailer hitch, as his had got bent on the way up to Packard's orchard. I stopped by a little red house on Taffe Road, where Pete was waiting for me. David Packard was remodeling his main residence and so, for the time being, lived in this little shack of a house.

Dave sat there, bigger than life, in a worn-out chair, in old jeans and a flannel shirt, "shooting the shit" (as Pete would say) with Peter. I was amazed. This was at a time when Dave had already served as Deputy Secretary of Defense in Washington.

We got to talking about apricots and then about how the area was changing. Dave was interested in my perspective, growing up in Santa Clara Valley. We talked for a few hours. Afterwards he said, "You ought to write a book about Silicon Valley, 'looking out.' It is a unique perspective that will be lost to history if you don't."

"I don't understand what I'm 'looking through' to provide a perspective on," I responded. "The business of high tech is over my head."

"It's really very simple," said Dave. "Technology makes it easier to accomplish tasks. That's it. It isn't more complicated than that. Sure, the microprocessor is complicated. The processing of the chip requires knowhow, and quality software requires creative work, but the whole point is to make tasks easier to accomplish. Companies that lose sight of this goal fail. Watch for yourself. You'll see this same pattern of successes and failures over and over again. This search for efficiency has world-wide appeal, and people world-wide are investing in our technology."

"But why here?" I asked.

"Because of the concentration of schools here training people and, most importantly, who want to stay in the area after they graduate."

It was then that Pete quoted my grandfather, who said, "Santa Clara is a great place to make apricots and make babies, and babies are going to win."

Suddenly, Silicon Valley didn't seem so mysterious to me. A place with great schools, a great climate, and the great California economy, where new technologies providing a simple promise of efficiency were being invented, and so with a tradition of innovation already in place, plus great financial institutions in San Francisco that had money for investment readily available, was the perfect place to incubate, nurture, and give birth to "Silicon Valley."

Although I ran into Dave Packard and Bill Hewlett and talked with them many times later, it was the simple connections within our farming community that gave me insights into the driving force behind the historically significant transformation of a simple farming community into the "ground zero" of information technology.

And what a transformation it was! The time when I first met Dave was when "memory" was something you lost with age, an "application" was for employment, a "program" was a TV show, and a "cursor" used profanity. My brother John, years later, would joke: "A 'keyboard' used to be on a piano, a 'web' was a spider's home, and a 'virus' was the flu." For me, a CD is still an account with the bank.

One last word about David Packard: He was a gentle, nice man, with a nervous tick, compulsively touching, or scratching, or picking at a single spot on the right side of his head. In some photographs, you'll see a bald spot, right where he picked. It was an odd quirk. If you ever see that bald spot on the side of Dave Packard's head, now you know why.

David Packard and his wife, Lucille, in 1986

A Brief History of the Family Business

Our family business history in the Valley was more evolutionary and opportunistic than strategically planned. Whatever we had on hand that was most plentiful we attempted to convert into some commercial value. Ironically, our business strategy was driven by having too much inventory. The genesis of this strategy was firmly rooted in our penny-pinching upbringing. The constant admonition was, "Never waste. Find a use for it, or a value." Spendthrifts we were not.

The Marianis, as a big family, were capable of doing a lot of work. Our hands were not to be idle. With hands aplenty, and no money, we gravitated toward agricultural enterprises that required many hands.

Without money, but with lots of time and a willingness to work hard, my grandfather (Djede) graduated from being a farmhand to contracting with farmers to buy their fruit (prunes, at the time) after blooming time each spring. He would do all the work for the farmer—harvest, sort, market, and ship the fruit—taking all the harvest risk. The farmer received a certain agreed price for the crop "as is" on the tree. After the harvest without the farmer incurring any harvesting expenditures or doing any of the work required to bring the crop to market, he would receive the agreed-on price (after taking into consideration all of these factors) of the crop on the trees. The basis for the price of the tree crop was a combination of an estimate on costs to harvest and the total pounds harvestable. If we harvested more fruit than the farmer estimated, and/or if we harvested for a lower cost than the farmer estimated, there was an opportunity to make money after the costs of coordinating all the work of harvesting.

As my father mentioned earlier in his memoirs, Djede had an inexplicable knack for estimating prune production from trees in advance—in fact, five months in advance—of the actual harvest. While driving through an orchard very slowly, he would stare at the trees with great intensity. He did this shortly after blooming time each spring, with the fruit still in its "bloom jacket," the stage when prunes are embryonic, with budding fruit still inside the bloom. Djede could accurately and instantly estimate the total harvestable tons of prunes after driving through an orchard. He was accurate within a few hundred pounds. It was an amazing gift. The success that resulted gave Djede the seed money to begin buying land.

Toward the end of his life, during one tender moment, he shared with me his secret.

"David, do you really want to know the secret how I estimate prune crops?"

"Yes!"

"Well, one year I went around from orchard to orchard—about ten orchards. I would stare in one spot inside the canopy of the tree and not move my eyes. I would count how many prunes I could see without moving my eyes. I wrote down how many prunes I saw in each orchard and then looked up the records of how many tons were harvested from each orchard. I compared the tons per acre with my prune-count per tree. Since all orchards in those days had the same number of trees per acre, all I needed to know was how much fruit averaged on the trees. If I saw five prunes, that would mean two tons to the acre; if I saw seven prunes, it meant three and a half tons per acre.

"The following year I tested my theory, and it worked. As time went on, after driving through an orchard and making my prune-jacket count. I compared it with the actual harvest later. From these comparisons, I knew by my fruit gaze the number of pounds of fruit for each tree—and by extension (knowing the number of trees in an orchard) the pounds for the orchard."

With this gift of crop prediction months before anyone else knew, the foundation of our enterprises began.

Having acquired plenty of land, we planted trees. The trees produced fresh fruit. We packed and shipped to fresh fruit markets all over the world. Overripe fruit, however, could not be successfully shipped without spoiling before it got to market. So we sorted out the overripe fruits and dried them.

Over time, we planted more trees, purchased more land in the Valley, harvested more fruit, shipped more boxes of fresh fruit, and sorted out more and more overripe fruit that couldn't be marketed and had to be dried; the dried fruit could be viewed as a salvaged waste product from our fresh-fruit packing business. We sold it to a local dried fruit company.

These dried fruit companies hired hundreds upon hundreds of people to process, clean, sort, and pack the fruit. It was all hand-labor at the time, with no possibility of automating or mechanizing.

As we produced more and more dried fruit, Djede figured out that we produced more of it than some companies that specialized in dried fruit. So we began our own dried fruit company, marketing directly to stores and other outlets—the "Mariani" brand. Again the pattern persisted: because we had so much dried fruit, we got into the dried fruit business.

As decades passed, we acquired more land and more capital. Again, we had too much inventory, so we got into real estate development and finance. Our real estate development created long-term lease and financial cash-flow financial instruments. With capital resources on hand, we got into banking, then investment banking. The same pattern, every time: "Never waste. Find a use for it, or a value."

Our family eventually split up our family enterprises, based in part on who was interested in what profession. Some members of the family stayed with the "mother ship," our dried fruit company. The automation and labor displacement in the packing industry in the last three to four decades alone has been astonishing: Mariani Packing now has optical color and defect sorters, magnetic screens, and air-plumes to separate debris or to separate by size. These sorting processes require only a few watchful eyes to make sure the machines are working properly. But the machines themselves sort fruit that would take an army of people to sort by hand. In Mariani Packing alone, hundreds of workers have, easily, been displaced by very clever technology that was unimaginable just a few years earlier.

These innovations were a continuation of the legacy and culture that began with my grandfather, Djede. He pioneered the creation of prune dehydrators. Bins, prune dippers, and tunnel dehydrators radically reduced the number of people required to receive and process prunes.

Many farmers believed success was based upon high prices and blamed their failures due to low prices.   Djede understood our business had small margins and thought success depended upon the ability to save money through innovations.   My father, who changed the industry forever with the introduction of moist pack fruit, often said, "Innovate or perish."

My Professional Career: The Early Years

1971–1979

The Secret of change is to focus all of your energy not on fighting the old, but on building the new.

Socrates

Lesson on Perceptions

After my college education I became responsible for our agricultural activities.

One day Nick Tickvica and I discussed the idea of growing grapes on marginal, rocky land along the road where prune trees would not grow. With little follow-up discussion, Nick, one day, just drove up to Healdsburg with his brother Lester and Mark Kettman[25] planted by hand to keep costs down. The Tikvica's charged nothing for their time and effort. They just did it. As a result, we ended up with a low-cost basis in the grapes planted there, giving us a low break-even point. With about ten percent of the Sonoma land in grapes, its income exceeded the net income on the ninety percent of the remaining land planted in prunes.

I was used to delegating or contracting out for our orchard or vineyard development work. The result was a higher marginal cost of development. In retrospect sometimes, you don't really save time through delegation; and through delegation it cost us more.

The lesson learned is that all delegation or always doing something yourself are not mutually exclusive principles. There are times it is appropriate to delegate, and there are times that it is just best to do it yourself.

After the successful vineyard plantings, I wanted to plant more grapes where prune orchards couldn't be planted due to the rolling topography in one part of the ranch; also, a small planting of pears failed to produce sufficiently on the rocky soil. We eventually did plant grapes after several years of debating the issue, in part because it made little sense to re-plant pears in such gravelly soil. On the lower ground, I wanted to pull some of the prunes and put more grapes in, because grapes had proven to be of high quality and profitable. Why not plant grapes since prunes were clearly not profitable? However, the rest of the family was too stuck in the mentality that "we are in the dried fruit business"—and the blindness caused by a closed mindset resulted in resistance. Years later, after Dad died, my brothers Mark and Rick ended up owning the Healdsburg properties and then sold them to the Jordan Winery. Jordan, of course, immediately bulldozed the orchard and planted grapes. The lesson is that sometimes the obvious can escape us if we become too rigid in our worldview. In our case, we were frozen in our thinking: "We are in the prune business."

Simarloo: A Lasting Legacy.

During the 1970's I was commuting back and forth to Australia – particularly during the harvest periods. But a few years earlier Dad realized there were not enough human harvesters to harvest the massive plantings of Simarloo's stone fruits, and the research and development engineering of practical mechanized harvesters was progressing too slowly. Also, during this same period, Australia was feeling a shortage of manpower, with its low population, and so it had created an interesting incentive program. They needed "breeders," as the Aussies would say. The Australian government offered to pay for a one-way ticket to Australia for any woman in the world (except for Asians—Australians at the time suffered from an unhealthy dose of Asian xenophobia) who was willing to stay and work for a minimum of two years.

My father, again boldly thinking outside the box, went back to Croatia, at that time under the hand of Tito, and where many wanted to leave. It was easy to convince an army of Croatian women to migrate to Australia, under our sponsorship, to harvest our crops. Our small army of all-female harvesting crews were legendary among the men of the upper Murray Valley. The large influx of Croatian women in a concentrated area had a long-lasting impact in South Australia. There remains to this day a very strong and thriving ethnic Croatian community in the valley near Simarloo.

Most folks driving through the Murray River Valley say, "Where or how did this Croatian group get here, in the middle of nowhere?" Now you know the story.

The foundation of my career was learning from both what we did right and what we did wrong. We were all born into a family of entrepreneurs. Growing up and watching and listening during family gatherings taught me many business lessons. Without being aware of it, just by living at the epicenter of family activity and family chatter, I was being educated in the art of business. The formal educational foundation to my career took a more circuitous route.

My undergraduate education began with studying theology, then changed, in my sophomore year at Santa Clara University, to a dual major in history and philosophy. Dad chided me about the questionable utility of my majors: "What are you going to do, give our boysenberries a pep talk after you graduate?" However, I was convinced that the ability to think and process data logically, and the ability to appreciate little details as well as the big picture (both of which I got through philosophy), were important for any process of decision making in business. And a knowledge of history gave me a context for interpreting the present. The disciplines of history and philosophy have served me well over the years. Upon reflection, I find it is amazing how reasonable and bright people can leap to illogical conclusions. Without training in logic and practiced conceptual thinking, many people simply live their lives reactively.

I went back to school in 1970 with a renewed sense of purpose, focused on business. Meanwhile, Arlene and I didn't have much of a courting period. We knew we were in love and meant for each other. We married in 1971.

During the day, I worked as a route salesman for our dried fruit company, calling on grocery stores; in the evening I attended USF night school, collecting credits for a bachelor's degree. Arlene worked at a local hospital. During our first year of marriage, we managed to save $8,000 and I made another $5,000 by selling options on the stock market. Although we were living rent free (I had added a bedroom to the guesthouse before we got married in exchange for free rent for two years), this was still quite a feat given that I only made $600 per month and Arlene earned $400 per month. We literally watched our pennies. We had $13,000 in savings on our first wedding anniversary.

At the period when I was selling dried fruit to mom-and-pop stores in San Francisco, Italian produce buyers could be brutal to salespeople; blunt and crude are words that come to mind. I was actually scared to go into some of the stores. Some yelled at me to get the #!@ out. One old produce manager would bark at me, "What does the Mafia want now?" I knew that, with a name like Mariani, people would assume we were Italian, but it had not occurred to me that people would think we belonged to the Mafia!

After months of insults, one day my most obnoxious produce buyer barked, "Come on, kid, your family are Mafia, right?" I had had enough of the verbal abuse. Something snapped, in my head. . . . . I remained calm and simply said. with a straight face: "Yes, we are. Now, exactly how many pounds of prunes are you going to buy from me today? . . . You don't want to make me angry." (To this day, I have no idea what got into me.)

His voice immediately lowered and cracked a little, and he said, very slowly, "How many pounds of prunes would make you happy?"

I slowly wrote down a number on my re-order pad (a modest quantity). He said, "It's a done deal." He didn't bark at me anymore.

I felt a little bad that I had lied about our being part of the Mafia, but I learned a valuable lesson about people and human nature: I learned about leverage, intimidation, and perception—though not everyone sees it there is a difference between a bark and a bite.

I didn't like using fear to accomplish my goals. However, understanding how people react to certain emotions was an important lesson for me. In business, I have found that all people are motivated by a combination of what I call the three horsemen: fear, greed, and need. I understood fear and how to use it; my dad taught me how to spot fear in others, but more importantly how not to abuse it. Dad taught me how to recognize leverage—and fear, greed, and need are, in truth, powerful points of leverage—but he also taught me not to abuse it. He taught me how to recognize leverage points only to gain insight into how to meet people's needs.

I also learned that perception was everything. It was the reference point, the alpha-and-omega of every business discussion.

Opportunities Seized—and Missed

Dad used to always laugh at missed opportunities and say, "Don't worry about them. You can't get them all." I learned to laugh at my mistakes—it was my coping mechanism, as I missed my share of opportunities.

While working in my teens on my second shift each day at night at our frozen food company, I had been taught how to operate our freeze-dried processing equipment. Our freeze-drying process used a chamber with a rack holding the frozen fruit: we would create a vacuum in the chamber and heat the racks to a very high temperature, and the product would go from frozen to dried almost instantly, reducing cell breakdown in the process. The feat was accomplished by forcing out frozen water, bypassing the liquid state; the frozen water was converted directly into vapor. At the time, there were only two such systems in the world: one was in our plant on Martin Avenue in Santa Clara, and the other was at Davis University. We had experimented with freeze-dried strawberries for Kellogg's, for their breakfast cereals. Kellogg's got excited, and we got excited, about this new line of business, so we invested in the expensive system.

A strawberry, once freeze-dried, can last for more than a year; a drawback is that the berry takes on the texture of cardboard. But, when re-hydrated properly, the berry tastes as fresh as the day it was picked—so it looked like a fabulous product for Kellogg's. The problem during consumer trials was that consumers either didn't wet the strawberry sufficiently with milk, and so bit into something that resembled a nut made of cardboard, or they let it sit at the bottom of the bowl and overhydrate and turn mushy. It was a consumer bust.

We ended up doing small contract jobs, from preserving important documents that had gotten wet to short runs for companies wanting to explore the commercial potential of freeze-drying without investing in the equipment. Our frozen-food operation was seasonal, operating only sixty days each year; I was hoping the freeze-dry business would help justify our keeping the plant in operation all year round. So I was single-focused on getting contract work.

One day a fellow from Nestlé's came to the plant while I was operating it. The company wanted us to experiment with freeze-dried coffee. We could either get a royalty on nationwide sales of all the freeze-dried coffee they sold over ten years (which at the time was zero), or they would pay us a premium to give them scheduling priority for six months to conduct a test. I got through to my Dad, who was in London at the time, to discuss it. We both agreed there was no future in freeze-dried coffee, so we opted to do the contract work and waived the offer of royalties. Boy, were we wrong! That was the beginning of high-end instant coffee.

I knew our frozen food operation could not make money operating only sixty days a year. The overhead was too big for seasonal use. Our freeze-dry business was shrinking as new technologies were designed and the process became more common.

In the 1970s we were leasing our frozen-food plant from the Cold Storage Company and its operations, which were contiguous to our building. We had a whopping twelve more years left on our lease. The lease rate per square foot was small, but the total annual rate was large because of the size of the building. Our rent was low in part because our landlord earned huge fees (called "in and out fees") associated with renting cold storage space for products placed there during the fresh-fruit summer months.

Everyone in our company saw this lease as a huge liability. The liability became the main motivation to continue operating the plant, year after year, even though at a small loss (it would have been generating no income at all, otherwise). I saw the lease as an asset or at least an opportunity.

I noticed there were buildings being built all around our frozen food plant and leased to high-tech firms. After doing some checking, I discovered that the rent around us was three to four times the rent we paid. I reasoned that our low lease rate had the effect of reducing the value of the building for its owners if we never used the adjoining cold storage services. If we just stopped operating, our landlord might want to buy our lease from us. It was a crazy idea, to turn a perceived liability into a cash asset. I analyzed our losses and concluded that we would lose less money by just paying rent and never operating the plant. The reason for this was that, by discontinuing the summer packing, we would be able to eliminate payroll and the overhead we carried year around even though our processing season was only sixty days long.

I convinced Dad not to operate the plant that coming summer, to allow me to set my strategy in place. Predictably, the property owners called me to meet to determine our intentions on the property. I told them that our lease rate was 5 cents a month per square foot and that I could sublease it at 20 cents for the next twelve years to high-tech users. Our 5-cent monthly rent was only 60 cents year, compared with the local market rate of $2.40.

After months of the landlord trying to make a case to terminate the lease, I reasoned with them that their building, with its low long-term rent, reduced the value of the building as a leased investment in the amount of $25 dollars per square foot. There was plenty of room to make a deal that made sense for both of us. I finalized a breakup fee with landlord, with the landlord paying us $6 per square foot to cancel our lease—a lease that was burning a hole in our pocket. This was more money than Mariani Frozen Food, Inc., had made in the previous fifteen years.

Somehow my part-time night job with the freeze-dry unit had turned into a real estate management mission. None of this would have been possible without the market appreciation in the Valley due to the technology explosion that was happening right before our eyes. Of course, I didn't really know what I was doing; I was just following my nose and instincts.

The following year I finished school, and Arlene was pregnant with our first child, Nancy. One of my duties in sales was to remove from retail-store shelves any of our branded products that had not been rotated properly by the store. Old products looked bad and reflected on the brand, not the storekeeper. Our product guarantee included a buy-back program of any products that looked old or poor for any reason.

Dried fruit companies commonly used "smoke houses" or "sulfur houses" to infuse products such as apricots and pears with sulfur; this helped to preserve the fruits' nutrients and color. Without sulfur treatment fruits lose their natural color quickly. But one problem with sulfured dried fruit is that, as the sulfur in the fruit dissipates, the fruit loses vitamins along with its natural color. The fruit eventually turns dark over time—consequently, it does not look appetizing to many people.

So, at the end of each week, I, along with all of our other salespeople, would fill my car with dark product "returns." We'd then take out the fruit bags and pour the returned fruit into big bins. There was actually nothing wrong with the fruit; it just didn't look very good after it turned dark. These "returns" were then diced and sold, for pennies on the dollar, to companies that used the fruit to flavor processed foods, such as juices and jellies.

One day I made a cold call on an "organic store" to sell our product. This was in 1973—just at the beginning of the organic food movement. They refused to buy our beautiful apricots and opted instead to buy from other sellers, at twice the price, unsulfured apricots, because they were "natural." The apricots sold in the organic stores were dark-brown because of the lack of sulfur treatment. I failed to make the sale of our premium apricots but realized the apricots we were selling into the secondary markets.[26] after the returns had lost all of their sulfur content, could be repositioned as "organic apricots." I discussed the idea with our national sales manager, Tierney Wilson. The answer was no. Organic was just a fad and the volume was too low.

Convinced that this organic idea was a missed opportunity, I asked our general manager, George Sousa, if I could buy the product returns at the same price we were selling to juice and flavor companies. The answer was yes, because it avoided the need to repack the fruit.

Next I designed a label and packaging, and negotiated a co-pack agreement for Paul A. Mariani Co. (PAMCO) to pack the returns under my own label, "Dave's Natural Fruit." Imaginative, aye? I quit working for the company and started selling Dave's Natural Fruit full time.

The short version of the story is that sales took off. My margins were about eighty percent net profit on gross sales due to my low purchase-price-point, a premium selling price, and virtually no overhead. But this bonanza to the David Mariani family didn't last long. On returning from an overseas trip, Dad called me into his office after he figured out what I was doing.

"I'm impressed with your resourcefulness and conviction with your ideas," he said. "I want you to come back to work fulltime for me."

"I'm happy with the present arrangement," I told Dad.

Then he made me an offer to buy my little company for more money than I had ever dreamed of, with a commitment to fast-track my career within the larger company.

"What do you like doing most?" he asked.

"Ag operations," I said (this meant managing the orchards and organizing the harvesting). "I really don't like sales that much."

Dad said, "O.K., it's a deal. You'll work under Florin Musladin, head of field operations, for two years to learn all aspects of our agricultural operations." Florin was a high energy guy with a formal education in agronomy and plant processing. Under Florin, I would learn the technical aspects of plant growth and processing principles.

Manual sorting lines in the 1970s.

(Sorting personnel, with the author, in the leather jacket, and a banking representative.)

I agreed to Dad's proposal and was soon at work. By now we had diversified far beyond prunes. Harvesting in the Valley began with cherries in May, boysenberries in June, apricots in June/July, peaches in July/August, prunes in August/September, pears in September/October, and grapes in October/November. In December, I got ready for harvesting in Australia: apricots in December, with the cycle repeating itself through April. It was a year-around harvesting cycle, often seven days a week that averaged easily

166

seventy- to eighty-hour workweeks. It was only upon reflection that I realize I have never taken a single course in agriculture, nor do I remember any instructions from either my father or grandfather regarding how to grow and harvest our different products. The knowledge all came from on-the-job training under Florin. I learned by osmosis. I was thrown into the business. I had a choice: learn it, and do it well, or end up pushing a broom in the warehouse. I decided to learn how to grow and harvest products well.

After two years I was appointed "head of field operations" and became the youngest member of the Dried Fruit Association.

I loved my work. As head of operations, I could actually spend more time with my family because I could delegate more; for example, I didn't have to go to Australia for an entire harvest season. Arlene was now expecting our second child. God knows when we had time to make babies. Nancy, our first, was a beautiful blonde, blue-eyed, sweet, and cooperative child. I was not prepared for our feisty, blonde, blue-eyed Molly. Having two girls with very different personalities was a handful, but such a joy. I had no idea what was in store for us in just a few short years.

No sooner had I got comfortable in my job as the ag department head than Dad called me into his office.

Another Career Change

"Son, your Aunt Mathilda will be retiring at the end of this year." Mathilda handled the banking and all the money for the company.

"I want a family member to handle the money," said Dad. "I want you to take Mathilda's place." I protested. I loved being out in the field and hated sitting behind a desk.

I was adamant. "I like agriculture, and the outdoors, I like the pressure of harvest time, I like the hands-on organizational challenges. Dad, you promised. You said to me, 'You can do whatever you are interested in,' " I said. "And what I am interested in is operations."

Dad lowered his voice and confided, "We really don't have a chief financial officer for our companies. Aunt Mathilda works hard, she is trustworthy, the bankers love her, but she is not a CFO, she was not trained to be a CFO. I am asking you to go back to school, get your MBA in finance and accounting, and become the CFO for all our companies. David, we badly need help in our financial management." I protested that I was not qualified to be a CFO and the company needed someone with experience.

After being out of school of two years, the idea of going back to night school again, with two children at home and working during the day, was not appealing. Again I said, "No, thank you." I was offered a substantial raise. I still said, "Respectfully, Dad, I appreciate your confidence in me, but no, thank you. I just don't want to leave a job I love doing."

Dad was a persistent and persuasive man. He said, "Look at it as a favor for your father. Go back to school at Santa Clara University for your MBA. I will even get the CFO of Santa Clara University to provide the experience to train you on the job. If you don't like it after twenty-four months, then you can go back to the ag department." I was struck by the thought, *Dad is asking me to do this as a personal favor. . . . He never asks for a favor from anybody . . . How do I say no to that!* Then I saw how to escape: *"There is no way Dad can pull off getting Mr. Marc Callan, the CFO of Santa Clara University, to come and give me on-the-job-training."*

So I said, "If you can get the CFO at Santa Clara to work directly with me every day for the next two years, I'll give it a whirl."

Monday morning came, and I was assigned an office in the main corporate office. Somewhat to my surprise, I was introduced to Marc Callan, eager to give me my first lesson in CFO'ing. Marc was retiring from Santa Clara, and Dad had learned about it. I found out later that, before I even said yes, Dad had already made the deal with Marc.

I was trapped. I went back to school.

During my first week on the job, around 1975, I discovered that money was tight. I became the go-to person to approve when money could be committed for every one of our companies, and every division within those companies, all over the world. Dad was virtually hands off. I sat down in an attempt to analyze the operations. I was in way over my head.

Dried fruit packing is a high-volume, high-leverage, low-profit-margin business. Our business was growing as much as twenty percent per year, and our cash-flow problems, partly self-inflicted, were a product of our very success and high growth rate.

By "high-leverage," I mean that we needed to take out large, short-term loans, using our massive fruit inventories as collateral. The money was used to pay our growers and carry the product for each year. The banks would only lend us seventy percent against the value of our inventory. I did the math: If we grew at twenty percent a year, our after-tax profits would be less than the additional equity needed to support the increased inventory requirements to support the increase in sales.

We began to borrow against our orchard land in Cupertino to support our packing operations. This worked well for a while because our land was appreciating faster than the borrowing-interest rate. Then the post-Vietnam inflation hit our economy. In the 1970s we saw a twenty-one percent prime rate. The combination of a high cost of borrowing and low profit margins made our business instantly unprofitable. We needed to borrow more money against our land to pay interest, with low-appreciating land collateral.

I found myself in a constant cycle of borrowing, paying banks back by refinancing other assets and repackaging our loans, or recapitalizing all our loans into bank participations. My learning was truly a baptism by fire. I learned that banks loved our business because we had huge compensating balances. We could at times owe a million dollars, but also have a million dollars in our checking account. So the bank could use the free money in our bank accounts and charge us interest when we borrowed from them. Suffice it to say that moving money from one bank to another, and refinancing, in order to manage the liquidity of our worldwide operations, became a full-time job.

I didn't need to encourage Dad to sell land to get our operations back into balance. Dad recognized that we needed to convert some of our land into cash and reduce our debt in this high-interest financial environment.

Marc proved to be a wonderful mentor, and I never went back to ag operations. I spent the rest of my professional career in the financial and business management world. By the time I was thirty, I was the CFO of thirty-two companies operating on several continents and managing related family interests.

Chapter 16

Dreams and Paradise Lost

Mid-1970s

Mariani Mall promotional material

Mall of Dreams

About 1950, during a period of widespread construction of state and national freeway systems, it was announced by the state that the Junipero Serra Freeway, or Highway 280, was going to be built through the Valley—and through some of our orchards. The highway was essentially cut through the heart of Silicon Valley and through the middle of much of our land holdings.

Along the western side of where the freeway was slated to be stood a seventy-acre orchard, half prunes and half apricots, which we owned. We decided to obtain commercial zoning for that land but doing this turned out to be a lot harder than we expected.

This was a time when land owners worked with the cities in true spirit of partnership compared to the political rules and legal gamesmanship in today's development environment.

At one time the city of Cupertino did not have the money or credit to bring additional water from Stevens Creek dam, a group of farmers, including my grandfather agreed to pay for the water line for the city provided we would have access to the water at no cost to the landowner. It was a deal written on a single piece of paper. It benefited everyone concerned.

When we decided to develop our Cupertino properties the city didn't have the infrastructure to support our development. The city gave us the commercial zoning to providing we agreed not to develop for ten years. We began to pay property taxes based on commercial property value that exceeded our gross income on our crops for 10 years but provided needed financing for the city.

The intervening 10 years saw many changes in municipal attitudes. In particular the working environment between an urban community and politics versus agrarian politics took hold. Specifically, pure politics won over good sense and the integrity of an agreement.

We were all set to go after ten years of planning to build a one million square foot enclosed shopping mall. The idea that the city after ten years would revoke our commercial zoning never occurred to us. Worse they issued no zoning by placing a moratorium on our property– meaning we were put in limbo for another 5 years. So the legendary partners like Ernie Hann, Al Taubman and Edward Debartolo were left at the altar with us. It was the beginning of our distrust of government, leaving my father to lament, "I would rather invest in dead metals over live politicians."

Mitel and Our New Bankers

About a year after our plans for a mall fell through, sometime in the mid '70s, Bank of America approached us to sell forty acres on De Anza Boulevard to a Canadian startup, a new and struggling telecommunications company. Bank of America was pressing us to take our asking price half in cash and half in stock at twenty-three cents a share. We had grown up with old-fashioned ideas that had seemed to survive the test of time—at least most of the time. A company that was fifty years old seemed a reliable investment; a company only fifty months old, not so much.

We were just not sophisticated enough to be able to evaluate startup companies. I was not in favor of the Mitel deal because the cash portion was insufficient to pay off our loans, pay our taxes, and generate what we needed for operations.

Bank of America pressed Dad hard. The Bank had invested a substantial amount of research and capital in Mitel and believed the stock was going to skyrocket, and we would be able to buy on margin accounts against the stock for our liquidity needs.

But the high-tech activity all around us made us nervous. In those days we didn't track the effects of deregulation or technology trends. We thought a wafer plant was making cookies! We were farmers and food processors. The exploding new technology seemed amazing to us. In truth it bewildered us.

Unfortunately, I argued successfully that we should not go forward with the Mitel deal. I reasoned that some startups were successful, and some were not. The professional venture capitalists get it right only one time out of six, on average. We couldn't afford the risk of a 1:6 chance of success on such a critical asset. We would be betting the farm with only a one-in-six chance of success.

Mitel went on to blockbuster success internationally. Another missed opportunity. Dad reminded me to laugh at the ones we let get away. Mitel was hard to swallow.

After we refused to take the Mitel deal, Bank of America said they would not renew our loan. Even though we had a personal friendship with three acting presidents of Bank of America, (the founder, Amadeo Giannini, with my grandfather, and Lorenzo Scatena and Tom Clausen with my father), it was a different matter when our credit was in question. Too much leverage (i.e., too many loans) was too much leverage.

We took the rebuff as a personal affront. We scrambled to assemble a consortium of banks to refinance our land holdings. It was strange dealing with an entirely new set of bankers and banks—in this case, mostly Japanese.

We tried to quietly sell several properties we owned all over Santa Clara Valley, with little success at our asking prices; except for our Almaden Mines property, which our partners wanted to sell but we did not—and then the government stepped in.

Almaden Mines

Dad, with a few of his buddies, had bought the Almaden Mines in Almaden Valley (which is part of the Santa Clara Valley metropolitan area). The mines had been known since the mid-1860s as New Almaden (after a famous quicksilver strike in Spain). The quicksilver strike at New Almaden has been credited by a recent historian as an event decisive for the winning of the American Civil war. The Confederacy had relied on cotton (a renewable resource) for currency to sustain its war effort; the Union had relied on gold. As the Union was running short of gold, the price of quicksilver (also known as cinnabar) became critical, because quicksilver is used to extract gold from raw ore. Due to the high global price of cinnabar during the early 1860s, the cost of mining for gold became prohibitive. With the discovery at New Almaden, global quicksilver (cinnabar) prices plummeted, and the Union could now mine for gold to finance the cost of the war. Without the New Almaden quicksilver strike, the Union might not have been able to continue the war to its successful conclusion.

By the time we purchased the property, the mine was still extracting quicksilver but only in small quantities. We bought it for the value of the land more than for the minerals.

The county purchased this historic property (which consisted of thousands of acres) from us under eminent domain, for pennies on the dollar. It is now a picturesque county park. There is no historical mention of our name at the park; I suspect this is because we resisted what we saw as confiscation of our property by the government. With the benefit of hindsight, the county got a bargain.

Prior to the county's "taking" of our property, Dad conceived that the miles and miles of New Almaden's underground tunnels could become the backbone of a compelling amusement park.

An amusement park that almost happened.

While at work, Dad was always near manic in his focus and energy. Dad would have his secretary set up and line up phone calls, then put them on hold, to avoid wasting time between calls. One day Dad asked his secretary to get

Walt Disney on the phone. By this time, in the early 1960s , Disneyland was a big success and Disney was an established celebrity. To my amazement, Dad's secretary managed to get Walt on the phone and on hold, waiting for my dad to get on the phone. Dad, confused for a moment, picked up the phone and said, "Walt, did you call me or did I call you?" Walt must have thought for at least a moment that my dad was a nut. Regardless, they ended up talking for months about the amusement park concept in Almaden. Although Walt's advisors decided against the concept due to the potential danger of cave-ins, Dad and Walt remained friends until Walt's passing in 1966.

Our idea for a kind of Disneyland North based on the New Almaden mines without Walt's backing finally died when the county condemned our property with the eminent domain acquisition.

When to Sell and Not to Sell, and the Need for a Poker Face

When Dad was not in a phone-frenzy, he was dictating memos and issuing directives. To third parties, he was a great listener. Internally, Dad was a sermonizer and a cheerleader. When it came to business strategy, Dad's Achilles' heel was his driving passion to maximize value at every turn, sometimes to our long-term detriment. The time he spent obsessing over estate planning to maximize the estate's after-tax value, or over avoiding taxes on profits (always done legally), was time spent away from making money by improving our operations so they ran smoother and smarter.

When real estate was booming, Dad didn't want to sell because he wanted to maximize appreciating land values by waiting, often until it was too late. During downturns, we would need to sell, but nobody wanted to buy. So we sold real estate often at discounts because we needed to sell during unfavorable market conditions. The result was we held on to our real estate longer than most, ending up with more appreciated assets than farmers who had sold their property earlier, but had not really sold properties at the best of times.

We had a lot of land, but also mounting land loans. I was worried. Dad explained to me that there are two kinds of sellers—those who want to sell and those who need to. Learning early in life the lessons about need, greed, leverage, and perception taught me the value of a good poker face . . . and boy, was a poker face needed!

While my stomach was churning with stress, Dad calmly explained his plan: "We need to be masters of our own destiny and not sit and wait for a developer to buy our land. We need to begin to develop our own land if we can't sell it to a developer at prices we need to get."

I didn't know what Dad had in store for me with this development idea, but I would soon find out with the launch of our business park a few years later: "The International Business Park."

Chapter 17

What is a Banco?

A group of Mexican-Americans approached my dad to invest in a *banco* they wanted to form. *Banco* means bank in Spanish. Dad was impressed that these immigrants weren't looking for a handout but just wanted to be "card-carrying capitalists," as he put it. I was called into a follow-up meeting with the "banco" organization committee. Before the meeting, I briefed Dad that we didn't really have spare cash to invest without shorting the existing budgets in our group of enterprises.

Dad, conflicted between wanting to help and mindful that we had a precarious cash management issue, straddled the issue by making a grand gesture, saying, "Look, I'm impressed that you're not looking for handouts but rather want to reinvest into the immigrant community. That's how a good friend of my father, Amadeo Giannini, got started with the Bank of Italy, serving Italian immigrants in San Jose, which is today Bank of America. So I'll tell you what: if at the end of your fundraising efforts, you are short on your goal to raise money to start the bank, I'll invest in the balance of shares needed to make sure the bank becomes a reality." Dad's thinking that this might avoid any investment at all backfired. We ended up owning seventy-five percent of the bank. I, of course, was the harshest critic of this deal. I was dead set against diverting capital away from our dried fruit company, which was consistently short of cash because money was being diverted to other activities.

During one organizing group meeting for the bank, Dad said, "To be proud of your success, you need to take on the responsibility yourself. *You* need to make the bank successful. I am not going to do it for you." Dad declined any board representation, even though we owned the majority of the bank's shares. It was an extraordinary gesture, brilliant if the bank was successful or catastrophically stupid if the bank was not. The demonstration over the ensuing years of the bank leadership's inability to make a profit, together with my scathing criticism of the investment and the bank's operations, surprisingly didn't get under Dad's skin; rather, it energized an insightful debate between Dad and myself about life, business, values, and aspirations.

One day Dad got a call from the California Superintendent of Banks. His office wanted a meeting with Dad. I happened to be meeting with Dad in his office when the call came through. He turned to me and said, "Son, we have a meeting with Carl Schmidt in San Francisco." Note the use of the plural "we." I should have been on the alert.

Schmidt opened the meeting by saying, "I am going to make this meeting short. Either you take over the management of the Banco de San Jose or we will." My dad, without any hesitation, turned and looked at me and said, "Good luck, son." It was a brilliant move; now that I was responsible for the bank's operations, I could no longer criticize them without criticizing my own stewardship. It silenced the critic.

I served as chairman of the board of the Banco de San Jose for about ten years. It was one of my most difficult challenges. Before this experience I had worked all my life in successful organizational teams, all of which had felt like "winners." But the entire staff at the bank felt and acted like losers and thoroughly emotionally defeated. The ability to attract quality executive staff in such a poisoned environment was nearly impossible. Really good candidates recognized the problems and attitudes and gave the opportunity a pass. Consequently I could only hire executive replacement staff that was only marginally better than what we had had before.

However, after ten years of reorganizing and re-staffing the bank, building a new headquarters, and re-branding as "California Security Bank," we eventually turned the bank around and sold it for two and a half times its book value. The turning point was when, after appointing one disappointing bank president after another, I had my personal CFO and confidant, Bob Serventi, hired as president. I had originally hired Bob away from Baron de Rothschild when the Baron owned Bank of California. Bob was an ex-seminarian and a Peace Corps volunteer, brilliant, with impeccable integrity and a fantastic work ethic. His leadership paid off.

It was a reminder that our businesses are only as good as our people.

Chapter 18

"To invent, you need a good imagination and a pile of junk."
Thomas A. Edison

The Valley in Transition

Roughly since the 1970s, the locals have referred to the southern part of the San Francisco Bay Area on the peninsula equally as Santa Clara Valley, the Valley of Heart's Delight, and Silicon Valley. This reflected the blend of the remnants of its agrarian history and its rising prominence in computer technology.

In the late 1800s, seven and a half decades before anyone had ever heard of a silicon wafer, Santa Clara Valley was that era's world center for inventers and manufacturers of farm machinery. In 1883, John Bean founded Food Machinery Corporation in Los Gatos. His first invention was a pump to spray orchards with a variety of materials, including but not limited to micronutrients, mold inhibitors, oils to stimulate bloom formation, and pesticides. This invention was followed by a string of innovative machines that saved both labor and money. Many innovations from other companies followed, such as the Philper peach cutting and pitting machine, and many farmer inventors began mechanizing and automating fruit processing (immortalized by Steinbeck in *East of Eden*). There was a blend of agricultural garage-based inventions and companies formed to specialize in agricultural-labor-saving technologies.

The company that best symbolized the technical innovation predating Silicon Valley was John Bean's aforementioned company, Food Machinery Corporation, which eventually became FMC, Inc. FMC was dedicated to making automated machinery for agriculture and food processing, from harvesting crops to equipment for canneries and packers. During World War II, the concentration of engineers at FMC was too attractive to escape the notice of our growing industrial-military complex, and FMC was transformed into a company that made military hardware.

Jim Hait

FMC's success was largely because of Jim Hait. Under the guidance of a brilliant engineer named Jim Hait, the Bradley amphibious tank was designed and engineered by FMC. [27] Hait was a kindly-gentlemen, schooled in engineering, but he knew very little about finance and management techniques, and so some say under his leadership FMC suffered from a lot of waste.

Nevertheless, Jim was an extraordinary engineer. Born in Brooklyn, New York, in 1906, Hait graduated from Rensselaer Polytechnic Institute in 1928 with a mechanical engineering degree. He worked at Emsco Derrick and Equipment Company, then at Peerless Pump as chief engineer. When FMC acquired Peerless in 1932, Hait remained as chief engineer, developing important innovations in pump design and filing more than twenty patents. (His designs covered a wide range of pump types, including centrifugal, discharge rotary, and lubricating oil pumps, multiple pump bearing designs, and well turbines.) At FMC, Hait ultimately served as president, chief executive officer, and chairman of the board. In 1971 he retired as chairman but continued to serve as a senior consultant and chairman of the corporate technical committee. In 1975 he retired from the board of directors. In 1983, Hait was inducted into the Ordnance Hall of Fame, one of the few civilians to be so honored. And in 1999, he was inducted into the Silicon Valley Engineering Hall of Fame.

Jim backed his son Paul in the dried-beef business. Paul was an Olympic gold medalist in swimming and founded Pemmican Beef Jerky. Paul licensed the rights to its formulas and processing to the Mariani family and sold his company to General Mills.

To this day, Mariani Industries carries on the business of making beef jerky in Australia.

We negotiated a deal to develop our own dried jerky business in Australia by obtaining a recipe license from Pemmican. Through the negotiations, Jim's marginal business acumen became apparent. Simple business concepts needed to be explained to him. From understanding the fundamentals of underwriting loans for his business to basic cost-accounting and strategy—these were concepts that eluded him. I learned that great engineers and stewards of integrity may make good chairmen, but they did not necessarily make for shrewd and perceptive small-business entrepreneurs and managers. I suspect that Jim's steady hand, his integrity, and his careful decision-making were responsible for his rise to the top.

But shrewdness comes in many forms. With a few of his friends, Jim owned about 10,000 acres over the eastern hills of Santa Clara Valley (in fact, the entire Isabel Valley). He spent most of his weekends at his estate there to relax. The problem was there were no services—no telephones, no electricity—because Jim didn't want to see power and phone lines marring his unspoiled vistas of this very special valley. The military generals during World War II were going crazy because they literally could not get in touch with him for two to three days at a time every week. So, compliments of the Department of Defense, miles of underground utilities and an airstrip were installed on Jim's property so the generals could have ready access to Jim during wartime.

FMC, a one-time agricultural engineering company, became a world center of high-tech engineering that invented and manufactured much of the technical hardware needed to support the silicon revolution.

With technology beginning to swirl all around us, I am reminded of Elbert Hubbard quip, *"The world is moving so fast these days that the man who says it can't be done is generally interrupted by someone doing it."*

I am also reminded of a character, my dear friend Lester Tikvica.

Lester Tikvica

Lester was the Son of Nick Tikvica Sr who was my grandfather best friend. Nick's career paralleled my grandfather's both independently and often as partners. They both were early 20th century orchardist in Santa Clara Valley and both were fresh fruit shippers of high-quality fruit all over the world; Nick Sr under the TIK brand and Paul Sr. under the Mariani Brand. Lester, as well as his entire family remained humble despite their accumulated wealth from hard work, good fortune and being in the right place at the right time by farming in Silicon Valley at a time when land cost no more than $ 10/acre.

During the late '60s and early '70s, if you seldom got from behind your desk for a drive around, you'd have been astonished, when you did, by all the new roads appearing, seemingly out of nowhere, buildings suddenly appearing on corners, and housing tracts seeming to grow right out of the ground. It was an intoxicating time for developers. Every topic of discussion seemed to end up about some "big deal," and more and more people I ran into were filled with self-importance. It was old friends like Lester and Nick Tikvica who kept me grounded.

I recall being picked up for a quick flight to Healdsburg from San Jose by Lester, a fellow flyer and owner of a Beechcraft Bonanza (an aircraft, at the time, costing more than the total price of ten average-sized homes). He was dressed in overalls and work boots and was driving a decrepit 1941 fruit truck called a bobtail flatbed truck.

Rather than parking in the local air strip's designated parking area, he pulled off the side of the road and jumped the airport fence to get to his plane. Lester's choice of parking was perhaps to avoid paying the parking fee in the lot. I complimented him on his nice airplane. His response was, "Big deal—it's just to get us to Santa Rosa faster." I asked, "Don't you love having a plane?" "No," he said. "I love flying. Be careful—don't fall in love with possessions or possessions will possess you."

Lester, a significant benefactor to Mitty High School in the valley in the 1970s, worked "undercover," so to speak, as a gardener at the school for years: Lester just showed up one day and started pruning, weeding, and clearing up the landscaping. Once, while Lester was mowing a lawn, an administrator came up to him said, "Lester, we don't seem to find you on our payroll roster." Little did they know that Lester was one of their biggest donors at the time.

The wit of Lester, his intelligence, humility, and generosity, were without equal. Nick, his brother, and I marvel to this day what a rare soul Lester was.

His world-class wit will never be forgotten. Once, after getting hit by lighting while on his D-4 tractor in Sunnyvale was scorched and rushed to the hospital. They scanned his brain for signs of damage. While getting wheeled from the scanning room, he declared, "They just scanned my brain but couldn't find anything." There are so many Lester stories one could write a book about him alone.

Chapter 19

From Fruit to Real Estate Development

1970s

The 1970s were in some ways analogous to the Wild West. The frenzy of new technology, new companies, new campuses, and new homes swirled all around us. Neighboring farmers were replaced with electrical engineers and software writers; fruit-packing plants were replaced with computer assembly lines and "fab plants"—facilities for fabricating silicon wafers.

As far as I was concerned, the place was turning into a concrete jungle of tilt-slab R&D edifices. We were paving over some of the richest soils in the world—top soil that had taken hundreds of thousands of years to produce and located in the most ideal climate for growing food. I longed for the days when we could drive for miles and see nothing but blossoms on trees lining both sides of the road. In particular, the trip from Cupertino to San Jose in springtime down Steven's Creek Road, as mentioned earlier, had been breathtaking. The blossoms on the orchards had seemed to explode with dazzling colors as we rode to school along Steven's Creek.

Nevertheless, despite my remorse that my beloved "Valley of Heart's Delight" was being transformed into "Silicon Valley," I was also curious; I wanted try to understand what all this technology fuss was about.

Politicians

Apparently, while Dad was a member of the California-Chile trade mission, he met a man called Ron, who was passionate about world trade as a means to build peace between nations. Dad was surprised when Ron asked Dad if he would make our guesthouse available for a member of the royal family in Egypt (unrelated to Samira); whose family was concerned about security. I remember Dad talking about this guy, "Ron," connected with the trade mission, and saying, "How in the world is this guy Ron connected with folks in Egypt?" Nevertheless, that was the beginning of our friendship with Ronald Reagan.

Along with my uncle Louie, we held fund-raisers for Mr. Reagan, who later became governor of California in 1967. Later still, as president of Mr. Reagan formed the Virtual Trade Mission Foundation International, demonstrating the consistency of his convictions. Dad's first contact with Ronald Reagan was the beginning of Dad's own passion for world trade as a means of building peace between countries. It was foundational to Dad's drive to develop overseas business and trade as public policy.

We hosted politicians on both sides of the aisle. Political philosophies ranged from conservative Republicans such as Reagan and Congressman Gubser to Republican liberals such as Congressman Pete McCloskey and Democratic liberals such as Leo McCarthy and Jerry Brown. What was common to these men was their integrity and their commitment to do the right thing ethically.

Dad told me one day that the difference between leaders and statesmen are their ethics. "Leaders can lead but may lead you into war or foreign genocide; but statesmen forge foreign policy by understanding the perspectives of others, by respecting foreign perspectives, then drawing upon their personal ethics to make decisions." It was then that I understood why we embraced both sides of the political aisle.

Although my father's magnetic personal presence drew a wide range of characters, the draw for many—to have a taste of Silicon Valley—was becoming evident. Visitors often asked, "What's it like to live in Silicon Valley?" I grew tired of bristling at the term, and tired of correcting our visitors—that it was called Santa Clara Valley—and began to listen to the deeper meaning behind the question.

My mother (center) with Ronald Reagan visiting Villa Maria while running for president

My brother John (at the far left), shaking hands with President Ford visiting our business park. (My father is next to John, in the middle.)

Charles Gubser   Ronald Reagan   Pete McCloskey   Leo McCarthy

Leaders on the both side of the aisle were visitors to the Mariani estate.

Dignitaries supporting our Industrial Park and the Foreign Trade Zone. Top left is President Ford. Top right , My mother and father are pictured here with President Ford, and bottom, is my father, Paul McCloskey, my mother and Norm Mineta.

Business Parks R US

One day Dad called me into his office. His office was actually a converted mobile home trailer, once owned by Mom's aunt and uncle and converted into an office at our Cupertino packing plant. It was cheap and efficient. Dad's humble office was in comic contrast to the scope of his business interests. Some people would call Dad cheap, others preferred thrifty, but Dad's attitude toward money can be best summed up by one of his favorite sayings: "A fool with money is only temporary."

"Son," Dad said to me, "it's now time to stop cultivating the soil and raising trees and begin cultivating clients and raising buildings."

"O.K." said I, "what do you want me to do?"

"I am making a big gamble by deciding to develop an Industrial Park on our Walnut Glen orchards. It is the only way to earn ourselves out of our mounting debt." It was counter-intuitive. I was working to reduce our debt while Dad was committing the family to more debt to develop the Park. My father theorized that we needed to create additional value rather than sell existing assets to pay off our overall debt load. To create value, we needed to incur more debt. It was a big bet with massive risks.

"Dad's briefing continued. " I've hired a guy to develop the business park. [The International Business Park or IBP]. I'm going to Washington, D.C., to see if I can get them to grant us a Foreign Trade Zone designation in Walnut Glen."

I scratched my head. "What the heck is a Foreign Trade Zone? Also, who's this guy you hired?" Dad seemed to be hastily embarking on a daring financial bet in a desperate bid to earn himself out of his mountain of debt. I thought of Mark Twain, who wrote, "Necessity is the mother of taking chances.

"Dad explained: "A Foreign Trade Zone is a special designation within the boundaries of the United States treated as if outside the U.S.A. for custom purposes, such as duties and tariffs." I said, "Who is going to run it?" "His name is Bill McKay. He's Monsignor McKay's brother in the San Francisco diocese. Bill will answer to you."

I protested. "I don't know anything about land development. I'm your CFO, not a real estate developer." Typical of my father management style of "baptism by fire," responded, "You'll do fine." End of discussion.

That was all the preparation he gave me: sink or swim. I quickly learned that Bill McKay was a nationally recognized, seasoned developer and the president of Coldwell Banker, which had developed the San Tomas Business Park in San Jose.

Bill McKay was fifteen years my senior, a lawyer with presidential experience at a large real estate company, and now he was reporting to me, a twenty-six-year-old guy who knew nothing about the business of development. The pro was reporting to the rookie. After thinking about this odd situation, I arranged for a meeting with Bill in our boardroom.

"Bill," I told him, "I understand you are reporting to me." He just stood there, giving me the "stink eye," so I continued, "In order for me to assess if you are doing a good job or not, you need to teach me everything I need to know about the development business. Because I don't know a thing about it."

Bill burst out laughing, "I promise to teach you everything I know . . . if you have ten minutes to spare!" We both began to laugh and somehow became instant friends. Bill took me under his wing and, true to his word, taught me everything he knew about real estate development. Bill was another incredible mentor to me. It took more than ten minutes to learn how to develop property. Decades later, I was still learning the nuances associated with the field.

Bill's first tasks were to design the Park's road, form the assessment district, and get the infrastructure of the Park installed and built. Most industrial parks are developed by insurance companies, but in the case of the IBP, our family was the sole owner and developer. Meanwhile, I worked on finding financing for the Park's corporate headquarters and for the facilities for what would become (after Dad got Washington's approval) San Jose Foreign Trade Zone #18. Somehow we got the bonds issued we needed, sold the bonds to build the roads, install the utilities, lights, intersections, gas lines, and extensive landscaping, and managed to have the Zone's principal buildings designed, financed, and constructed, all within forty months.

Before I knew it, we had the President of the United States, Gerald Ford, pay us a visit, along with up-and-coming politicians Congressmen Pete McCloskey, Jr., and Norman Mineta.

President Gerald Ford (far left). Second and third from the right: My father, Paul Mariani, and my brother John.

It was a whirlwind time for all of us. My learning curve was straight upward. Now it was a race for time to sell the lots and construct buildings fast enough to make the bond payments and make a profit. I found myself a long way from farming and the dried fruit business.

During the beginning stages of developing the IBP, I was called into Dad's office to sit in on a meeting with an "important developer." I was used to the polish of the regional mall developer Ernie Hawn, with his private airplanes and his fancy thousand-dollar suits. Expecting no less, I encountered the infamous Carl Berg. Carl wore an open-collar shirt, casual khaki pants, and scuffed shoes. He was already in Dad's office talking when I arrived at the meeting.

Carl had information in his car he wanted to give Dad, so Carl and I went out to his car to get a needed document. Carl drove an old, broken-down Chevy.

The back seat was piled with boxes of papers. Carl, like a magician holding his hands out, hesitating only a moment, dove through the stacks of boxes, then reams of papers, until he found what he wanted. It was amazing—there must have been a thousand sheets of paper in big piles in the back seat, and he knew where everything was. No filing system—it was all in his head.

Carl's partner finally arrived. He was a thin guy dressed casually in a tennis outfit. He explained that he was late because his tennis match had gone on longer than expected—but no apologies. Meanwhile, the tie I had put on was choking me, and I wondered why I had a tie on at all for these jokers—but first impressions can be deceiving. Carl's partner was a young guy in his thirties who drove a flashy car. He was very sure of himself—almost cocky. His name was John Sobrato. Between Carl and John, they had energy like an atom bomb. It was Carl's and John's energy and decisiveness that accelerated and dictated the direction of the conversation and eventually an agreement to sell some of our prized property to them. They were the first guys I ever witnessed who could out-maneuver and out-negotiate my father. My father was usually able to dictate the tempo and direction of a negotiation and discussion, but Sobrato-Berg were in a league of their own. They were electric together as they dictated the discussions.

A deal in principle was struck during that first meeting with Sobrato-Berg. Just like that, Sobrato said we would have a purchase contract with a good-faith deposit of $100,000 delivered the next day. I sat back at my desk later that day and considered that it appeared Sobrato-Berg were willing to pay us millions of dollars for an old forty-acre apricot orchard. I could not help but wonder, "*Here we are, beating our brains out, working seven days a week, and these guys are throwing millions of dollars around like water and playing tennis in the afternoons! Where are they getting all their money from?*" They were going to construct a building for a company called "Four Phase" (which now no longer exists) for $20 million. We had millions ourselves—we worked hard, but I could not conceive of just writing a check for $20 million to construct just one building. These guys were putting up buildings all over Silicon Valley. I realized there was another world out there that I didn't yet understand. I wanted to figure it out.

Carl and John could not have been more different. John wanted to build buildings that were stylistically memorable in the belief that, in the long term, they would be more valuable, and Carl wanted to construct buildings that were down-and-dirty cheap, producing more profit immediately. Carl was heavy, John slight; they were both intense personalities, but Carl was affable and easy to get to know, whereas John had two moods—serious and more serious. I worked mostly with Carl during the close of our forty-acre transaction in Cupertino. He was one of the funniest, brightest, and most energetic guys I've ever known. Carl amicably parted ways with John a few years later. It was not a surprise.

Eventually, both Carl and John became billionaires. However, Carl seemed to be driven by a relentless pursuit of the deal—he was great at creating value and accumulating money, though his shrewd business acumen exceeded his organizational skills. He was successful because of his extraordinary memory and business instincts rather, I suspect than his skills as a manager. His bookkeeper once bilked him out of some $20 million.[28] He didn't even know the cash was missing until the IRS tripped up the bookkeeper. The IRS noticed the bookkeeper had purchased a jet airplane but reported only a modest income on her tax returns. Oops.

Carl would have worked 24/7 if he could have; he slept only because he needed to, and he played hard when he wasn't working hard. However, forty years later, he is still the old Carl— I am reminded of Thomas Edison who said, "Show me a thoroughly satisfied man, and I will show you a failure." For Carl, his success illustrates the opposite might be true: Carl's success is a combination of a hard work, a brilliant mind, and being forever consumed in the thrill of chasing deals.

There is a Shinto saying: "A man is only wealthy when he has no wants," which is a little different from being satisfied. Another prominent developer, John Mozart, and a close friend of mine, has one of the finest vintage car collections in the world. Despite all his collections, like Carl there is a restlessness about him; he never seems really content, driven by the chase, with an inability to fully enjoy the moment. I suppose there are life trade-offs that come with success. However, developers like Dick Peery, John Sobrato, Carl Berg and John Arrillaga can be proud that, collectively, they developed more commercial and residential properties than anyone else, and more than any other group of individuals shaped the landscape and skylines of Silicon Valley.

Someone told John Sobrato that I taught tennis professionally. He asked me to give him a few lessons, and I said sure. I quoted him the going rate for lessons I charged at Los Altos Country Club. He pushed back, saying he thought it was too much. I didn't want to get ground down by John, so I said, "O.K., I'll give you a few lessons for free, but you have to give a generous donation to my favorite charity based on my going rate." John immediately agreed. John's donation was more than generous. I became curious about a guy who could be so hard-nosed in business and yet be so generous to charitable causes. This guy had a giving heart. Even with this early sign of generous giving, I had no idea John would someday become one of the biggest philanthropists in the Valley.

Once, in the early 1980s, Arlene and I joined John and his family on a chartered yacht on the Italian and French Riviera. After a long trip by plane, we excitedly looked forward to boarding the yacht, but as soon as we got there, John spent more than an hour passionately arguing over the cost of the wines he had ordered. The sumptuous yacht cost a small fortune in chartering fees, but that meant nothing to John—the cost of the provisions he had ordered on board incensed him because he believed he was being overcharged. It became clear to me that John was hyper-sensitive to people taking advantage of him. It might have been a childhood experience that set the mold for his sense of value and justice.

Regardless, one quickly learned that, while John was tough as nails in business, people were willing to work with him because he was fair. John, as mentioned, also eventually became a billionaire. No doubt the thrill of success drove John. But was he happy? I would say yes. Although driven by business and his two extreme moods, serious and more serious, I have seen John really smile, really relax his facial muscles, when describing something done by a particular charity he supports. His legendary philanthropy, I suspect, has given John a certain completeness in life.

John embodied the lesson my dad taught me about *why* you work hard in business. Dad's view was that hard work enabled you to do things for, and give to, worthy causes. John was a living example of the philosophy I learned from my father.

John and his wife Sue Sobrato raised three amazing people who could have been selfish and spoiled rotten, given the availability to them of more money than they could ever spend. Yet they are not self-centered; they did not live off their father's legacy of wealth; rather they embodied a different legacy from their parents, one of hard work and a giving spirit. They created a massive amount of value from their own accomplishments and generously gave away their bounty. They are a testament to John and Sue's good hearts and fundamental ethical values. John is a hard-driven, hard to get to know, hard on the edge, man. After spending many vacations with John and Sue, it was evident to me that, while John could roar like a lion, Sue could make him purr like a kitten. John is soft as cotton inside. Clearly, John and Sue's love for each other served as a "grounding" force and a model for their children. John has shaped the texture of Silicon Valley not only with his buildings but also with his legacy of giving throughout the entire community.

The Homebrew Computer Club

Don Pezzolo

At one point during those years, I met an interesting fellow named Don Pezzolo. Don was a neighbor of ours in Los Altos Hills and later a neighbor in Carmel Valley. Don is not a household name, nor is he one of those guys books are usually written about, but someone someday should do a book about him. He was an incredible talent. Don was one of Silicon Valley's enigmatic characters and early pioneers in electronics.

For example, Don created the first digital calculator from scratch. In another case, while working as an electrical engineer at Fairchild, he invented a bipolar gate that he cobbled together to make integrated circuits. But Fairchild's marketing department said his invention had no practical utility. Twenty years later, Don's process had been adopted by the entire semiconductor industry.

Those are just two examples of his work. The full list of his accomplishments is astonishing. One day, I asked Don if I could interview him about his fascinating life in Silicon Valley. I sat down with him about a year before his passing, and concluded from my interview that the Valley, in addition to its well-known personalities, was full of lesser-known people whose collective brilliance helped create the foundations of the Valley's success.

The Homebrew Computer Club

While writing down Don's story, I was reminded of the days of the "Homebrew Computer Club" (HBCC). The Club started out as a hobby club for local computer programmers during the pre–personal computer days. One of the rules of the Club was that everyone in it shared their computer ideas, discoveries, code, etc., with the other members. They began meeting at a community center in Menlo Park, but a meeting at SLAC (originally called the Stanford Linear Accelerator Center) was particularly memorable, at least for me, who was not really involved with the club, but happened to be attending out of curiosity and a desire to watch and learn.

A couple of programmers named Paul and Bill wrote some cool programs in Basic (a computer language of the time) and put them on tape.

I sat two seats away from a quirky, short, heavy-set guy whom everybody called Woz. This guy was typing code into a funny-looking little machine faster than I could type on a simple transcription machine.

I could type pretty fast (English words, that is), but this guy typed furiously in programmer's code, based on his own handwritten notes laid out on at least twenty pieces of paper. He kept up this frenzied pace of writing code throughout the entire meeting.

At the end of the meeting, Woz stopped typing, sighed a little, and gave everybody a look. The rest of us stopped and looked back at him. I had no idea what it was all about, but something was definitely in the air. Then he fired up his little machine . . .

But first a little background: Those who write code for a living know that, if you make a mistake in coding in a primary software language, it becomes a huge "bug," and the overall program usually will not work at all. All of the code to work the machine had been either inside Woz's head or on those twenty pieces of paper; Woz typed it all in without a single key-stroke error. He fired up the machine . . . and the damn thing worked.

It was, in effect, the first prototype personal computer. As the machine was only a Basic interpreter, and had no way to store the code at the time, the entire code was lost when he shut off the machine. I sat there after the meeting, stunned. His entire, flawless code was lost—except in Woz's head.

Remarkably, Woz had been typing code for what would one day become the third-generation forerunner of the "Lisa," which would eventually morph into the "Mac," as in Macintosh.

When my contemporaries went to school and took computer classes, we learned to write in primary programming languages, such as Basic or Pascal. Today, our kids' idea of a computer class is to learn how to use an "Excel" spreadsheet or "Word" word-processing programs. It's startling how fast the world has changed. What Woz did that day was truly amazing.

HBCC was a funky club composed of technology cowboys during Silicon Valley's Wild West technology explosion. The sharing and learning and forging of new frontiers soon started to fracture the relationships between the Club's members, however. Don Pezzolo, in my interview with him, recalled that Bill, one of the members, after writing some code, accused another programmer from Albuquerque of stealing *his* code. Lee Feltonstein was the club's moderator at the time; he conducted the meeting with a big stick and an abundance of humor. Bill's emerging possessive behavior was met with catcalls. From that point on, Bill stopped sharing his ideas and didn't attend any more meetings.

Steve Jobs and Bill Gates

But everyone else continued to either share their ideas and discoveries or promoted concepts to the group. At one meeting, Woz's buddy, Steve, did a show-and-tell about a pint-size computer for consumers. Next, Herb Goshen (a manufacturing guy) got up and told everyone they were idiots for sharing everything and that nothing was going to come of any of their ideas: "You are all stupid and dumb."

Woz is better known these days as Steve Wozniak. Steve was Steve Jobs, who, with Woz, started Apple Computer. Paul was Paul Allen and Bill was Bill

Gates. (Bill, at least in those days, received a lot and gave little. Today, we see a complete reversal in a man dedicated to giving his life and resources for the benefit of others.)

The Homebrew Computer Club soon became a fuzzy memory. However, HBCC was the breeding ground for ideas that laid the foundational technology both for what would soon become household names like Microsoft and Apple and for many other notable companies, some of which have come and gone, such as Tandem and Four Phase

With my modest understanding of technology, it was not obvious to me that the personal computer was going to be successful. I was used to "dumb" terminals connected to a centralized computer center filled with punch cards. The growing technological advances enabled computers to move beyond centralized repositories of data and processing capabilities; we were about to be untethered from central computer rooms.

Don Pezzolo, however, did see the potential in PCs. Long before the phrase "killer app" was coined, Don, along with Tim Barry and Ed Engler, created, in 1977, a company called "Pragmatic Design." Don's simple idea was to create useful things for the PC—a memory card was their first brainchild.

Fast-forward thirty-five years, with a steady stream of technological advances, and we seem to have come full circle. It is ironic that some of us are now tethered again to a central computer called "the cloud," a fancy name for a giant computer center made up of thousands of smaller computers called "servers." The CAT5 hardwiring of the past has been replaced by fiber-optic cables via the internet to a central computer or data center "in the sky."

When it comes to starting companies out of garages, or boot strapping at home, the Homebrew Computer Club may have been the club, but guys like Steve Wozniak and Don Pezzolo were doing the brewing. Although I became fascinated with technology, it also became a distraction for me because we still needed to develop our properties.

Chapter 20

A Passing of an Era

1970s

Gnashing of Teeth and Tender Moments

The 1970s were a decade of extremes. It was a time of confusion and clarity, of stress and success, a time of quiet, tender moments and of the clamor of the boom in Silicon Valley. It was a frenzy I began to think of as normal life. It was also both the happiest and the saddest period of my life.

Early on, as mentioned, I got married to my beautiful wife Arlene, who gave us three children in rapid succession: Nancy, Molly, and Janna. I loved every aspect of being married and being a father; it provided my life with its quiet and tender moments. I was fascinated by how different each of our children, et loved them each the same.

Then, in 1976, I was wakened up by a phone call in the middle of the night from our family doctor, Rex Bigler. He asked, "Is your father traveling out of the country?" I responded in the affirmative; he was in Central America looking for sources of new fruits for the company.

"What country is he in now?" Rex asked.

I was now fully alarmed. "Why are you asking?"

"Because I got a call from a nurse in Trinidad that your father was in a car accident," Rex replied, "and they need me to get on the next available plane, immediately. I'm trying to figure out if the call was a hoax." I confirmed that Dad was in Trinidad. I called Mom to let her know that Dad had been in a bad traffic accident. Then the scramble began, finding passports and arranging flights.

Mom and Rex flew out the same morning to find my dad and his assistant, badly injured, inside a little tropical hospital with few staff and no windows, though it did have access to water from an adjoining well. If Doctor Bigler hadn't arrived when he did and performed surgery to correct the broken ribs and punctured lungs, both Dad and his assistant might not have survived.

Dad arrived home a few weeks later. There was no time to rest. We sat precariously between a mass of assets and a mountain of debt, and stress was beginning to take its toll on Dad.

His empire was starting to crumble under the weight of crushing interest payments. Young people today would have a difficult time believing the interest and tax rates during the post-Vietnam era. The ill-conceived and poorly financed war in Southeast Asia ushered in raging inflation, a twenty-two percent prime interest rate, and a top marginal tax rate of about <u>ninety percent</u>. These high rates are hard to believe in today's world, but they are all true.

Looking back, the 1970s, culminating in '79, were the best of times and the worst of times for the Mariani Family, with land values skyrocketing because of high inflation, the boom in Silicon Valley, and the demand for land, while at the same time we were beginning to accumulate a portfolio of debt caused by crippling interest rates.

The nature of the dried fruit industry required the purchase of long-term storage facilities for huge fruit inventories. Our land position and developments required a massive amount of cash flow. I was at our business's ground zero, managing our global cash balances and needs; all of our business interests were interrelated, so if I made one serious mistake, everything would come crashing down. The pressure to find money to keep our operations functioning properly was on me. I was a kid in my mid-twenties, moving cash all over the world, working ninety- to a-hundred-hour weeks. The concept of going public was an alien idea within the family. We were a private company—period. So capital needed to be generated either from operations or borrowed.

Between 1975 and 1979 I missed every family dinner during the week. At some point, Arlene quit waiting for me to come home; the family just ate when dinner was ready. I came home when I came home, to find a plate in the oven waiting for me.

As described earlier, Dad made a strategic decision to purchase Angas Park Fruit Company in Australia. We couldn't afford this without taking money from other operations. But Dad's gamble paid off. Angas Park was profitable, whereas our parent company was struggling.

Then there was the International Business Park, which had yet to break even, let alone turn a profit. However, by 1978, IBP sales activity began to pick up. It was beginning to pay off. Also, John Sobrato's all-cash purchase of a large parcel of land from us in Cupertino gave us some financial breathing room.

By the end of 1978 I could see Dad wearing down with worry, and I was wearing down with stress and exhaustion. Every day, six days a week, for four straight years, the weekly question was often "What do we need to do to make payroll this week for our companies?" Money had to be moved around the world efficiently and wisely.

However, by the end of 1978, though money was still tight, we turned a corner: IBP looked terrific, with a mature landscape where I had once picked walnuts on my hands and knees; buildings were beginning to sprout, and high-tech companies began to flock to our business park; and our family enterprises would remain private—we wouldn't have to go public, with the risk of losing family control.

It was a time when we could actually focus on discretionary investments, and we had the luxury of time for estate planning and life insurance. In January 1979, I pestered my dad, who had never had time to even get a physical, to get a proper amount of life insurance. So, three days before he and Mom were set to leave for New Zealand, I arranged for a doctor and our insurance broker to show up at Dad's office, and they gave Dad a physical while he sat behind his desk, including a blood pressure test and listening to his heart.

He passed the physical, and we completed a purchase for Dad of "key man" life insurance (a type of coverage for persons of exceptional value to an organization) from New York Life Insurance Company. In February 1979, the paper work was completed, and Dad was off to New Zealand with Mom. I made his first, and last, life insurance payment in February.

On March 14, 1979, I got a call from Mom. With a trembling voice, she told me that Dad had had a major heart attack but was in stable condition. He needed surgery for a pacemaker. Dad, through Mom, told me, "Just in case the surgery doesn't go well, do whatever you need to do for estate-planning purposes." He also told me he was signing and arranging for a "witnessed" modifying his Will, but it will be blank. It was up to me to amend my father's will in any way I saw fit, or as I believed appropriate. (Mom later hand-carried to me this blank amendment to Dad's will.) Dad's use of the word "appropriate" meant: "Change whatever needs to be changed to minimize inheritance taxes."

Two days later I received another call: while in the cardiac ward, Dad had had a massive heart attack (his third that week) and was in surgery. My life came crashing down two hours later when Mom called me to inform me that Dad was gone. I was to tell my brothers and sisters. I was stunned, life became a fog and I cried hard. This man, bigger than life for everyone who knew him, a man who was also our father, was gone. He never lived long enough to know his empire was safe and going to survive.

The shock of losing my dad affected our business partners all over the world, and unfortunately created a fair amount of insecurity in our business relationships. There was an immediate demand from all corners of the world to know whether we could carry on and manage Dad's far-flung business empire. The combination of questions and demands came crashing in from all directions. My brothers and I hardly had time to grieve. To this day, with unresolved closure, I still have dreams with my father in them.

Dad's ultimate trust in me to do the right the right thing for the family is best illustrated by his signing an amendment to his Will and Testament and signed by witnesses but left blank for me to fill out as I felt appropriate. It was his last communication to me. I kept that blank piece of paper, with Dad's desire to amend his will as I saw fit, all these years as a reminder of how much Dad trusted me with the family's affairs. I, of course, had no intention of filling out the signed and witnessed blank amendment to his will. What Dad was asking me to do, and entrusted me with doing, was not legal, but I humored his drug-clouded request by not arguing with him at the time.

I arose early the day after Dad died. For some reason, I just began to drive aimlessly. I drove through the International Business Park, a place Dad had worked so hard to develop and had constantly worried about whether it would be successful, since, for financial reasons, we needed the Park's success to help shore up our other enterprises. As I drove through the Park, I realized there had been an explosion of activity in the Park after Dad left for overseas. I saw buildings under construction. All the trees in the Park were in bloom. . . . Then it hit me hard: the stress we were working under was almost over. The industrial park was going to thrive, and as a result there would be relief from the intense financing pressure I had been under.

Uncontrollable tears came streaming down my face as I realized Dad had not lived long enough to know this and see the Park thrive. I cried, knowing that, for Dad, through all the years of unimaginable amount of worry, the stress was about to be over—but he had died without being relieved of his worry . . . without knowing his empire would survive.

Dad's death and funeral made the front-page news as well as editorials.

Dad's obituary in the *Valley Journal.* (Courtesy of the *Valley Journal*)

Although grief stricken, we had no time to grieve. Vendors, customers were all concerned about our business affairs now that our leader was gone. Life became a blur . . . I suppose it was a grief-induced blur, if there is such a thing. The task of dealing with lawyers, accountants, and bankers, which began immediately, plus an investigation by a suspicious life insurance company, created a pressure-cooker environment. The life insurance company was understandably suspicious about the timing of our taking out a life policy on Dad shortly before his passing. The formal investigation began before Dad was even laid to rest. It was the largest life insurance payout relative to the length of the contract in the history of the life insurance business. We made one payment, and only a few weeks later Dad died. I would have preferred having our Dad back.

Losing Dad also changed the family's dynamics. Unknown to me, Dad had appointed me head of the family businesses; when Mom informed me of Dad's wishes, I told her I didn't want the job. I reasoned that I was a middle child, and my older brothers and sisters were being passed over. The consequences of this could not be good. But Mom insisted . . . it was what Dad had wanted.

Reading some of the editorials about Dad reminded me of the big shoes that needed to be filled.

Valley Opinions

A valley-grown genius

The untimely death of Paul A. Mariani Jr. deprives the Santa Clara Valley of a leader who uniquely symbolized the valley's growth from a specialty crop center to a significant force in world trade.

Mr. Mariani's heritage was similar to that of many another prune and

EDITORIALS

apricot orchardist's son who grew up during the Depression. What he did with it was very distinctive.

From the family fruit-processing company in Cupertino, where golden orange apricots drying in the sun still cover great patches of open earth in mid-summer, the Marianis grew an empire. Paul Jr. was its patriarch and agribusiness genius. It now extends eign Trade Zone, wmu...

In a notable twist, the firm has become America's largest importer of apricots.

Mr. Mariani was a pioneer in two technical aspects: the use of freeze-drying for fruit preservation, and the development of "moist" packaging of dried fruits. But beyond his ability to apply technology in a field where processes had long been static, he was a businessman blessed with exceptional foresight, acumen and hankering to enterprise. With his skills he parlayed a land base in a fast-growing region and a grasp of that same region's specialty-crop farming into one of the largest, most far-flung agribusinesses on earth.

A family man whose breadth transcended his occupation, he gave generously of his time and talent to many charities and church activities. He

A sample editorial about my father shortly after his death
(Courtesy of the *Valley Journal*)

In preparation, I began reading a number of biographies of famous American families. I was struck and alarmed by a consistent pattern of the destructive effects of wealth on families. I reasoned that our family was too close for such things to happen to us,. But too often, once loving and close families degenerated into a group of hostile strangers filled with distrust, hostility, and greed. Dad used to say that, without family, you have nothing . . . it is the ultimate form of poverty, the poverty of spirit. The danger we were facing I thought of as "the poverty of affluence."

I sought advice from people I respected. One day I met with Dick Peery, of the development firm Peery Arrillaga. Dick told me the story of his family: with their different financial needs, objectives, and desires, he had thought it was impossible to serve all of them, and so he had recently sold some prime Sunnyvale property and distributed the proceeds among the family members. This freed him to begin building a development firm with his partner, John Arrillaga, with little or no debt.

Richard "Dick" Peery ended up building a real estate empire in Silicon Valley with his business partner as the high-tech industry in the Valley. Their firm, Peery Arrillaga, bought farmland in the 1960s and turned it into office parks. The duo sold about 120 buildings for $1.1 billion in 2006; this represented only a fraction of their holdings.

Dick Peery and John Arrillaga are another team of incredibly charitable individuals, as their philanthropy is legendary, with Dick's focus being on his Church and John's on Stanford University. Their example pounded home to me my father's words about why he labored so hard in business: "The question is why you are a businessman. Do you accumulate capital as an end in itself, or do you work hard to provide cheaper goods and services, provide jobs, and earn money for the ultimate purpose of giving back to the community? If it is the latter, then your whole life becomes a selfless act of love."

Regrettably, I did not follow Dick Peery's advice, and developed most of the family lands for the benefit of my extended family. Dick's advice, and his implicit warning of family discord to come, was heard by me but not believed. I was blinded by our tradition of "acquiring and accumulating land, and only selling if you have to sell" philosophy. The flaw in that philosophy is that the worst time to sell is when you have to sell. And discord came sooner than I thought possible, but not before a heartbreaking loss that was caused by outside forces.

It was an end of an era with my father's passing. The entire family dynamics changed. Dad was the indisputable man in charge. The rule was, "we did as he said." Now without his energy, his spirit, his leadership, his presence, there were no rules. The void seemed to scream in our heads.

Part IV

Chapter 21

The real significance of crime is in its being a breach of faith with the community of mankind.

Joseph Conrad

The Great Villa Maria Robbery

Shortly after my father died, in 1979, my mother purchased a home in Santa Cruz, at Pleasure Point, as a getaway for weekends and brief vacations. For security, when Mom was not in residence at Villa Maria, she made arrangements for a Stanford football player to house-sit, joining our Doberman pinscher on watch. The estate did not yet have an alarm system. With fourteen glass French-doors, on the ground floor, the home was at the time an easy target for burglars.

As the months passed following my father's death, we needed to open up Dad's safety deposit box at the bank in the presence of state-inheritance tax auditors and lawyers. At the same time, we decided to get an itemized appraisal of our mother's collectibles of significant value. One Friday, in the presence of the auditors, we opened the safety deposit box. Now, it had been Dad's custom to buy gold coins in every country he ever visited; he had done this for over thirty-five years. We had never been able to figure out where he kept his collection. Now we knew: inside the safety deposit box were three old airline flight-bags full of gold coins. Two bags were filled to the brim; the third was half full.

The two full bags weighed some twenty-five pounds each, the third about ten to twelve pounds. The estate auditor inventoried the coins and took pictures. When he was finished, we brought the coins back to Villa Maria for the appraiser to do itemized evaluations the following Monday morning.

Additionally, we gathered all of Mom's jewelry, ivory carvings, silverware, and original seventeenth-century silver sets, and ancient artifacts given to us or collected from all over the world, and placed them in grocery bags alongside the gold coins. The bags lined the inside walls of my father's now vacant dressing room in order to facilitate the appraisal of the inventory or itemized insured items. Although the room included a secret floor safe, it was too small to be used to secure 99% of the items.

Mom had planned to stay home for the weekend but changed her mind on Saturday afternoon, called our house sitter, and left for Santa Cruz for the rest of the weekend.

Our house sitter ended up being a no-show because he chose to attend an all-night frat party instead of house sitting as promised. Early Sunday morning, I got a call from my brother Mark, who said, "Villa Maria was robbed" and told me to get over to the Villa because the police were there.

After inspecting a broken pane in a side glass door, I walked through the house to help identify what was missing. We proceeded upstairs to my father's dressing room. Our hearts sank as we saw the door open and the room empty.

After discussing possible suspects with the detective outside in the driveway, we all seemed to notice, at the same time, a small pool of oil in the driveway. The detective said, excitedly, "Most of your cars are late models and unlikely to be leaking oil, right?" Mark and I said, "Yes," in chorus. We then noticed tiny drops of oil circling our drive and out the front gate. I think it was Mark who jumped into the police squad car, with his head hanging out the window as the car followed the trail of oil drops. The oil drops led them to a gas station miles away, in the Rancho Shopping Center. After fishing out the only used oilcan in the station's garbage bin, with fingerprints clearly visible on the can, the detective brought the can back to the lab for identification, but were unable to get a positive identification.

Miscellaneous news coverage of the Villa Maria robbery (from the
San Jose Mercury News)

The robbery was, at the time, one of the largest home robberies in the history of Santa Clara Valley, and likely one of the largest in the state. The news spread quickly, and newspapers and television stations were soon featuring the story. However, with one dead-end lead after another, the television stations lost interest in the story. With only one set of unidentified fingerprints, the case turned cold after a year. Not one piece of silver, gold, or uniquely carved ivory or jewelry ever surfaced in any pawn shops or known fences that year.

Meanwhile, Los Altos and Palo Alto were experiencing a spate of home robberies— mostly precious metals, as in our robbery, though on nothing like the same scale. Even an Olympic gold medal was stolen, in Palo Alto, making the news as well.

About a year after the robbery, my brother Mark got an anonymous phone call from someone who claimed to know where all of our stolen goods were being stored. He stated that, if Mark met him at a specific time on dark corner in east Oakland in the early morning hours with $10,000 in cash, he would tell Mark where the stolen goods were being stored. If we called the police, the deal was off.

Mark called me to update me on the development, and with characteristic good sense, made the observation that people kill for $10,000. We both agreed to call the investigating officer in charge of the case.

An undercover cop showed up in Oakland in place of Mark at the appointed time and place, with a dragnet of supporting local police officers. One of the Oakland detectives recognized the blackmailer almost instantly.

The blackmailer (we were told) had been found about a month earlier up in the Oakland hills by hikers. He had been stabbed multiple times and tortured, with his hair scalped, and left for dead. While he was in the hospital recovering, detectives had interviewed him. He refused to say anything about what happened or by whom and was eventually released from the hospital.

Now back in jail for blackmail, he began to relate a bizarre story: He was part of a family gang of house burglars. The mother of one of the gang members had a small foundry in her backyard. Their simple plan was to burgle wealthy homes of jewelry and precious objects, then conceal the identity of the stolen goods by melting them down and selling the metal as gold and silver bars. The boys did the stealing; the mother made the bars and sold them for industrial and commercial uses. She, of course, got most of the profits.

The gang could not believe their eyes when they opened the door of my father's dressing room—a room full of treasure collected over a lifetime, all bagged up for them in grocery bags ready to be hauled away.

The boys were petty thieves with scores in the tens of thousands, not millions, of dollars. They were unwilling to share their bonanza with the mother, a tyrant who took most of the profits. So, keeping her in the dark about the size of the haul, they gave her two bag-loads of loot, of the dozens of bags of stolen goods, and hid the balance in a public storage unit without the mother's knowledge.

At some point, our blackmailer decided to steal all the goods for himself and moved the goods to another public storage unit. The rest of the gang confronted him about the now empty storage unit, then tortured and left him for dead in the Oakland hills after he gave up the details of the location. The only way the blackmailer could get revenge for his torture without putting himself again in jeopardy, and still make money on the deal, was to reveal the new location to the original owners for a price, depriving his fellow gang members of the goods.

After taking far too long to get a search warrant issued, a warrant for the new storage unit was finally obtained. On inspection, the unit had apparently been cleaned out days earlier. But detectives now knew the identity of the gang members and raided the house of the mother and arrested the gang.

They found magnificent, Baroque-era silver sets half-melted down; the criminals not realizing that one set in particular was an original casting that all other modern-day sets have been based on; it was worth far more than the value of the metal. Some of the collectible coins were worth, in some cases, a hundred times the metal value. But they had all been melted down.

We couldn't claim the molten result as our property, since the melting process prevented us from making any positive identification—but we knew it was ours. The clincher was that the gang mother's son had taken a liking to an intricate ivory-carved finger stand, used to place and store rings on my mother's dressing table. It was one of kind; a marvelous work of art, with pictures documenting it. It was found hidden under the son's bed. We also discovered that the fingerprints on the oilcan had been his.

The young men and the mother were all convicted and given extensive prison terms. All but a fraction of the stolen goods was recovered.

Later, we installed an elaborate security system at Villa Maria. Our security system became a symbol that Santa Clara Valley was changing. In a short period of time we went from never locking our front door to security and surveillance systems.

The Family Splits Up

Siblings are often very different from each other. My brother Mark, for example, was a sequential-type thinker and a morning person, up at the crack of dawn and fading in the afternoon. I am a parallel thinker and do my best work late in the day. Mark wanted 6 to 7 a.m. breakfast meetings, when I was barely awake; I wanted 6 to 7 p.m. evening meetings, when he could barely keep his eyes open. [29]

On top of that, since our thinking processes were very different, we asked completely different questions when evaluating a business issue, and this grated on both of us. It sounds petty, but the truth is we were not mature enough to respect, celebrate our differences. We lacked the wisdom to take advantage of our differences to gain a richer mosaic of business insights by cross-pollinating our thoughts. Instead, Mark could not understand me when I pursued parallel business strategies and viewed my approach with suspicion. Nor did I understand Mark. I viewed Mark's focused, and rigid business approach with disdain as too simplistic. The truth is that both Mark and I were too young when we were thrown into running a multinational family business. Because of our immaturity, we resented each other's differences rather than celebrating them. Had we been older and more mature, the combination of our respective talents would have carried us further working together than when we were apart.

We decided, as a group, to separate our business interests along areas of personal interest. It was an enormously complicated balancing act to separate operating companies, capital accounts, valuations, equity, and hundreds of related notes payable and receivable. Finally, we decided to break up MGC [Mariani Group of Companies] by creating "pots" of equal value. This was very difficult to do due to the wide range of asset classes. I did the best I could to be fair and offered to take the last pot of assets after everyone else had chosen theirs.

It worked. We separated our family interests. To the outside world, nothing seemed to change. Mark and Rick got the farming and dried fruit business, and the rest of the family got land and other enterprises.

Mark passionately wanted the legacy family business, Paul A. Mariani Company (the dried fruit company, commonly known as PAMCO). I feared that Mark didn't fully understand the deep problems the company had associated with to the industry's massive ongoing consolidation. In 1950, there had been over fifty dried fruit companies in the US; by 1980, there were only ten left. The cutthroat competition between the remaining companies made most of the companies unprofitable. In the decade of the1965 - 1975, our dried fruit company struggled to make money for ten years. It was clear that the dried fruit industry was also suffering through major changes globally.

Additionally, PAMCO both benefited and suffered at the hands of our long-term employees. Many were fiercely loyal to my dad, but many, regrettably, possessed outdated skills and were unable to meet the modern challenges facing the industry. The education of many of these dear, loyal souls had largely been on the job; many were ill-equipped to adjust to new ways and new technologies. Suddenly, circuit-switch boards replaced operators, voice-mail replaced the receptionist, tractors were driven and guided by GPS, and prune-, walnut-, grape- and boysenberry-picking machines had become part of everyday life.

With Mark's less than ideal understanding, at the time of finance, balance sheets, and unit-cost reports, combined with problems at key managerial positions and the deep-seated problems in both PAMCO and the industry itself, I feared the worse.

A few years later, the family bail out the dried fruit company. We voted to raise enough money, securing a debt against our Cupertino homestead, to lend to the dried fruit company.

Mark, however, proved to be a quick learner and made dramatic and needed organizational changes, forged critical alliances with major customers—notably with Kellogg's—and created new product lines and new strategic directions. These were skills I hadn't guessed Mark had. He did a great job turning the company around to profitability. However, his efforts were too little, too late. PAMCO was unable to pay back the family loan in full.

Faced with either taking over the company, I agreed to largely accept noncash payment, by trading Angas Park (the dried fruit company in Australia, mentioned earlier, that PAMCO still owned) in return for retiring PAMCO's debt. This decision would eventually haunt me. My brother Paul acquired Angas Park in return for a smaller interest in MGC and some cash; since he lived in Australia, he would be able to look after this investment. In short, MGC ended up with the debt and a smaller asset base to support the debt - debt compounding at an alarming rate. This was the single biggest strategic mistake of my professional life. I was blinded by a desire to make "everyone happy"—in this case, Paul and Mark and Rick—but left MGC in a compromised position.

For Mark, his fortunes turned for the better. We were all delighted with his success and cheered him on. He purchased the Del Monte Packing Plant in San Jose and moved his operations there. About ten years later, he sold the property for enough money to pay off all his debts, invest in a new plant in Vacaville, and diversify the company's interests, buying commercial income property. Amazingly, Mark was able to change the culture of PAMCO, and modernized and streamlined its operations. Mark went back to school to Harvard graduate school. He did a remarkable job; a job he should be proud of work well done—the rest of the family, for sure, were very proud him and admired his accomplishments. Today, his boys continue the family legacy within Mariani Packing Company of hard work, honesty and a healthy dose of charisma.

Paul, in Australia, also flourished and eventually sold Angas Park to Chiquita Banana at an attractive price.

Unfortunately, MGC's fortunes didn't do so well. MCG eventually developed the Families heritage property in Cupertino for residential use. The inordinate time delays to get approvals from the city of Cupertino resulted in excessive debt on the property caused by compounding interest. Worse, the delays resulted in bad timing for the project. Shortly after beginning construction, the first Gulf war began, and the savings and loan crisis emerged.

I have prided myself on carefully managing risk. The two major risks I missed were not predicting the Gulf war and not predicting or considering that my bank would go broke. The latter thought had never crossed my mind as a project risk. Our bank did go broke and stopped funding a project, called

Portofino, even though we were under budget and selling units at our target prices and projected profit margins. The FDIC now held our erstwhile annually renewed construction loan, which matured. But banking rules treat renewing a loan has the same thing as making a loan, and the FDIC does not make loans— so it called in the loan in the middle of our project. The result: MGC, and our family, had to let go of its legacy property—it was a tragedy on multiple levels.

Through all of this turmoil, I kept thinking about my dad. I kept thinking about some of the more enduring values he had imparted to me, rather than the temporal assets, which, throughout history, have always been fleeting. I sometimes think to myself that I am the last of my kind. Dad expected honesty and integrity in all aspects of life. I was told to hold the doors for women and children, to shake hands with a firm grip, to remember people's names, and to always give the customer more than expected. His rules, I realize, were more than a philosophy; they said everything about who he was.

In my mind, he was not the International Man of the Year, as declared one year by the Santa Clara County World Trade Club of the San Jose Chamber of Commerce; rather, he was a man of integrity, grit, kindness, and respect. I also learned that, because Dad believed in honesty and integrity, he also believed that others did as well. He believed in human decency and assumed that others were just like him. He believed that most people, when given the choice, would do what was right, even when it was hard, and he believed that good almost always triumphed over evil. He wasn't naïve: "Trust people until they give you a reason not to" was also something he told me. More than anything else, it was not Silicon Valley, but my father who shaped me into the man I am today.

Plaque at the base of Dad's International Businessman of the Year award

Although my dad had a great influence on my life, my cousin George Sousa also helped shape me as a man. I could tell many heart-warming stories about how George influenced my life, but the most important impact was the way George encouraged me by gently asking me, "What do you think?" This made me feel that my opinions were valued. Little questions like that gave me confidence in my convictions. While Dad rarely gave you a compliment to your face, George was quick to say, "Good job!" or "Congratulations!" Without the combination of my dad and my cousin George in my life, I would never have the courage to one day venture out on my own.

Chapter 22

The Roaring '80s and '90s

1980—1999

Mariani Financial Company

My business career had formally begun when I served as the chief financial officer for our family's agribusiness interests and thirty-two related operating companies, active on three continents, in the 1970s and '80s.

After the reorganization of our family interests following my dad's death, I was free to form my own company for the first time. I founded Mariani Financial Company in 1982. This entity managed our financial business interests in California Security Bank and my real estate development business, American Western Banker (a leasing company that specialized in lending to the agricultural community).

The 1980s were a dynamic time for both my financial company and Silicon Valley. I found myself serving on multiple boards, including as chairman of California Security Bank, for fifteen years, and co-founder and chairman of the board of Presidio School of Management, now a premier MBA program in San Francisco.

I became the managing partner in Glenborough, an SEC-registered $400 million real estate master limited partnership. Glenborough was the predecessor of Glenborough REIT, which was later sold to Morgan Stanley for $1.8 billion. I found myself consumed with empire building. Then I awoke one morning to the echoes of my father's words of advice.

Dad once related the following story to me: "I came home one day from an overseas trip to a house that seemed strangely empty, and I asked your mom, 'Where are the kids?' She looked perplexed and said, 'Paul, they are all gone, they are all out of the house now.' " Later, Dad lamented how he had missed so many years of being a father because of his empire building. He stared at me for a long time and said, *"Don't you dare make the same mistake I did. The most precious thing you can give your children is your time. David, it is our time that is irreplaceable. Do not make the mistake I made . . . Spend time with your children, go on vacations, play with them, go to their sporting events, be involved. Your kids will grow up seemingly overnight. You may think they will be kids forever, but it is just a phase and before you know it, they will be all grown up and out of the house."*

I tried to be faithful to Dad's advice and made a point to attend as many of my children's extracurricular events as possible, although I still could have done a better job being there for them. Fortunately, Arlene was a terrific, attentive, loving mother. She effortlessly picked up the slack and, on many occasions, single-handedly attended to raising our family during the busiest of my days. I never forgot my father's words, which helped me moderate my ambitions, though not my passion to build and create.

Apple Computer and an Unlikely CEO of the Millennium

Not long after Dad died, Steve Jobs (whom I had first met in the 1970s, when he was a young computer programmer, with his partner Steve Wozniak at the Homebrew Computer Club) heard through a broker that we were planning to build an office building in Cupertino. He contacted me and told me he wanted us to construct a building for his new company on one of our apricot orchards on De Anza Boulevard in Cupertino. I looked at their business plan and was shocked at how sophomoric and unsophisticated it was. I gave them a polite no, as we were not willing to invest two cents to construct a custom building for his company—particularly a company with a really dumb name: Apple Computer, Inc. Maybe it was a play off the fruit trees in the area—but if so, it seemed inept, as nobody had ever commercially grown apples in the area.

Thank God Michael Markula was brought into the picture. Michael did all the heavy lifting on Apple's business plan. If memory serves, to get the company started Michael actually signed a bank guarantee for something like $500,000 (perhaps even less). Now, with just enough funds raised to launch his company, Steve took me aside (I believe without Michael's knowledge) and asked if we would consider giving Apple free rent for six months in exchange for stock valued under a dollar a share. Jobs didn't want to go back to Markula for more money; he thought that, if Michael put more money into the deal, his own shares would become even more diluted.

I thought about the proposition. I was thoroughly impressed with Steve Wozniak, and I liked Michael Markula and his wife Linda a lot, but Steve Jobs was another story. Steve was self-absorbed, abrupt, brash, demanding, and almost always rude, with an abundant ability to be cruel to subordinates. I thought, "How can a guy like Steve Jobs lead a successful startup? No way." So we politely turned down the offer of shares for free rent.

At a nickel a share, we could have received about 13 million shares of Apple stock. At the value of Apple shares at the time of this writing (Spring 2019: $ 171.26) . . . well, we can all do the math.

On December 12, 1980, Apple launched the initial public offering of its stock to the investing public. When Apple went public, it generated more capital than any IPO since Ford Motor Company in 1956 and instantly created more millionaires (about 300) than any company in history. Several venture capitalists cashed out, reaping billions in long-term capital gains.

A month later, in January 1981, Apple held its first shareholders meeting as a public company, in the Flint Center, a large auditorium at De Anza College, which is often used for symphony concerts. Previous Apple meetings had been held quietly in smaller rooms, because there had only been a few shareholders.

Before the De Anza property was converted to a college, it was a walnut orchard with a grand, abandoned Georgian home on it. I remembered, as boy, walking on my way home from school, cutting through that walnut orchard. I would look in awe at the grandeur of the Georgian home.

Even the walnut trees were stately. When I didn't cut through the orchard on rainy days, I walked along the side of the orchard down McLennan Road. I'd look at the grand home while kicking cans down the road. I had no clue that our relatives who also owned the walnut orchards, would become one of the world's largest independent walnut packers (Mariani Nut Company). Nor would I guess that, while attending the Apple meeting, I would be witnessing someone who would one day become "the CEO of the Millennium."

I learned many years later that the business of this meeting had been planned (or choreographed) so that the voting would be staged within fifteen minutes or less. At most shareholder meetings, voting proxies are collected by mail and counted days or months before the meeting. In this case, after the IPO, many shares were in new hands; as a result, the meeting had more shareholders present than otherwise would have been expected.

Steve started his prepared speech, but after being interrupted by voting shareholders several times, he dropped his prepared speech and delivered a long, emotionally charged talk about betrayal, lack of respect, and related topics. I left the meeting so glad that I hadn't traded rent for stock with him.

Today, looking back, I recall my dad saying, "Mistakes are valuable for the lessons you learn from them. And never brood over mistakes. Don't take on your mistakes like armor; never identify yourself with your mistakes, just like you should never define yourself with your successes. So take both your successes and failures with a sense of humor, to avoid taking yourself too seriously." The mistake not to invest in Apple can be measured with many decimal points. Was it a stupid or bad decision? It's hard to say. Apple was at the brink, at one moment in time, of going broke. My inclination is that, given the facts as I knew them at the time, I would probably have made the same decision. I suppose we can write this up as a "missed opportunity."

I am still puzzled to this day how Steve Jobs morphed from a brash young man to the executive of the millennium. I have long suspected that Steve might have had a mild case of Asperger's syndrome due to Steve's marginal people skills, and fixating to an extreme on projects and issues. I suppose what Steve lacked in people-skills was overshadowed by his intense focus, drive, demanding standards, and fiery spirit. I did not appreciate until many years later the real secret to Apple's success, which Steve brought to the company: an unyielding commitment to product simplicity, usefulness, and quality. He may go down in history as the greatest product developer of all time. There is no question that Steve matured into an outstanding executive and a legendary leader. I did not see any hint of Steve's destiny when he was in his early twenties. Michael Markula saw it—good for Michael!

Other Silicon Valley Legends

Some influential Silicon Valley personalities were less well-known than others but still characters in their own right. Jack Belleto, CEO and co-founder of VLSI Technology was a wild man in a good way. Jack was edgy, driven, focused, with an endearing sense of humor and marvelous leadership abilities. He was terrific at reading people. "Very-large-scale integration" (VLSI) is the process of creating integrated circuits combining thousands of transistor-based circuits into a single chip. The early 1980s ushered in a new era of chip design.

VLSI Technology specifically designed and manufactured customized and semi-customized integrated circuits. The company was headquartered at our McKay Drive location, in our International Business Park (IBP). VLSI Technology's main competitor was LSI Logic; together, they defined the leading edge of the ASIC chip sets, which ushered in a new era of affordable programmable systems.

LSI Logic was founded by Wilfred "Wilf" Corrigan. Unlike Jack, Wilf had no sense of humor. Wilf was driven, like Jack, but rude with everyone around him. Corrigan once told me, "If you want me to locate LSI Logic in the International Business Park, you will have to give me free rent for five years." This was his way of bullying people prior to commencing negotiations. I suspect it surprised him that I never called back. LSI Logic eventually purchased VLSI Technology, so he eventually ended up, partly, in the International Business Park. I saw Corrigan on a few occasions—at a distance; though worth millions, I never saw him smile; he was admired by some, feared by most, and nearly universally not well liked.

Jack, on the other hand, went on to serve with top-tier venture capital firms that earned him shares in many startups. He did as well as, or better than Wilfred, but remained affable. Jack was a happy man.

Gordon "Gordy" Campbell was another character. We built a world headquarters in our Park for his startup company, SEEQ Technology; constructing a "build-to-suit" building for Gordy. The facility was a fab plant, for the fabrication of silicon wafers. SEEQ made programmable chips.

I lost track of Gordy. He was a polite, gentle soul. I suspect the venture capitalists wished he'd ruled with a firmer fist. But he got the job done, not because he pushed his people, but because people wanted to work and get the job done "for Gordy."

I found the contrasts in style interesting: soft-spoken Gordy and Michael Markula at Apple, or the gentleness of Andy Grove at Intel, or Gene Amdhal, founder of the now forgotten Amdhal super computers; brilliant pussycats—all of them quiet, smart, articulate gentlemen—contrasted with the pushiness of Steve Jobs and Wilfred Corrigan. They all seemed to be successful, though for different reasons; but one group seemed happier than the other. Those who thought and cared about their team of people exuded a peaceful spirit, an inner peace that spilled over into happiness.

We built and financed special-purpose buildings ("build-to-suits") for these startups which, at the time, had no track record. At one time, I believe we built more semi-conductor, or "fab," plants in Silicon Valley than any other developer.

I was asked on multiple occasions why I would risk five, ten, fifteen million dollars at a time to finance and construct a building for a company with no operating history or history of success. My reasoning was simple. Other developers shied away from the risk-financing of building fab plants, which left that market underserved. Mariani Financial Company built and paid for buildings costing millions, but venture capitalists who were financing the companies we built for were making even bigger bets, with capital and lease guarantees for equipment: it was not unusual for them to invest $30 to 40 million in equipment for use *inside* a building that we constructed. In the event of a bankruptcy, I reasoned a judge would always reinstate the lease to protect the estate assets inside. My theory worked.

However, one day I asked my executive development group to figure out why our company seemed to be the only one building fab plants. I wanted to make sure I wasn't missing something. They came back a week later to inform me that other developers didn't do fab plants because they were really hard to develop. The complexity and coordination took up a tremendous amount of time. So while I would be laboring over the design and construction of a single fab plant, my competitors would be constructing five to six easier to construct buildings, with the same amount of effort. So I stopped building fab plants.

Venture Capitalists and High-Tech

Most people might think that Silicon Valley is all about innovations in semiconductors. Certainly, it was from silicon wafers and chips that Silicon Valley got its name. However, Silicon Valley is more about innovation than it is about silicon.

For example, Apple Computer, with all of its legendary consumer products, is more about astonishing innovation, software, and imagination than it is about the chip sets inside the box. It was innovation that made the company, not just silicon.

Another source of Silicon Valley was "venture capital," a one-time financial novelty that emerged at the time into a mature industry. Without the brave investors willing to take on extraordinary risk for the prospect of extraordinary gains, many an innovation in Silicon Valley would have remained just an idea. What makes Silicon Valley different is that an idea is perceived as potentially the "next big thing" and is greeted with excitement, curiosity, and a sense of possibility, whereas in most parts of the world, a new idea is often met with skepticism, and a person with an idea is viewed as just a dreamer.

The Sand Hill Road Gang, the VC Hill Gang, and VC Clustering

Sand Hill Road, in Menlo Park, became known for the Sand Hill Road Gang, as most of the biggest and most important venture capital firms (VCs), such as Cypress and Kleiner Perkins, came to be located on or near the road. But the clustering of VCs was not limited to Sand Hill Road.

Venture capitalists were changing not only the Valley, but also the hills in Los Altos, where I lived. Slowly the open meadows had given way to nice homes owned by farmers, professors, doctors. Then, within two decades, many of these new homes began to be torn down and replaced by mini mansions. Nuclear scientists, entrepreneurs, and venture capitalists replaced the neighborhood of teachers, poets, and merchants. The VCs also lived in small, upscale hamlets such as Atherton, Woodside, Menlo Park, and Los Altos Hills.

Within a few short years, Loyola Drive soon became "VC Hill." Sam Collela, B. J. Cassin, and Bob Todd, to name a few, surrounded us as neighbors.

Sam is the managing director of Versant Ventures and a legend in the healthcare and biotechnology spaces. B. J. Cassin lived up the street; he started Xidex Corporation, which became a Fortune 500 company, then began investing in such companies as Lasercope, Maxtor, PDF Solutions, Symphonix Devices, and Cerus Corporation.

B. J. is a soft-spoken, kindly gentleman. I asked him once, "What is the secret to venture capital?"

He answered, "You have to have your first investment be successful."

I asked, "Why?"

"Because it will cover all the losses in the next six investments until you find another winner!"

The truth is that B. J. is enormously bright yet a genuinely humble person. Interestingly, his core passion, much like John Sobrato, is rooted in "giving money away." Making money for them now is really just a means to enable them to help our community be a better place with better opportunities for the most needy. B. J.'s peaceful grace is contagious, and his joyful self bespeaks a rich spirit.

Bob Todd, Jr.—also a VC—lived practically across the street from us. He was the general partner at Red Rock Ventures LP. Bob began his career with operating experience as founder and CEO of Flextronics and went on to invest in dozens of startups.

We eventually sold our family home, where all our children grew up, to Vivek Mehra. Vivek cofounded Cobalt Networks and sold it in less than sixty months after its founding for to Sun Microsystems. He joined the venture capital firm August Associates. With that, "VC Hill" became complet, and included our historic family home.

The interesting profile of the VC Hill Gang in Los Altos, unlike that of many professional VCs, is that they all first started their own companies, operated them successfully, then sold them, prior to becoming venture capitalists. This gave them a distinct advantage—of being able to identify business plans worthy of investment, looking beyond the spreadsheet numbers; of being able to identify leadership personalities, product niches, and other business fundamentals, based on firsthand experience, all of which no doubt helped lead to their success. This is unlike many modern-day VC firms, which are often filled with MBAs with Wall Street experience but with little or none of actually running a business. There are advantages in both backgrounds for successful venture investing—which, I suppose, is the reason these VC firms include a mix of professional backgrounds on their staffs. I do find it ironic that I began my career as a farmer, in foggy wonderment over where all the new companies in my beloved Valley of Heart's Delight were coming from, how they got started, and who had all the money to develop them—and now find myself literally surrounded by the venture capitalists who were essential in making Silicon Valley a reality.

Another interesting trait of my neighbors is that they are all very bright yet also very humble and appreciative of their opportunities. They all seem to understand their roots and how lucky they have been to be in the right place at the right time. Clearly, their sense of gratitude has translated into their becoming giving souls. Perhaps it was their being thoughtful and giving souls that made them leaders, inspiring others, and building great companies. Universally among them, there's a certain twinkle in their eyes that conveys a joy in life. I suspect it is their charitable giving that makes them complete.

All of the VC Hill residents are notably active in various charitable works, giving of both their time and their money.

Much like the Shinto saying I quoted earlier, there is a similar saying in Indian culture: "A rich man has no wants." It does not say that a rich man has many possessions. In Christian and Islamic cultures, we talk about the joy of giving. And there is a similar theme: we can't buy enough to make ourselves happy.

My theory of "having no wants" is that it frees, or releases, the human spirit to give generously, leading to philanthropy. It is the recognition of having "no wants" that leads to a richly contented soul. Some people believe that philanthropy makes you happy. But I don't believe that is true. I believe philanthropy is a manifestation of a happy contentedness not possible without first being grateful for one's good fortune.

Andy Grove

Part of my duties in the early 1980s was going to business dinners. Dining with many of the CEOs who were my tenants was unavoidable. I never asked them to dinner at home as I figured they were busy running their companies, and I was busy and preferred to stay home and spend time with our growing family. However, they often wanted to meet and get to know their landlord.

Although he was never a tenant of mine, I saw the legendary Andy Grove—co-founder, with Robert Noyce and Gordon Moore, of Intel—at Akani, a hole-in-the-wall, but very good, Japanese restaurant in Los Altos, famous for its sushi. Seeing Valley legends dining there was not unusual.

Andy Grove was an interesting Silicon Valley luminary. Andy was slightly built in stature, with a quiet voice and a gentle soul that belied the weight of his words. The power of his thoughts roared as if spoken from a megaphone. Although retired for some time, he wrote interesting articles that give us a peek into the dynamics of Silicon Valley as we now know it. He too was spiritually centered, with an inner peace, while Silicon Valley was reeling from manic growth that some said was out of control. Andy's insights are things our politicians and policy makers would be well-served to understand. If the history of the Mariani family in Santa Clara provides a view from inside Silicon Valley at its birth "looking out," Andy Grove provides an interesting perspective. He clearly articulates why money invested in startups in Silicon Valley produced few manufacturing jobs in the USA. In sharp contrast, our politicians and talking heads in the newsroom lament over the loss of jobs, and promote job creation through technical innovation. Andy described, in lucid clarity, why America is losing manufacturing job. Due to an unbalanced playing field with China, America defaulted to becoming the "designers", and the Chinese the "makers."

To give perspective of our job loss in America, in 2010, Foxconn of Taiwan manufacturer employed over 800,000 people making products for Apple, Microsoft, and Dell with $62 billion in over-all sales. Foxconn's sales are more than Apple, Microsoft and Dell combined. Meanwhile Apple employed 25,000 people in 2010. Andy clearly understood something is wrong with this picture.

Andy Grove 1936 - 2016

Other Silicon Valley Luminaries

There were many CEOs in the '70s and '80s who were enormously important contributors to Silicon Valley but were never heard of by average people unless they lived in the Valley and were part of its culture.

Folks like Al Stein and his wife Arlene. I particularly enjoyed spending time with them. Al was the CEO of VLSI Technology after Jack Belleto. He came from Texas and was different from our homegrown Silicon Valley legends: he was polite, well-mannered, thoughtful. We would on occasion have calm, low-key, and enjoyable dinners in Los Altos; it was quite easy to talk to a gentleman like Al Stein, who nevertheless had influence over hundreds of millions of dollars.

By contrast, one of the, strangest, as well as one of the most memorable dinners I had was with Gene Amdahl, founder of Amdahl Computer, which made supercomputer mainframes.

I was having an enjoyable dinner with Gene and his chief operating officer Joseph Zemke. The Joe and I were engaged in a wide variety of subjects, while Gene just sat in silence, like a bump on a log. I thought to myself, "*And this is the genius who invented Amdahl's law?*" Then, suddenly, during dessert, Gene blurted out, "Wait!" as he stuttered and stammered: "I see an apparent logically inconsistency in what was just said." I thought to myself, "*Who talks like that?*" With a quizzical expression, I asked, "What do you mean? What are you talking about?" Gene was perplexed because a comment made by one of us three hours earlier he had reasoned through a series of seven logical steps (if X is true then

Y must be true, and if X and Y are true then . . .), leaping across three hours of our conversation to perceive a logical inconsistency from a comment on an entirely different subject, though connected, in some obscure way.

It suddenly dawned on me that Gene had not just been sitting immobile throughout dinner; rather, he had been silent because his mind was racing with input overload, thinking through the implications stimulated by a wide range of topics and analyzing and cross-analyzing each comment in depth. I never observed before, and doubt if I ever will experience again, such an extraordinary mind. Gene was a delightful and kind man, but he lived largely in his head at the expense of common social skills. I couldn't tell about his spirituality or his relative happiness, since most of the expressions of his life were consumed within his brain.

American Council on Germany

In the early 1980s I was asked to be a U.S. delegate at a week-long meeting with German leaders in Hamburg—the American Council on Germany (an outgrowth of the Marshall Plan). The group consisted of relatively young leaders from a broad spectrum of German society, including business leaders, political scientists, economists, bankers, and politicians. Part of my role was to deliver a speech there giving my perspective on Silicon Valley. People around the world wanted to learn the ingredients that had gone into the making of the Valley. Civic leaders all wanted clean, high-paying industries in their countries; they wanted to duplicate the Silicon Valley phenomenon. I was judged to be someone who could provide relevant insight. But my only credentials were that I had lived through the phenomenon since its beginning and knew the Valley when it was better known for its agricultural industry.

During my time in Hamburg, I attended a cocktail reception at the Warburg mansion. Mr. Eric Warburg[30] was a gracious host. I happened to sit down next to him and began discussing banking concepts and theory. However, it was not long into the conversation when I realized that, while I was talking about banking various companies, he was talking about the merits of banking different *countries*. It all became clear to me when he stated, "It is better to be a king-maker than the King,"

Before this reception, I had never made the connection between Daddy Warbucks in the musical *Annie* and a real-life character like Mr. Warburg. Warburg, being of Jewish descent, had escaped Nazi Germany to the U.S., leaving behind his banking interests in the hands of a trusted friend. While in America, he was trained by the U.S. air force to fly and later to lead raiding missions in Germany, due to his intimate knowledge of the country's geography. He led the Allied air force attack on his beloved Hamburg. With a twinkle in his eye, he said, "I, of course, made sure we didn't bomb any of the buildings I owned!"

I gave my speech and listened and participated in geopolitical discussions at a high level. It was one of the most fascinating weeks in my life.

The German delegates attending the meeting seemed to be intensely interested in the "inner dynamics of Silicon Valley," meaning what were the main social and economic drivers propelling the Valley's success. As a landlord for silicon chip makers and companies that supported the chip-making process, I could see clearly that simple measures such as investing in the necessary infrastructure for industrial parks in Germany, or providing tax breaks, were not going to create another Silicon Valley. Silicon Valley was the result of a unique combination of venture risk capital providing seed money for startups, world-class universities providing intellectual capital, cheap land, cheap labor, and literally thousands of small companies providing a broad range of specialized technical capabilities: machine shops, model makers, specialists in handling various gases, electrical engineering companies, test-equipment makers, clean-room HVAC specialists, so-called "masking" companies (providing services to build clean-room functions for the manufacture of plates needed to make silicon chips), etc.—the list goes on and on. Without these support companies and resources, the new startups cannot move efficiently from innovation to production. It would be very difficult to duplicate this set of dynamics.

It wasn't until Silicon Valley real estate and labor became too expensive that local electronics manufacturing began to be off-shored, first to China— which strategically focused on producing components under the theory that, if they made the components, no one else in the world would be able to successfully compete against them to assemble the components. Today, China has the manufacturing advantage. It will be structurally very difficult to reclaim assembly jobs back to the U.S., now that essentially all the parts are made an ocean away.

My big takeaway from being a U.S. delegate at the Hamburg meeting [American Council on Germany] was philosophical. America, throughout its history, has encountered other countries that, for one reason or another, did not agree with our foreign policies. Diplomacy sometimes worked; cynically speaking, it worked when the other side finally agreed with us. Teddy

Roosevelt's concept of "speak softly, but carry a big stick" resonated with Americans, because that is the way most Americans think. When diplomacy, threats, intimidation, and embargos didn't work, force became the solution.

In preparing for war, Washington has sought the high moral ground to gain the support of us, the American citizenry, to wage war against those who do not agree with Washington. In the psyche of America, there is an unstated but well-understood notion that "might makes right." Our politicians mix the "might makes right" principle with moral justifications for their actions.

The American Council on Germany served as a laboratory test case on a better way to identify problems and find solutions, through personal interactions between its respective citizens. The problems were the political, economic, or trade issues and debates "de jour": we debated economic theory, tax-rate effects on expanding economies and why sometimes lower tax rates can increase revenues for the Treasury, and why at times such strategies don't work. Through the process of discussion, with Germans becoming friends with Americans, and Americans with Germans, there comes about a fundamental understanding of the differences in perspective between our respective countries and cultures. It is a lack of understanding of problems concerning such things as trade, resources, etc., that can separate great democratic nations and eventually lead to conflict. Since World War II, the American Council on Germany has sent young American and German leaders in business and politics visiting and conferring with their counterparts in their home countries; one year the Americans visit the Germans, vice versa the next. This process has been going on (as of this writing) for sixty two years. The kindergarten lesson when faced with differences: it was better to talk than to fight.

As one result of these yearly meetings, German-American relations, in the face of fierce economic competition with each other, have remained friendly and peaceful. Some say that Germany's alliance with America is the strongest of our European alliances. The key is that the trust and understanding between our cultures are based on real friendships and mutual understanding. Perhaps American leadership will someday learn from this real-time geopolitical laboratory and apply the principles of mutual understanding and respect to our broader foreign policy. Our foreign policy would become proactive rather than reactive and crisis-based.

As Silicon Valley's economic reach is now global, U.S. foreign policy and foreign-trade policies have become critically important to the Valley's concerns.

Because the politics of fear and force seldom end well, we are thus already seeing Silicon Valley becoming more assertive in national politics.

America's foreign policy is inextricably mixed with our role as "the world's policeman." But this position is fundamentally flawed because it is laced with contradictions. As a consequence, the wisdom of our role "policing the world" deserves reexamination.

We Americans clearly see tragedies unfold around the world. As a nation, we often step in to make peace when other nations are unwilling to participate in "might makes right" conflicts. Although our motives might be noble, the irresolvable contradiction is that we often insert ourselves into conflicts only when it is deemed in our economic or strategic best interests. The United States, as the world's policeman, exercise force often when it is self-serving rather simply because force might be necessary on pure moral grounds to stop barbarism. As an affluent country, we let a poverty of the spirit pollute our good intentions. The unavoidable consequence for those we defeat is resentment. There are other conflicts resulting in unspeakable atrocities that we don't care about because our interests are not immediately at stake; those victims are ignored. This type of foreign policy produces ill-will all over the world: both from those we meddle with, and from those we ignore.

Washington's political motives are obvious to the world but often difficult for us Americans to see. At one extreme there is Iraq, which is strategically important to America for many reasons, so we have spent over a billion dollars to "nation-build" there, and many Iraqis have resented us and want us out. At the other extreme, there are many African nations where we have no commercial interests, and so we stand idle, witnessing butchery at the hands of dictators.

Most Americans see ourselves as an internationally philanthropic nation, championing the good and protecting the weak. While this is no doubt true in many cases, most of the world sees us for what we are: acting principally in our own interest. It is this disconnect that breeds the view of the ugly American; more so than the loud-mouthed, gaudy, fat, culturally insensitive American tourist.

Our foreign policy is more than a Silicon Valley concern. The world would be a better place if our role as the world's policeman were based upon of the moral principles of mutual understanding and respect.

Chapter 23

Empire Building

1980s–1990s

Silicon Valley was booming throughout the 1980s and '90s. I threw myself into my work developing real estate and lived life on a large scale, collecting exotic cars, yachts, prop-jets, ranches, and vacation homes in Tahoe and Aspen.

I had the good fortune of having a good-natured, flexible, down-to-earth wife who kept me grounded every time I thought I could walk on water. My excesses gradually (very gradually) evolved into more common-sense pursuits through her gentle guidance

After Dad's death, I was left with a legacy of fond memories, new professional challenges, stress, and a mass of assets, along with debt. Historically, we had borrowed against appreciating properties that fueled our growth. Alternatively, we traded into more and more properties in so-called 1031 tax-free exchanges. After decades of borrowing against our properties to satisfy our voracious equity requirements to acquire more properties and more companies, or for the purpose of supporting our operating companies, we ended up with an unenviable amount of debt secured against real estate. Most of these properties had a very low tax-cost basis.[3132]

As long as real estate continued to appreciate, our asset mix was stable. However, even a small downturn in real estate presented potential trouble. Most of the other large developers, such as Peery Arrillaga or Sobrato and Berg, at one point sold properties, paid down debt, paid their taxes, and developed properties using their own cash reserves rather than borrowing from the banks. It was a great way to manage risk and fuel their own growth. History has proven the wisdom of their strategy.

For our family, to manage risk, it made sense to sell property to pay off or pay down our over-all debt and to begin accumulating cash reserves. However, as a result of an eighty-year-old business philosophy to avoid paying taxes whenever possible by borrowing and trading for our cash requirements, we were trapped. It was a trap I needed to deal with head on.

The trap was that our debts exceeded our cost basis, creating so-called "phantom income," or a "boot." This simply means that, in many cases, if we sold a property, the total gross proceeds would be less than the amount needed to pay off both the land debt *and* the taxes triggered by the sale. In most cases, we would receive little or no net cash from the sale; in some cases, the net sale proceeds were less than the combined taxes and debt payoff. We were stuck holding the properties even if the market suggested it was the right time to sell. It was a bizarre set of circumstances.

Even though I loved every minute at home and playing with our children, it didn't stop me from charging forward to build, build, build. It was the imprint of my father who worked hard and long hours, for the example of his entire life drove me, subconsciously yet relentlessly, to build assets to create value. I became obsessive, not unlike many Silicon Valley CEOs, though in my own way.

Ford Motor Assembly Plant

After developing millions of square feet of commercial buildings, and buying about a quarter of a billion dollars of foreclosed properties from banks, my first really big bet was purchasing the 157-acre Ford Motor assembly plant in Milpitas, California, located on the eastern edge of Silicon Valley (this was the same plant in whose parking lot the young lady my mother had tried to help— Roxy—had been found murdered many years before). Price tag: $70 million dollars. It was a big deal for me because it was an uncomfortable concentration of assets and a sizeable risk.

Prior to the close of escrow, our soil tests for compaction analysis turned up an unexpected trace element of solvents. I flew out to Ford's headquarters in Dearborn to meet with the then-sitting president of Ford Motor Land Company, Wayne Doran, to advise him of our reservations. Wayne insisted that we rely on the advice of his environmental vice- president's report. Wayne stated that we could rely, one hundred percent, on Ford's environmental closure-plan and assessment as being complete and comprehensive. On the strength of a two-sentence letter to that effect, we closed on the property three weeks later.

Consistent with Silicon Valley growing pains, communities were quickly discovering that, from Stanford business parks down to Milpitas, clean-tech was, in fact, not so clean. After three and half years of developing the Ford property into an industrial park, we discovered an undisclosed massive ground contamination, apparently from solvent tanks used by Ford while in operation; unknown to Ford, the tanks had cracked upon installation in the mid-1950s and leaked steadily over the following three decades. The cost of remediation was estimated in the tens of millions. More devastating was the time delay in developing the property.

I asked my secretary to retrieve the Ford letter that stated we could rely on Ford's environmental assessment as a condition of close of escrow. The document could not be found!

I few out to Dearborn to have a chat with Wayne, terrified because we could not produce the document that could, potentially, protect us legally against loss.

Upon entering Mr. Doran's office, and after some pleasantries, I asked Mr. Doran to ask his secretary to pull the environmental reliance letter from the Mariani property file to read it for the sole purpose of refreshing his memory. He said, "Sure, but what is this all about?" I said, "I would like you to just read it." Two minutes later his secretary entered the room and gave Wayne a copy of the original document (the document we could not find). He read it. I then showed him our environmental report that documented the contamination.

I simply said, "Wayne, this is not our deal." Wayne asked to interrupt our meeting and called in his environmental and legal team. I was asked to return in an hour. Although I was outwardly calm, by stomach was doing a back flip. Upon my return, Wayne simply said, "You're right. Ford will deal with problem honorably." Ford purchased back the property from us for $97 million, in recognition of the work we had performed on the property and the value of the national credit tenants [33] that we had already built for and leased on the property. I was amazed how honorably Ford dealt with the whole issue. They could have buried us in litigation for a decade if they wanted to. I have nothing but respect for the Ford Motor Company and Wayne Doran. Ford eventually adopted our redesign criteria and converted the site into what is now called The Auto Mall.

For many reasons the purchase of the Ford Motor plant led to a second, but not lesser, seminal moment for me. It was a lesson my wife taught me.

I recall excitedly coming home to tell Arlene all about the great deal I just made with the purchase of the Ford Plant. She smiled, acknowledging my excitement, and followed with, "That's great, honey, but can you take out the garbage for me? . . . That would be a great help." I was momentarily deflated, but I could not help begin laughing inside about how unflappable Arlene was. At the time I didn't understand the deeper meaning of her reaction. It was not until the development of the Ford Plant ran into problems that I understood the deeply spiritual and wise core of Arlene's spirit. During the tense moments of resolving the Ford matter, Arlene merely said, "David, it's O.K. Don't worry. We love you. You have your family." The pressure of success or failure melted away instantly through Arlene's unconditional acceptance of life. Events, whether good or bad, were not going to affect her inner peace and happiness. Her centered soul was happy—regardless of my relative successes or failures.

I began to understand why she reacted so mildly about the exciting purchase of the Ford property and reacted equally calmly when its challenges emerged. Successes or failures were not at the heart of Arlene's happiness. It was hard to wrap my head around this reality. It is easy to be happy during good times, but to be happy during bad times? That was difficult for me to grasp. Arlene was truly a grounded, spiritual person, and I was not. I evolved through her example into who I am today because of her.

Through the frenzy of empire building, I had forgotten my father's words: to take time for your family. My pursuit of affluence took away my time to be spiritually centered, , to be introspective, to examine myself and open up my heart. I am reminded of Michael Singer's words in his book *The Untethered Soul*: "When you are done playing with the temporal and finite, you will open to the eternal and infinite."

Glenborough, Losing the Homestead, and World Odyssey

The near disaster of the Ford Plant deal renewed my fears over our portfolio debt load. After studying potential solutions, I came to the conclusion that forming an MLP might make sense. An MLP is a "master limited partnership," a special organizational class that the IRS permits to contribute properties in lieu of marketing securities, tax free. If we formed an SEC-registered share offering and went public, we could hold share units debt-free and convert our illiquid real estate into liquid, tradable shares. It promised to be an elegant solution to our liquidity problems.

In 1985, I partnered with the late Robert Batinovich. Robert at the time was the acting general partner of Glenborough in a dozen or more real-estate partnerships. We combined forces and formed Glenborough MLP. As co-general partners with Batinovich, I was the sixty-percent general partner, holding forty percent of the total limited shares as well.

We went public just in time for Reagan's tax simplification act to pass Congress. Contrary to the name of the tax bill, the legislation greatly complicated our tax system, adding thousands of pages of new regulations. Most importantly, the bill shifted the tax system regarding real estate ownership from having tax advantages to having penalties. Our MLP was market dead on arrival. It reminded me of my dad's fond saying, "I would rather bet on dead metals than on live politicians."

With most of my assets tied up in the MLP and no means to raise money in the capital markets to pay off our mortgages, I needed to wait out the market and babysit our portfolio.

I refocused my efforts on the last significant family lands that were left to develop. This property we called the homestead ranch; it included our original dried fruit packing plant, together with our original family home, built in the early 1900s. It sat on sixteen acres on De Anza Boulevard in the heart of Cupertino, across the street from Apple's headquarters.

I have told the story of this development, called Portofino, earlier, in chapter 23. As a result of our lending bank going broke during the savings and loan crisis, we were stuck with a half-built project and no more funding. The loan maturity period expired and we were foreclosed out of our homestead property. Painfully, I ended up personally writing a multi-million-dollar check to pay off all the project creditors. However, it was more painful knowing that my brothers, sisters, and widowed mother lost a significant inheritance, because it happened under my supervision. I feel overwhelmed with guilt to this day. This quickly taught my once prideful self a serious lesson in humility.

During this same period, I began to diversify and branch out into entertainment. I focused on a specialized technology called large format films and related technology, commonly known as IMAX films and theaters. In reality, IMAX, before it was converted to a digital system, was a film format: 15/70 (each image is 15 perforations long and 70 millimeters wide). I formed a company called World Odyssey to develop the specialized commercial cameras and projectors, as well as films and destination theaters and a feature film industry using this technology.

This enterprise led me down an interesting path, including a joint venture of World Odyssey with the French government and *La Geode* (an extraordinary institution in a section of Paris called *La Cité des Sciences*), focusing on museums and exhibitions, with additional ventures with Goto Optical in Japan. Most of our success was in the Japanese market. The pomp and ceremony associated with opening specialized educational theaters in Japan was beyond description. It was culturally educational for me and gave me a great respect for Japanese culture and the Japanese people. We developed new technologies with so-called "Ultra 70 projectors." Eventually, we developed a novel design for 15/70 projectors[34] and patented a large-format projector called "The Maverick," later introducing the system in association with Crown Theaters in the U.S.

Keith Merrill, an Oscar award–winning writer and producer, was my partner. Through this experience, I met a host of notable personalities, including Steve Young, the San Francisco 49ers' quarterback, who was a close friend of Keith's. Steve ended up being a tenant in one of my buildings. Steve's public image is just the way he is: humble, smart, articulate, and friendly and one of the thriftiest people I have ever met.

Max's Tea Room and More Interesting Personalities

In the sleepy town of Los Altos, in the late 1980s there used to be an old restaurant and bar on Main Street called Max's Tea Room that had operated for at least thirty to forty years. One evening, Bob Serventi (my CFO), Keith Merrill, my partner in World Odyssey, and I were meeting at Max's with singer Donny Osmond; we were working together on a potential project. We were sitting in a dark corner of the room, and no one recognized Donny. A piano player was playing songs with amateur singers using a portable microphone; it was a sing-along, pre-karaoke style. One member of the audience after another would sing a song, then pass the microphone along, and it slowly moved around the room. You guessed it: the mic was suddenly handed directly to Donny Osmond. There he sat in a dark corner of the room, with a smirk on his face, telling me he was tempted to belt out a tune; after five or ten seconds, we all thought better of it, because it would have resulted in ending our meeting for the evening. However, I often wondered, if Donny had begun to sing, there would have been a legend about Max's Tea Room that would still be living today.

I remember meeting with actor Louis Gossett, Jr., on a project, again meeting at Max's Tea Room. The interesting thing about Louis, who was at the peak of his career at the time, was that he had a singular passion. All he wanted to talk about was helping inner-city kids break out of the cycle of violence and ignorance. There was an inner glow and a sparkle in his eyes when he talked about the inner city programs. This same passion seemed to die when Louis talked about the art of acting, his movie roles, film opportunities, and money.

My life path has connected with so many amazing people that sometimes it feels like I'm just name-dropping. But the truth is that each person I connected with gave me a certain insight about life, about values, about what made him or her rich in spirit. Each person I connected with became part of my life and therefore part of my story.

A Ranch in Mendocino and Darkness in Davos

As the 1990s roared on, Silicon Valley became more congested with traffic and the pace more frenetic, with people in restaurants filled with self-importance talking too loud on cell phones. It became a place I didn't know anymore. It was no longer what I remembered. But yearning for a bygone era was useless.

I decided to buy a ranch in Mendocino, in Round Valley, to recapture the rural environment of my youth and to expose my kids to nature. We didn't want our kids to be affected by having lots of "things." Connecting them with nature and sports was a good way to root them in the essentials of life. It was a wonderful place, with 4,000 acres and two and a half miles of frontage on the local river. The whole family was involved in organizing sports camps at the ranch for many memorable years.

Not long after purchasing the property, I was invited over for lunch by a mysterious landowner across the valley. The ranch was called the Diamond H Ranch and comprised 11,000 acres. It was owned by Baron Steven Bentinck. I accepted the lunch invitation, and we became friends. The Bentinck's family fortune included Swiss banking concerns.

One winter, the Baron invited my wife and me to his mountain estate in Davos-Klosters, in the Swiss Alps. Davos-Klosters was hosting the annual World Economic Forum and its gathering of dignitaries and heads of state from all over the world.

We skied, played, ate, drank, hung out in the sauna (it was funny how those big shots all looked the same in a sauna!), and partied with gusto. One evening, back at the Baron's estate, we ate and drank more than what might have been prudent. The wine was wonderful. The Baron drank sufficiently to loosen his tongue to reveal the dark side of the Swiss banking system. How the Swiss banks handled Jewish flight money that remains forever unclaimed suggests that a moral compass had gone missing. His poverty of spirit overshadowed his considerable wealth.

One cannot really tell the Silicon Valley story without including the Bohemian Grove, even though the Grove is not in the Valley. The Grove is a rural mountainous property with a spectacular grove of giant redwood trees, just north of San Francisco.

There are many wild and sordid stories about the "goings on" at the Bohemian Grove. As a frequent guest, I can say with confidence that such stories are mere legends and speculations; nevertheless, the Grove is an astonishing place filled with amazing people and experiences. Although the parties at the various encampments buzzed with energy all night, they were not sordid in anyway. Each spring there is an event at the Grove called the "Spring Jinx," a gathering of men from all over the world, including leaders in politics and industry, artists, poets, musicians, painters, entertainers, magicians, and writers; it is an extraordinary group of luminaries. If one could imagine a secret society of Freemasons of the highest order gathering together, it would look like the Bohemian membership and guests.

The first time I attended the Spring Jinx, Ronald Reagan was in camp along with his secret service entourage. So-called "skit night" at the Grove is, by any measure, a Broadway-scale production performed on a stage set at the edge of a forest lake. On one occasion Frank Sinatra crashed the party and began singing. Another time, during one of the skit nights, there was a spoof on NFL owners. The actors wore custom-made masks with the likenesses of seven or eight NFL owners, the onstage imposters cleverly impersonating the owners. The edgy show, filled with sarcasm and ironies, was hilarious. When they all came back on the stage, a switch had been made backstage . . . the group of actors had switched with the real owners of the NFL teams. The owners took off their masks, which were likenesses of themselves, to reveal the real owners underneath.

I recall one evening, during dinner, debating with a guy across the table from me about theories concerning the human past based on scant fossil remains. I felt that anthropologists read too much into their findings from a few bone fragments. After I got more than one smirk around the table, a fellow sitting next to me finally leaned over and whispered that I was debating anthropological theory and practice with Donald Johansson, the guy who had discovered "Lucy." That's the kind of place the Bohemian Grove is.

Silicon Valley minted many millionaires from the high-tech revolution, ranging from inventors to investors. But one would probably not expect the town barbers to benefit from the high-tech boom.

But Al and Louie, the barbers in Los Altos, did. They cut the hair of David Packard, of Steve Jobs (when he had hair), of Microsoft executives, and others. Al and Louie simply asked what their hair customers were doing. Conversations in the chair inevitably led to descriptions of new products.

So Al and Louie, who were interested in their customers and the products they made, went out of their way to try out the new products. If they liked them, they would buy the stock in those companies. Over the years those simple, down-to-earth barbers became millionaires. Regardless of their fortunes, accumulated over a life time, they kept at their jobs, cracking jokes, and listening to their customers well into the late seventies, because they loved what they did—cutting hair. This reminds me of advice my father gave me:

Don't choose your work based upon what you will make. Find your passion first, then follow that passion to find your profession. If you love your work so much your back molars ache [I know, it's an odd expression], you will never work another day in your life. [Meaning when works becomes a passion and a pleasure, it is no longer work.]

My dad's advice must have been the reason why Al and Louie kept cutting hair until they couldn't stand up anymore.

Knights of Malta

The Knights of Malta are a Catholic-affiliated order that goes back to the time of the Knights Templar during the Crusades. Their special focus is on supporting hospitals around the world.

I was honored to become a Knight of Malta in the 1990s, in part because of my earlier work in the leper colonies. After being knighted, my family would tease me, calling me "Sir David," which I took in good humor.

As a Knight, the ego boost was wonderful: the pomp and ceremonial processions, including all of the Knights dressed in lavish capes and ancient costumes made me feel special—the formal events somehow made me feel like I was more important than others, when I didn't feel I was any more special than anyone else on the street, navigating through life the best we know how. I just couldn't get out of my head that the lavish robes I wore, and the pomp and ceremony of the events, made me think I was just an old guy playing dress up and the events I attended were just ego boosters.

So I chose another path to spend my free time on, directly giving back to the community—such as the thankless job of coaching youth sports, and, as of this writing, currently working with abused and neglected children as an officer of the court as a court appointed special advocate [CASA]. These are great extremes, but it is a path that makes me feel more complete. But I think no less of the Knights of Malta, as they are a source of good works.

During this time, our children seemed to be growing up fast. I treasured every moment with each and every one of our children. Before having children, I had wondered how you can love a child, then have another, and still love the first one, and love them both the same. It's like loving art. I love Picasso, but I also love Rembrandt's paintings. They are very different, but I love them both, for different reasons.

My way to spend more time with our kids was to involve them in sports and coaching. (It's a tricky business, coaching your own kids.) This began with my oldest daughter Nancy, because her soccer team had no coach. I was tapped to coach because I was, at that time, the only father who had actually played the game. (I learned the game during my year in Chile.) The coaching continued for twenty-two more years, with about ten years in highly competitive youth soccer programs.

Initially, I fiercely resisted the idea of coaching and viewed it as a chore because it took me away from my empire building. However, my chore soon became my joy. The joy that comes from seeing confidence where there was once doubt in the eyes of the young girls warmed my heart with a satisfaction unmatched by simply making business deals. Watching the skills of our players, sharpened by hard work and determination, become lifelong attributes of determination and self-confidence and a good work ethic brought more meaning to my life than accumulating "things."

It's a funny thing about life: of all my "toys"—my cars, boats, planes, ranches, and multiple second homes—nothing gave me more pleasure than seeing the joy in the eyes of a young soccer player accomplishing and perfecting a soccer technique for the first time. Observing these young girls become young women, maturing with confidence in themselves, was a far more satisfying life experience than my accumulations. In fact, the toys of affluence distracted me from the activity that made me happy and satisfied—a giving spirit rather than a consuming spirit.

Nevertheless, my passion for building a portfolio raged on unabated, with one eye to finding long-term solutions for my family and my company by reducing our debt and our risk, and with my other eye on the soccer field, watching out for who was having a difficult time on the field and thinking what practice drills we should to add to their routines. Unlike most coaches, my primary goal was to build a good work ethic and self-confidence in the players. With skills and self-confidence, winning takes care of itself, as, with our talent base, we won our share of games.

Chapter 24

"Failure is instructive. The person who really thinks learns quite as much from his failures as from his successes."

John Dewey

The Millennium:

Time for Reflection

2000—Today

As the new millennium approached, the pressures of business mounted, and I felt myself headed toward burnout. "Building one building after another mindlessly," I thought, "does not quench the soul's thirst." The tedious nature of babysitting the emotional ups and downs of a large staff of people and motivating them began to seem, in the long run, an endless and meaningless effort.

During my "empire building" years, I often worked eighty-hour workweeks, including weekends and holidays. We enjoyed skiing at homes in Snowmass and our waterfront properties in Tahoe, and I flew our prop jet wherever we wanted to go, or ran around in my Rolls Royce, but mostly I worked, and worked hard. But I also began to reflect on the changing world around me.

Silicon Valley: Its Benefits and Dangers

As I continue to reflect back and take a hard look at Silicon Valley, I can see that there is no doubt the Valley has risen to world prominence and created thousands of millionaires and minted an impressive list of billionaires. The affluence in Silicon Valley can be seen by everyone, from the houses we build to the cars we drive, from the clothes we wear to the quality of our schools and universities, and so on.

The essence of Silicon Valley is innovation, with a companion feature, like agriculture and the presence of water—automation. First, we automated the function of adding up data, then we automated virtually every aspect of our lives and how we live our lives. There is a benefit to automation, by reducing costs and helping labor become more efficient; more efficient labor by definition means less labor. This creates a human cost and a kind of poverty that is difficult to measure. It is a kind of poverty that results when certain jobs are permanently eliminated resulting in permanent unemployment; people who spent their lives mastering difficult skills are suddenly without work. They are told their skills are no longer useful or needed.

Our politicians tout that technology creates jobs without understanding that, *by definition,* the jobs being created by technology must be fewer than the jobs the technologies displace; if not, the innovation would not be cost-effective. So, on a net basis, technology and automation eliminate jobs, or the technology will not be adopted.

At the turn of the twentieth century about half of all Americans were involved with agriculture (along with twenty-two million workhorses). By 2002 less than two percent of Americans worked on farms, while massively increasing food output. The displacement of farm workers was quickly absorbed by manufacturing jobs. Now automation has, over the last few decades, largely eliminated manufacturing jobs. The U.S. today is becoming more and more a one-dimensional economy: a service economy. But automation is constantly chipping away, even displacing service industry jobs.

There is no doubt that, automation will eventually eliminate many high-skilled jobs, jobs that were thought until recently to be immune to automation. Automated online legal advice is already more accurate than human legal advice. Online medical advice competes favorably with human consultation and diagnosis. Imagine an economy that can provide all the goods and services needed in America but required less than 30% of Americans to produce. Will a seventy-percent unemployment rate become the new norm? What kind of financial and psychological poverty will people endure because they have skill sets that nobody wants? What kind of poverty is being created by the affluence created by our wonderful technology? This is not a theoretical question. The relentless march of "progress" through innovation in technology and automation could eventually result in massive permanent unemployment. Our political leaders have been too slow to recognize the unintended consequences of technological change. The natural progress of the fruits of Silicon Valley is likely to have unintended consequences if we as a society don't address this "future shock."

Another unintended consequence of the Valley's success: I discovered that beneath the wealth of the nouveau riche there was sometimes moral bankruptcy, with wealth poisoning the hearts and souls of the newly enriched. To repeat what I said before: when folks get all wrapped in themselves, they make very small packages. On the other hand, very successful Silicon Valley luminaries who have used their wealth responsibly as an act of love have become giants. Silicon Valley is a study in contrasts; one cannot cast everyone who has succeeded there in the same mold.

Despite the problems created by Silicon Valley's successes, we have every reason to believe that the technology bursting from the Valley portends a very bright future for humankind. But it is also a cause for concern if society does not begin a national dialogue on how to address our social structure in the future.

Learning to value people for who they are rather than for what they do, redefining safety nets, and restructuring capital priorities in a society, all begin with a national dialogue.

What if the new norm for American society is hypothetically a permanent unemployment rate as a result of innovation and automation? How do we handle the vast inequalities of wealth and income that are being generated by our very success? The politics of greed too often lead to the bitter politics of envy. How do we address these looming possibilities today?

It seems to me that we start with our corporate culture and capitalistic imperatives. Our corporate world and capitalistic system created opportunities, unimaginable 100 years ago. There is much to be grateful for what our system has created over the last 100 years. But corporations are inhuman, amoral, artificial entities that need to grow or perish. A company must grow, or the capital markets will punish them. Giant corporations can vanish overnight unless they continue to grow, which means we, as a society, must continue to consume.

But we live in a finite world. Locusts will mindlessly multiply until they consume all available resources. Homo sapiens are credited with mass extinctions that are destroying our biodiversity, a process that eventually will endanger our own survival. In modern times we are slowly destroying our planet's biodiversity, all in the name of growth—growth because our economic system demands it. Our corporate and capitalistic system is a type of locust. Unless we imbue our corporate world with a broader purpose and sense of mission as a requirement for incorporation, we are in danger of extinguishing ourselves by the way of the locust.

Our technology and affluence portend poverty on many levels of human existence unless we begin a national dialogue and a new narrative by changing the corporate rules to deal with the brave new world ahead of us.

Of all my years of empire building, I realize now that it was at the expense of spending time with my family. Dad, with all his flaws, had an enormous pool of sage wisdom. He pulled me aside shortly before he died and told me, "Stop pursuing your fortune as you already have a treasure at home." He implored me not to make the same mistake he had. I listened and modified my behavior. My grandfather, Djede was fond of saying, "Live like you are going to die tomorrow and work like you are going to live forever." Suppose a doctor told us, we have 30 days left to live. How would we live our lives, and what priorities would we embrace? I think this is what my grandfather was trying to tell me.

The truest advice Dad ever offered me was when he made the following point: "The greatest lessons you can learn from me is not from what I did right, but rather from what I did wrong."

Wouldn't all of us be lucky if we paid attention to what people do wrong, and learned to avoid their mistakes? The things you do right will take care of themselves.

Retirement, the Dot-Com Bust, and Back to Relevance

I decided to slow down and enjoy life. It's not only the scenery you miss by going too fast—you also miss the sense of where you are going, and why. After raising our children, and they had all moved out, except our youngest daughter, Tracy. Arlene and I sold Villa Maria; and I sold all of my real-estate holdings and moved into a retirement community in Carmel Valley (about ninety miles south of Silicon Valley) at the early age of fifty-two.

The buyers of our home were a young couple. They were freshly minted multi-millionaires from the dot-com frenzy. I remember meeting them for the first time. We dreaded the meeting, as I anticipated a couple of arrogant nouveau riche.

Both husband and the wife had started two, separate companies of their own within the previous twenty-four months and had sold their companies for eight and nine figures, each; such was the fantasy bubble in Silicon Valley at the time. What we found were two very humble and appreciative people who recognized that they had been very lucky. They could have worked twice as a hard a year earlier or a year later and could have flopped. Their sense of perspective and their grounded moral sense were pervasive. They had a sense of goodness about them that transcended any effect that their fabulous wealth might have had on them. Their true wealth was in their heart and spirit.

The timing of our sale was lucky, as it was on the very eve of the unforeseen dot-com bomb in 2001. Afterward, home and commercial real estate prices plummeted. But, though I sold at the right time, I too fell victim to "smelling the roses" of the dot-com mania.

A friend of mine was the founder of American Scientific; he theorized that a dot-com address was like a real estate address; therefore, the streets with the most traffic would be the most valuable. The logical conclusion was that one ought to own as many street corners and intersection properties as possible. These enormously wealthy, very smart people had me convinced to bet the farm on high-tech stocks. I was "drinking the Kool-Aid." Even in retirement, I couldn't help but dabble in business—but this time I was dabbling outside my area of expertise.

I didn't heed my grandfather's advice to stick to land and tangible assets rather than printed paper (that is, stock certificates) from Wall Street. My heavy investments in all these new startups saw a significant amount of my investments get wiped out as a result of the dot-com collapse. Fortunately, not all of the investments tanked.

This setback didn't kill me; it was retirement that was killing me.

All men and women need to feel relevant. Retirement, without goals and a dynamic plan for the future, is an empty existence focused on the bodily functions of eating, sleeping, and the like.

Fortunately, during the ensuing decade and half, I was able to rebound with strategic investments. But so what? I say all this a little cavalierly, because success and money or lack of success and lack of money meant very little to me—to my soul, to my community, or to the world. Relevance, I discovered, is a central element needed for human contentment.

I was given a quiz recently:

1. Name the five wealthiest people in the world.

2. Name the last five Heisman trophy winners.

3. Name the last five winners of the Miss America pageant.

4. Name ten people who have won the Nobel or Pulitzer prize.

5. Name the last half-dozen Academy Award winners for best actor and actress.

6. Name the World Series winners over the last decade.

I didn't do too well. I couldn't remember the headliners of yesterday. These aren't second-rate achievers; they are the best in their fields. But the applause dies. Awards tarnish. Achievements are forgotten. Accolades and certificates are buried with their owners.

Then I was asked:

1. List a few teachers who aided your journey through school.

2. Name three friends who have helped you through a difficult time.

3. Name five people who have taught you something worthwhile.

4. Think of a few people who have made you feel appreciated.

5. Think of five people you enjoy spending time with.

6. Name half a dozen heroes whose stories have inspired you.

The people who make a difference in your life are not the ones with the most credentials, the most money, or the most awards. They are the ones who care. If you want to stay relevant, then care for other people.

After my failed retirement, Arlene and I moved back to Silicon Valley. I found it to be a strange place. Cupertino, ground zero in Silicon Valley, had been transformed from a place of rural farmers of Slavic, Italian, and Japanese descent to a high-tech mecca, with dramatic ethnic and demographic changes. Cupertino is today called by the locals "Chinatown," complete with a growing number of billboards and retail shop signs written in Chinese characters only.

I felt like a character in Robert A. Heinlein's novel, *Stranger in a Strange Land.* But this is where most of my children and grandchildren live, and I cherish our time with them. I love my work, my volunteer time, and my wife.

However, I can't help but take a step back, in my twilight years, witnessing the hustle and bustle of Silicon Valley, bumper-to-bumper traffic, the frenetic pace and, most disagreeably, the growing hubris and arrogance, the consuming self-importance, of many of the nouveau riche.

Money can buy a house but not a home. With money you can buy a clock but not time. With money you can buy a bed but not sleep. With money you can buy books but not wisdom. With money you can buy a doctor but not your health. With money you can buy a position but not respect.

Envoy: The Seven Greatest Marvels

As a society, we give extra weight to things that are manmade. We humans pride ourselves on the wonders of our civilizations. Throughout the ages we have marveled at our ancients: Stonehenge, the Coliseum, the catacombs, the Great Wall of China—to say nothing of the Porcelain Tower of Nanjing, the Hagia Sophia in Istanbul, the Leaning Tower of Pisa. But it seems to me that the most precious things of all can neither be made, nor purchased, by man.

It's astonishing, the natural wonders of the world: the Great Barrier Reef, Victoria Falls, Mount Everest, the Grand Canyon, the Auroras Borealis and Australis, Paricutín volcano, and Ayers Rock are all marvelous wonders that are not manmade.

As amazing our world is, our universe is even more astonishing.

As we ponder the universe with other beings like ourselves, or muse about our place in the overall scheme of things or ponder muons and gluons or the space between electrons, I can't help wondering about the place of humanity in the overall scheme of things.

Although the marvels of human invention give us a certain sense of place,

the seven greatest marvels are right before us: the marvel to see, to hear, to touch, to feel, to taste, to laugh, and to love. As our paths cross with wonderful people, we are enriched indeed. As Yeats remembered his absent friends,

> "Think where man's glory and most begins and ends.
> And say my glory was I had such friends."

By sharing my family history and perspective on the growth and change in Santa Clara Valley over the last half of the twentieth century, I hope I have provided readers with a glimpse of the development of Silicon Valley "from the inside, looking out." As the Valley continues being a historic center of innovation and prosperity, my hope is that we will also benefit by finding here a perspective on the even grander pursuit of a healthy heart and soul.

About the Author and the Mariani Family

David W. Mariani

Mr. Mariani grew up and has lived most of his life in Santa Clara Valley, now better known the world over as "Silicon Valley." His life has spanned three major technological revolutions in the Valley, covering agriculture, information technology driven by the silicon chip, and the rapid adoption of the World Wide Web at the turn of the twenty-first century. Mr. Mariani is married to Arlene Mariani and father of five beautiful daughters.

Although a published research author, Mr. Mariani has pursued his professional career primarily in business. He currently serves as the chief executive officer of Mariani Capital Partner and Mariani Investments, LLC. He has a broad background in finance, real estate development, and investment banking. Mr. Mariani was the co-founder, chairman, and managing partner of Glenborough MLP, a real-estate firm he helped found in 1986, the predecessor of the Glenborough REIT, which was sold to Morgan Stanley in 2006.

Over the past thirty-five years, Mr. Mariani developed, and subsequently managed, more than five million square feet of commercial real estate and numerous residential developments. In the 1970s and 1980s, Mr. Mariani was the chief financial officer of his family's agribusiness interests, managing thirty-two operating companies on three continents. He earned his B.A. from the University of San Francisco and completed undergraduate and postgraduate work at Santa Clara University. Mr. Mariani's broad background has led to his serving on twenty-seven corporate, industry, agency, and public boards, including as chairman and a founder of the Presidio School of Management, chairman of American Western Banker, and chairman of the board of California Security Bank, of which he was the majority owner.

[2] These titles come from Venetian documents, where I found mentioned "*dux Marianorum Morsticus*," "*iudex Marianorum*," and "*rex Marianorum*"; also "*dux Morjana Morstika*."

[3] Marianovic(h), in Croatian, means "son of Mariani."

[5] Antoinette Svilich, Victoria's sister, subsequently married Steve Lobrovich, and they had three children: two girls, Mary and Irene, and a boy, Archie, the youngest. Archie was born at roughly the same time as Paul, Jr. (who would one day become my father) and so were the same age

[7] Djede, my father and myself were all married at age 22 in the same Mission Santa Clara Church, 64 years apart between Djede's marriage and my own.

[8] The 19th Amendment, affirming a woman's right to vote, was ratified in 1920, and suffragists introduced an equal rights amendment to the U.S. Constitution in 1923 as the next step for equal justice for women under the law. This amendment, another version of which was circulated for passage by the states in the 1970s, has yet to be passed.

[10] I believe this was awarded by the San Jose Chamber of Commerce.

[11] The most common reason why dry-away ratios differ is because of the content of fruit sugars or solids. Some fruit varieties tend to have more sugar than others. Climate and soil conditions and the ripeness of the fruit when picked all affect the amount of sugar solids in the fruit.

[12] The University of California Davis were developing different varieties to adapt to climatic conditions in California. The Sacramento Valley had great growing conditions but often the summers got too hot, resulting in "pit burn": the pits would heat up and burn the flesh of the fruit. The new varieties of prunes, when combined with better pruning techniques, were less susceptible to pit burn.

[13] Alfalfa was planted to fertilize the land through its nitrogen-fixing properties.

[14] The skin of a cherry has an extremely thin, cuticule-like membrane that transports substances into and out of the fruit. The fruit surface also has microscopic cracks invisible to the naked eye but large enough for water to flow through them into the cherry. If the fruit is rained on, the surface expands, splitting the skin in the process.

[15] The Bracero program was a diplomatic agreement between the United States and Mexico that began on August 4, 1942, and ended in 1964.

[16] The coffee grounds were a waste byproduct from the making of instant coffee.

[17] PH around 5.5-5.8 is optimal to enable plants to absorb nutrients. This is the same range of average rainwater – or slightly acidic. Worm castings are neutral – neither acidic nor alkaline.

[18] "*Force majeure*" literally means "superior force," but in the legal world, it means that parties can free themselves from obligations if circumstances arise that are out of their control.

[20] Piece rate was a system of payment to farm workers. The more they picked, the more they got paid. This system was in lieu of an hourly wage. But there were too few "dropped" prunes to pick at piece rate, to make it worthwhile to attract any pickers.

[21] Like most packers in the 1960s and early 1970s, we grew only a fraction of the fruit we processed and sold. Networks of growers were critical as supply sources for our business.

[22] Years later, the discovery of thousands of miles of tunnels crisscrossing throughout the war zone. explained how the Viet Cong's were able to release rockets, at close-range, yet seldom be found during search and recon missions.

[23] These slicing and pitting machines were called Philpers, from a design by James Hait of FMC (originally Food Machinery Corporation) in 1963. FMC was a hotbed of innovation serving the agricultural community in Santa Clara Valley.

[24] Discing is a method to remove weeds that compete for nutrients with a farmer's crop and to aerate the soil, among other benefits. A tractor pulls a set of large steel discs, set at an angle, up and down the rows of crops, pulling the rotating discs along, and the discs dig deep into the soil and turn the soil over.

[25] Mark Kettmann had worked with the family for over 50 years beginning as young boy.

[26] The secondary markets included juice and flavoring companies and the confection market.

[27] This was the same engineer who held the patents on our peach-pitting machines, the Philpers, mentioned earlier.

[28] According to multiple newspapers at the time.

[29] Modern science now understand circadian rhythms' are very different from one person to another. Without an understanding these differences, they became a source of friction.

[30] The Warburg family, partners in Kuhn, Loeb & Co, a multinational investment bank. Eric was influential in restoring German-Jewish relations and rebuilding German economic ties after WWII.

[32] Real estate is not an asset allowed to be depreciated in the calculations of tax accounting. The original price paid for the land stays on the books as your "tax basis." If you purchased a property for $1,000 forty years earlier and now the property is worth $500,000, you are taxed on sale based upon your tax basis, or $1,000

[33] The value of a lease is affected by the quality of the credit of a tenant. The moderate credit of a local company is worth less than the much larger credit of a national company with a very large positive balance sheet; such a tenant is known in real estate parlance as a "national credit tenant."

[34] The challenge was that a very large film format 15 perforations long had to make a loop and move into the projection window onto a film flattener, remain absolutely still for a nano second for two shots of light to project the image, taken off the film window with another frame to follow, 24 times a second. Only two companies in the world were able to accomplish this feat. IMAX and World Odyssey, our company.

ISBN #

978-1-7331461-3-5

POVERTY OF AFFLUENCE: THE STORY OF THE MARIANI FAMILY IN CALIFORNIA

My highest recommendation for this wonderful memoir—a beautifully written tale of a very large and successful family from Croatia in whose progress one can see the magic of resettling in America for a brighter future. The Marianis were farmers in their old country and became very successful fruit farmers here—and eventually they spread their empire overseas to Chile and Australia as well. A very tight family with a couple of exceptions, they were successful beyond their dreams and, in part because of large land holdings--essential to farming, they were major players in the conversion of the "Valley of the Heart's Delight" into "The Silicon Valley." The exciting adventures of the Marianis resulted in considerable affluence, renown and the attendant problems of too much success and too much fame. Along the way we meet a three-legged horse (and experience a couple of beheadings.) An exciting book and very well written. David Mariani has been years in the writing of this well told tale, and the result is a superb book with a very interesting and very California story.

John Swensson
Retired Lieutenant Colonel US Army
Emeritus Professor of Literary Chair